F*CK THE ARMY!

PERFORMANCE AND AMERICAN CULTURES

General Editors: Stephanie Batiste, Robin Bernstein, and Brian Herrera

This book series harnesses American studies and performance studies and directs them toward each other, publishing books that use performance to think historically.

The Art of Confession: The Performance of Self from Robert Lowell to Reality TV
Christopher Grobe

Realist Ecstasy: Religion, Race, and Performance in American Literature
Lindsay V. Reckson

The Queer Nuyorican: Racialized Sexualities and Aesthetics in Loisaida
Karen Jaime

Black Patience: Performance, Civil Rights, and the Unfinished Project of Emancipation
Julius B. Fleming, Jr.

F*ck The Army!: How Soldiers and Civilians Staged the GI Movement to End the Vietnam War
Lindsay Goss

F*ck The Army!

*How Soldiers and Civilians
Staged the GI Movement
to End the Vietnam War*

Lindsay Goss

NEW YORK UNIVERSITY PRESS
New York

NEW YORK UNIVERSITY PRESS
New York
www.nyupress.org

© 2024 by New York University
All rights reserved

Library of Congress Cataloging-in-Publication Data
Names: Goss, Lindsay (College teacher), author.
Title: F*ck the army! : how soldiers and civilians staged the GI movement to end the Vietnam war / Lindsay Goss.
Other titles: Fuck the army!
Description: New York : New York University Press, 2024. |
Series: Performance and American cultures |
Includes bibliographical references and index.
Identifiers: LCCN 2023038599 (print) | LCCN 2023038600 (ebook) |
ISBN 9781479821846 (hardback) | ISBN 9781479821860 (paperback) |
ISBN 9781479821877 (ebook) | ISBN 9781479821884 (ebook other)
Subjects: LCSH: Free Theater Associates—History. | American drama—20th century—History and criticism. | Vietnam War, 1961-1975—Literature and the war. | Literature and society—United States—History—20th century. | Theater and society—United States—History—20th century.
Classification: LCC PN2297.F695 G67 2024 (print) | LCC PN2297.F695 (ebook) | DDC 792.09—dc23/eng/20231115
LC record available at https://lccn.loc.gov/2023038599
LC ebook record available at https://lccn.loc.gov/2023038600

This book is printed on acid-free paper, and its binding materials are chosen for strength and durability. We strive to use environmentally responsible suppliers and materials to the greatest extent possible in publishing our books.

Manufactured in the United States of America

10 9 8 7 6 5 4 3 2 1

Also available as an ebook

For Martin and Lisa, my parents

CONTENTS

Introduction: Scenes of Solidarity	1
1. Seeing the Antiwar Soldier	17
2. Staging the Movement	39
3. Say It! Solidarity Without Guarantees	69
4. Enlisted Audiences and Emancipated Spectators	113
5. The Actor and the Activist	152
Conclusion: A Refusal	191
Acknowledgments	199
Notes	203
Index	219
About the Author	227

Introduction

Scenes of Solidarity

In early 1971, a handful of celebrities got together to crack jokes about the rising casualty rates of US soldiers in Vietnam. Led by Jane Fonda and backed by Hollywood money, they called themselves the FTA, or the Free Theater Associates. To roars of laughter and applause at their inaugural performance on March 15 in Fayetteville, North Carolina, actors Donald Sutherland and Peter Boyle, as the sportscasters Red and Red, delivered a vaudevillian, rapid-fire blow-by-blow of an imagined battle between the Viet Cong and an Army detachment. Red and Red watch as the Americans accidentally drop napalm on their own 101st Airborne Division ("And there are penalty flags down on the field!"), then include an unfortunate herd of bystanding water buffalo in the tally of enemy combatants killed.[1] The scene concludes with the sportscasters scanning a lengthy list of American dead before declaring that casualties for the day were "light to moderate."[2] The routine would remain a popular mainstay as the FTA toured its antiwar cabaret to a dozen cities and towns in the US and Southeast Asia. Over the course of ten months, the group played to tens of thousands of enthusiastic young spectators, whose "raised fists, V signs, and cries of 'Right on!'" punctuated every performance.[3]

At first glance, the FTA appears to reinforce a persistent perception of the antiwar movement during Vietnam as "anti-soldier."[4] Ridiculing military incompetence and mocking lockstep patriotism, the show's content and all-star cast might well conjure Vice President Spiro Agnew's view that the antiwar movement was a crisis of "national masochism encouraged by an effete corps of impudent snobs" trying to pass as intellectuals.[5] Certainly, the involvement of Jane Fonda encourages us to set the show alongside the infamous image of that actress perched atop enemy weaponry in North Vietnam, and the claims (however thoroughly debunked) that she deliberately prompted the torture of American prisoners of war.[6] Seen through this lens, the FTA fits a well-worn narrative that imagines the era's activists spitting on soldiers and calling them "baby-killers," as it is just such an audience of civilian spectators that the sketch's warm reception appears to suggest. Yet the remarkable truth is that at every stop the FTA's audience was composed almost exclusively of active-duty soldiers, sailors, airmen, and Marines. Far from an attack on American soldiers, the show was an act of solidarity—a civilian-led effort to support the growing number of servicemembers who were fed up with the war and, increasingly, inclined toward organizing against it from within the military's ranks.

If you're unfamiliar with the GI movement, that's because you're supposed to be. While draft dodgers and disgruntled veterans have come to hold an enduring place in our image of the era, efforts to downplay and obscure the existence of the active-duty, antiwar soldier (which began but did not end with the Nixon administration) have been exceedingly successful.[7] This explains why, in 2006, when I attended a screening of David Zeiger's *Sir! No Sir!* at the International Film Center in New York, I encountered a history about which I had previously known almost nothing: between 1967 and 1972, thousands of GIs organized against the military from within its ranks, circulating underground newspapers, collectively refusing orders, and participating in acts of public protest. These coordinated expressions of dissent transformed what was already a profound crisis of morale and discipline into a powerful challenge to US imperialism. Through interviews with participants, Zeiger documents many of the key uprisings during this period, from the Fort Hood 43 (Black soldiers who refused riot-duty at the 1968 Democratic National Convention) to the Presidio 27 (prisoners in the stockade at San Francisco's Presidio Army Base who refused to work after a mentally ill prisoner was killed) to the Armed Farces Day demonstrations that took place across the country in 1971.[8]

Encountering the history of the GI movement was one thing, as it suddenly revealed a wing of the antiwar movement that understood the incredible power of the soldier-as-worker—to strike, to sabotage, to slow down. But there was something else as well. Among the footage from earlier films Zeiger had included in *Sir! No Sir!* were scenes from *FTA!* (1972). The documentary feature, directed by Francine Parker, follows the FTA's tour in the fall of 1971 to US bases overseas and the enthusiastic reception it was given by active-duty servicemen and women. Despite my twin interests in activism and theater, and the considerable time I'd spent exploring their intersection in US culture, I'd never heard of the FTA. That this might've been due to some objective assessment of the show's insignificance is unlikely, as a brief outline makes clear: between March and December 1971, the FTA toured to over sixty-four thousand troops, playing near, but never on, bases in North Carolina, California, Washington, Texas, Idaho, New Jersey, Okinawa, Japan, the Philippines, and Hawaii. Besides Boyle and Sutherland, the first show, near Fort Bragg in Fayetteville, featured prominent comedian and civil rights activist Dick Gregory. In New Jersey, near Fort Dix, Nina Simone performed. The show's participants and content reflected not only the growing resistance movement within the Armed Forces, but also the extreme levels of sexism and racism that compounded the experience of repression for women enlistees and non-white GIs. From its beginning and almost without exception, the FTA drew standing-room-only crowds, was covered positively in underground GI newspapers, and found its audiences eager to talk after every performance, even as its run time could stretch to three hours or more. David Cortright, in his comprehensive account of the GI movement, directly credits the FTA with contributing to major events within that movement's history, and Colonel Robert Heinl references it in the "Society Notes" section of his 1971 article "The Collapse of the Armed Forces."[9] Mainstream news sources featured articles describing the popularity of the show, noting the roars of applause and approval following comic scenes of insubordination, musical numbers, and dramatic readings from antiwar texts. In November, before it departed for a tour of bases along the Pacific Rim, the FTA appeared at Lincoln Center's Philharmonic Hall before an audience of two thousand. The evening would earn it a "Special Citation" Obie for the 1971–72 season.

Despite the show's popularity and impact, the FTA appears nowhere in the historical narrative of 1960s and '70s political theater. The reasons for this are likely several. The first, and most obvious, is that the GI movement itself has been effectively excised from the history of the Vietnam War. While some progress has been made toward excavating the history of the GI resistance—notably via David Moser's *The New*

Winter Soldiers (1995), the reissue of David Cortright's *Soldiers in Revolt* (1972, 2005), the release of Zeiger's documentary (2005), and, more recently, David L. Parsons's *Dangerous Grounds: Antiwar Coffeehouses and Military Dissent in the Vietnam Era* (2017)—it is still a phenomenon of which the general public is largely unaware. However, the reasons for the FTA's absence from a narrative of the era's radical performance practices have just as much to do, I would argue, with the ways in which "political theater" has been defined and redefined in the intervening decades. The FTA, both its project and its performers, does not fit readily into an investment in and emphasis on the experimental, the aesthetically innovative, or the process-oriented, all characteristics considered representative of the various forms of political theater produced during the 1960s and early '70s, including those connected to the antiwar movement, such as Bread and Puppet Theater and the San Francisco Mime Troupe. Nor was the FTA a collective in the sense associated with groups like the Living Theatre or the Open Theater. Its form was decidedly popular, in keeping with the format of Bob Hope's USO programming, on which it was modeled, and it deliberately harnessed star power. Much of its ability to attract an audience at each stop depended upon the fame of its performers—especially Fonda and Sutherland, whose feature film *Klute* (for which Fonda would win an Oscar) was playing at the time in local cinemas. The scripted material was straightforward, and although its authors included experimentally inclined writers such as Jules Feiffer and members of San Francisco's The Committee, the focus on producing a routine that would be broadly relatable while also explicitly political in its message meant short blackout sketches—consisting of a brief setup followed by a punch line—dominated.

In other words, the FTA was built to serve a movement, and this singular focus dictated its form and content. As a result, and unlike many of the groups and collectives most closely identified with the period, the FTA dissolved and disappeared at the end of its brief, spectacular run, leaving nothing that might be identifiable as an artistic legacy, because it produced no notable aesthetic innovation or experimentation. The performers went their separate ways and the feature film documenting the group's Asia tour was pulled from circulation. More to the point, the sense of political urgency that had given rise to and been sustained by the GI movement was deftly spirited away by the end of the war and the end of the draft. With it went the radical character of the FTA's vaudeville variety show, which appears radical only in its original context.

In contrast, many of the political theater groups most associated with the 1960s continue to make work in the present, a fact that informs how contemporary scholars understand the significance of the work they did in the past.[10] The resulting historiographical emphasis upon continuity and legacy in discussions of the era's political theater sidelines a group like the FTA, an omission that obscures key contours of the era's artistic and political radicalization. Whereas political movements from the period in question in many cases articulated and acknowledged failures, a different afterlife attended artistic practices that located success not exclusively in political gains and social change, but equally (or increasingly, as the former became less tenable) in artistic practice itself. What happens, remarkably, is the production of a sense of continuity between the work a given group did in the 1960s and the work that they do today. And although continuity certainly exists—in the artists involved, in the form and content, in the beliefs or values of the participants—continuity in the context of radical social and political transformation *is not continuity*, but rather obscured transformation.

Strangely, then, a narrative of political theater that emphasizes legacy, continuity, and compatibility, between past practices and contemporary contexts, obscures the profound shifts in political ideology that have played out in the intervening decades.[11] While shifts (and intensifications) in conservative ideology are relatively well discussed by those who might align themselves with the left or identify as progressive, the corresponding shifts in progressive or left-wing perspectives and strategies are not. The result is that they appear as a natural or inevitable development—the progression of left ideas away from revolutionary idealism and toward a more practical or academic approach—as opposed to the direct product of historical and political events, most especially the sense of defeat and failure coming out of the 1960s and early '70s.

For example, a significant shift in political circumstance pushed groups like El Teatro Campesino and theater artists like Amiri Baraka to reconsider their approach to making performance. In his consideration of "social protest theatre" during the 1960s, Harry Elam, Jr., identifies the potential efficacy of a political performance as tied to the existence of "urgency." He asks, "What happens to social protest theatre, then, after the urgency dies?" Activists and performers "had to determine for themselves, individually, whether their greater commitment was to the theater or to the social cause."[12] Even as Elam references the conditions that gave rise to the "search for new strategies and solutions after the immediacy of the liminal, revolutionary times had passed," he does so in keeping with a narrativization of the 1960s that renders its aftermath the "evolution" of the "naïve, absolutist arguments of earlier times." While, on the one hand, this is an entirely necessary acknowledgement of the limitations, particularly around issues of sexism, of the politics of both El Teatro and Black Revolutionary Theatre, it is equally, I would argue, in keeping with a desire to foreground a continuity between past and present practices, to celebrate successes, and to delay or prevent altogether a confrontation with (political) failure.

The transformation of a retreat into an "evolution" obscures the political consequences of the impact of the failures that devastated the left and prompted a flight into academic spaces. The FTA, then, reintroduces the fact of the failure of the *revolutionary* project of the 1960s, which is obscured by a history that emphasizes continuity even as it acknowledges a changed and changing political landscape. This is not to say that the only outcome of the 1960s was failure, for unquestionably the movements of that period achieved significant and lasting changes, particularly in securing an expanded recognition of the legitimacy of the claims of historically oppressed groups to self-determination, protected rights, and greater representation within cultural, political, and educational institutions. We have seen, however, in the ongoing rollback of the rights and recognition won on each of these fronts, that the underlying economic and political structure remained and remains intact.

The fact that a continuity can be claimed between the practices of political theater groups during the 1960s and their work today is evidence of a radical shift in the perception of both the means by which and the extent to which a radical transformation of society might occur. Yet this established continuity goes largely unquestioned, suggesting, even if implicitly, that the adaptation of political theater groups to a context in which the possibility of revolutionary change is perceived as off the table is the logical, inevitable, or even desirable outcome of that period. The FTA challenges this presumption. What, its example encourages us to ask, of groups that chose not to take aesthetic risks, because the political context called for a mainstream practice? What of practices that disappear from the historical record because they failed to register as aesthetically radical? What would a theater history of the 1960s look like if it centered (or even simply included) the work of groups that undertook to make theater *only when* they perceived it to be the most effective political weapon in the given circumstances? Such a shift in focus would complicate the tendency to construct our political theater historical narrative by working backward from what we can point to in the present, revealing other ways of thinking about theater and theatricality as sites of political potential. Whereas existing narratives tend to understand formal experimentation, spectator participation, and collective creation as evidence of radical politics, this book proposes that their absence might, in some cases, equally reflect a commitment to a revolutionary project.

These are questions for theater historians, of course, but they are also questions for anyone interested in better understanding the forces shaping our perception of activism and activists during the 1960s and '70s and, by extension, our perception of activism and activists today. In failing to register as sufficiently aesthetically radical, we might also say that the FTA failed to register as sufficiently *authentic*, in a manner that has come to define the era's political theater and its emphasis on breaking down the line between reality and its representation. The FTA certainly pursued something we could call authenticity—in its insistence upon drawing its material from GI newspapers, in its careful efforts to highlight the particular power of the soldier to end the war—but it did not do so, arguably, on the level of its aesthetics. It was not interested in pressing against traditional conventions of theatrical representation and so, in a sense, it barely counts as theater at all. In light of this, we might adjust my previous question and ask what of practices (and activists and movements) that disappear from the historical record because they failed to register as *authentic*? What of antiwar soldiers recast as merely activists, activists recast as merely actors? What of political theater that is merely political theater? What of movements that reimagine the world so radically that a discourse of authenticity becomes meaningless? When might a movement's *absence* from the historical record indicate that its example is one we ought to consider following?

Against a theater historiographical emphasis on legacy and continuity, I identify an alternative political and performative legacy, one that positions theater as a *tactic*, with, therefore, specific advantages and limitations relative to its associated political project and its immediate context. Critical to this undertaking is the acknowledgement that the FTA is not the central story of the GI movement, but only one tactic among many. To suggest otherwise would be to risk indulging in a kind of disciplinary myopia, reading the era's radical politics through the lens of theatrical practice simply because that's what I know how (or want) to do. Such a reading takes us further from any useful cultural or political analysis of the 1960s, if in the process we neglect the way in which movements *actually related* to specific instances of theatrical practice. Theater from then that is politically interesting to us now may or may not have had anything to do with other kinds of activist practice. An attention to theater as a tactic forces a question we ought to apply to any kind of activist activity, or, indeed, scholarship: why this, why now?

The FTA forms the basis of this book, then, not only because its recovery offers a critical addition to our picture of the era's political theater, but because its existence and erasure raises directly the question of the tactic and its relationship to theatricality. The FTA's existence and impact demonstrate how theatrical performance, both on stage and off, made space for a reconsideration of the "authenticity" of the soldier, insofar as this was based on an assessment of his attitude toward the war. Drawing its form from comedian Bob Hope's Christmas tours to bases abroad, the show sought to provide an alternative to what some troops increasingly perceived as an out of touch, culturally conservative routine, performed by a man who had more than once expressed his support for the war in no uncertain terms. As critically, in addressing antiwar soldiers, the FTA exposed and responded to the dominant image of the soldier as an unsustainable fiction, by recognizing an alternative image, and amplifying, circulating, and legitimizing this image. The show produced, both on stage and in the auditorium, evidence of the existence of the antiwar soldier, retaining that soldier's legibility *as soldier* by making sure the show itself was legible as soldier-oriented entertainment. For their part, soldiers, individually and collectively, undertook forms of theatrical protest and sought an audience willing to validate and recognize these performances as legitimate expressions of patriotic dissent. Theatrical performance, in a broad sense, at once made possible forms of recognition that were otherwise precluded by military discipline, but also exposed those who participated in these performances—soldiers and civilians alike—to accusations of inauthenticity and illegitimacy, that is, of being someone other than who or what they claimed to be, which is to say, an actor.

The problem of acting as it haunts activist discourse and practice, then and now, sits at the heart of this book and motivates its historical reconstruction of a little-known theatrical event that had profound implications for a little-known radical movement. The "little-known" in either case reflects how efforts to produce a sense of continuity between the politics of leftists then and progressives now (as well as political theater then and now) have led to the erasure or forgetting of projects that challenge this narrative. As a popular theater practice that was premised entirely upon the possibility of significant political impact, the FTA offers a means of shifting, however slightly, the terms of debate surrounding the relationship between politics and performance. My argument is not that the FTA is a model for contemporary theater practice, nor that it should serve as the basis more generally for an explicitly or overtly political approach to performance. Rather, through its unapologetic and tactical intervention into a critical movement, the FTA draws our attention to the knots and breaks in the clean line often (if implicitly) drawn between the political investments of theater practice in the 1960s and '70s and those at work in contemporary discussions of radical or activist performance. It suggests we look differently at how theater and theatricality work within and on political discourse, and reconsider the ways in which contemporary movements for social change navigate ideas of authenticity and legitimacy.

My approach is not dissimilar to that of Andreas Malm in *How to Blow Up a Pipeline* (2021).[13] Malm considers the ways in which the narrative of "non-violence," particularly as wielded by climate activists, has conveniently forgotten the violence that often facilitated pacifism's impact—the armed defenders of Dr. Martin Luther King's work; the arson committed by the suffragettes; the bloody rebellions of enslaved Africans. The problem with this erasure is not simply that it distorts our understanding of the past and of the ways in which the gains won by these movements were achieved. As importantly, it leads us to draw the wrong *lessons* from the past and to misunderstand what it means to apply the past to the present. The lesson fits the narrative, but the narrative excludes that which might contradict or upend the lesson.

Whereas Malm focuses on non-violence, I focus on the central role that theatricality played in the movements of the 1960s, specifically through the lens of the GI movement and the performances, both onstage and off, that participated in growing that movement and sharpening its impact. I am interested in how what I identify as the necessary and tactical theatricality of radical activist and protest movements in general and the GI movement in particular has been re(in)scripted into the historical narrative as evidence of these movements' illegitimacy, inauthenticity, and flagrantly irresponsible pursuit of a project doomed to fail. That the idea of performance, and more specifically of acting, continues to shape political discourse is evident in the recent discussions of "ally theater" and "performative activism" playing out on the left. A concern with the ways in which "inauthenticity," whether perceived or "real," can undermine the foundation upon which movements are built has risen up, I would argue, in part as a way of anticipating right-wing attacks that similarly leverage the claim that activists are making demands to which they are not entitled, either because they are the wrong people or because they are making those demands in the wrong way.

It is precisely because the GI movement sought to mobilize the profoundly legitimizing identity of its participants that it offers such a rich site for examining how accusations of illegitimacy and inauthenticity work by relying upon a discourse of performance and what possibilities exist for fighting against them. Not only did the GI movement leverage the authority of servicemembers in criticizing or denouncing the war, it also undermined efforts to paint the civilian antiwar movement as anti-soldier. For anyone who has been involved in protesting any of the many US foreign interventions over the last fifty years, this will be a familiar trope—that to be against the war is to be against the troops. In fact, it is such a potent premise that some antiwar groups protesting Operation Desert Storm in the 1990s recirculated this narrative about Vietnam-era antiwar protesters (no doubt believing it to be true) in order to identify themselves as a more enlightened kind of activist. Tellingly, this position meant that as soon as boots were on the ground in Iraq, protests against the invasion dried up almost immediately. The specter of the anti-soldier antiwar activist was sufficient to dissuade anyone from trying to argue that it is possible to be one without the other.[14]

The FTA, as a particularly concentrated and spectacular instance of civilian support for the GI movement, helps to undo this persistent misperception, and its historical recovery here, like the vignette with which this introduction began, points backward to reveal the remarkable events to which it constituted a response. Perhaps even more critically, for our contemporary moment, the FTA, *as theater*, quite literally "stages" solidarity and suggests that we might reexamine our investment, on the left, in using a discourse of authenticity, so well-worn by the right, in our efforts to hold allies accountable for their words and actions. To what extent is some kind of "acting" always necessary, when the relations or conditions we seek to make visible are refused legitimacy by the existing terms of representation? Can we hold allies accountable without foreclosing the possibility that we might, of necessity, be engaged in a representational practice that is not (yet) officially seen as "real"?

Consider that the official line from the show's actors and organizers was that "FTA," as the name of the show, stood for "Free the Army." This phrase, however, was the polite interpretation of an acronym the performers had borrowed from the soldiers themselves, who had appropriated it in turn from the US Army's slogan "Fun, Travel, and Adventure." During performances, when the troupe came to the line in their signature song that featured the phrase "Free the Army," spectating servicemembers would regularly offer a gleeful correction and encourage the performers to take it up—which they did, shouting "Fuck the Army!" from the stage. Extra letters and words were added as needed, depending upon the composition of the audience, such that FTA would become "FTAF" or "FTN," or "FTM," or all four at once, spelled out in a triumphant, expletive-filled list.

*F*ck The Army!* is, finally, built upon the simple premise that it is useful for activists today to understand what made it possible, in 1971, for a group of civilians, including Jane Fonda, to join an auditorium full of soldiers in shouting "Fuck the Army." While the premise is simple—that there is something useful to be learned here—unraveling the event itself is more complicated, insofar as it requires us to *use* theater, and theatricality, and acting (as an actor acts) as analytics. That is, the problem is not merely a historical or historiographical one, though solving it certainly depends upon including the GI movement and the FTA in our picture of the period. Rather, the problem lies in seeing that which is not meant to be seen and hearing that which is not meant to be heard. Theater, I argue, is a relation or a structure that lets us do this, and so it becomes, in what follows, the *way* we understand the antiwar soldier's efforts to attain and also navigate visibility; the mechanism by which civilians participated in supporting and amplifying the GI movement; the precarious construction of solidarity; the emancipation of the spectator; and the radical acting of the activist. Thus, while the book roughly follows the trajectory of the FTA, each chapter uses the group's history to consider a particular facet of acting and/or theatricality and examine its relationship to the pursuit of a political project.

Though the military privately acknowledged (and tried to stem) the flood of dissent within its ranks, publicly they continued to portray the American servicemember as obedient, clean-cut, patriotic, and proud to serve. Chapter 1 explores how this required the antiwar GI to *stage* his status as soldier, because being antiwar automatically called this status into question. Moreover, as GIs came back from Vietnam, radicalized, and headed into college on the GI Bill, they could merge with the activist tide in ways that diminished their visibility as veterans who had a particular authority on the matter of the war and whose opposition to it was downplayed by the administration. As a result, GI and veteran protests frequently featured imagery and activity drawn from the soldier's repertoire but bent toward a critique of the war, a creative reinterpretation that allowed participants to ground expressions of antiwar sentiment in the legitimacy of their identity as soldiers, refusing the premise that the former invalidated the latter. Theatrical tactics such as medal-returning ceremonies and marches that ended in the ceremonial breaking of plastic weaponry destabilized the military's claims that supporting the troops required supporting the war. However, such performances also always opened GIs up to accusations that they were not "real" soldiers. Precisely because "staging" was necessary, antiwar soldiers contended with efforts on the right to discredit the legitimacy and authenticity of antiwar GI s by claiming that they were "merely" activists in disguise. Under constant threat of misrecognition, antiwar soldiers required an audience of civilians willing to validate as "real" that which was officially characterized as not real or not "really" happening. I consider how existing institutions and practices that validated the established pro-war GI identity, such as Hope's show and the USO, were challenged by parallel structures and events organized by civilians, which provided critical yet also precariously constructed "sites of recognition" for the antiwar GI.

Chapter 2 examines the FTA as a particularly potent site of recognition, constructed deliberately (and through much debate) in such a way as to encourage antiwar activity among soldiers and facilitate identification with the movement. The FTA responded to a rhetoric of (in)-authenticity by strategically aligning itself with the established tradition of "entertaining the troops." Building on the previous chapter's attention to theatricality as a feature of activist practice, I focus on the FTA as an example of theater that makes tactical use of its form, principally by taking the choice to make theater not as a given but as a contextually determined answer to a question of political strategy. By positioning soldiers as spectators and relying upon celebrity status and a familiar form of entertainment, the FTA gathered interested but as yet uninvolved GIs together as audiences and smuggled the GI movement's own antiwar content onto the stage. Where the military had begun to offer troops spaces and forms of entertainment that more accurately reflected their tastes, the FTA, in its continually denied requests to be allowed to perform on base, revealed the political conservatism of these culturally "radical" efforts. The shows themselves, while pitched like Hope's as "just entertainment," expressed support for escalating acts of insubordination and drew connections between the war and other forms of oppression. I examine the efficacy of the FTA as a site of recognition, as well as efforts to undermine its effectiveness and legitimacy, by tracing the domestic tour of the show and noting the critical events within the GI movement that the show helped to promote or even spark. Relying heavily upon original research, including interviews with participants, I reconstruct not only the conditions of each performance, but also the debates that shaped the show's form, content, and changing cast.

Chapter 3 develops a theory of solidarity as a performative political relation that depends, paradoxically, upon precisely that which is supposed to invalidate the performative: the theatrical frame. This theorization proceeds from an analysis of the way the FTA negotiated gender, nationality, and race in preparation for and during the group's tour of the Pacific Rim. If sites of recognition provided the basis for the visibility of the antiwar GI, one of the central debates surrounding the GI movement was what, precisely, should be visible. Which political positions were compatible with the legibility of the GI, and which threatened to obscure his legitimacy as a political actor against the war? The third chapter continues the roughly chronological account of the FTA's history begun in chapter 2, in this case toward drawing out and focusing on the show's production and negotiation of an anti-imperialist counternarrative to Bob Hope's annual visits to bases abroad. I discuss the careful arrangements, both logistical and political (and sometimes quite funny), that preceded the group's arrival in each location, and which facilitated a remarkable level of communication between the show's cast, GIs stationed at a given base, and local activists resisting US military presence, impact, and expansion. A trove of correspondence provides much of the source material for this chapter, as well as interviews with performers. I argue that the FTA's content and presentation carefully navigated and activated solidarity as a performative political relation, and I explore how an added and fledgling emphasis on international solidarity complicated, challenged, and reinforced the show's established goal of connecting GIs and civilians across differences in race, gender, class, and enlisted status. By continuing to perform for a single audience (GIs, though in different locations) while increasingly including material about struggles apparently, if not actually, external to the audience's primary concern of reforming the military and ending the war (e.g., women's liberation, anti-racism, national self-determination, workers' rights), the FTA put into practice a successful model of solidarity in performance. At the same time, I discuss how these efforts often provoked accusations (primarily from other civilian activists) that the group or, more particularly, Fonda possessed an insufficiently authentic connection to the GI movement or to the other issues raised by the revision of the show's content.

Chapter 4 builds on the concept of solidarity developed in chapter 3 by focusing on the question of spectator activity and the actor-spectator divide. To do so, the chapter covers the history of the *FTA!* film, originally released in 1972 but almost immediately pulled from circulation and destroyed; this was reportedly due to a call the head of the production company received from the White House. Alongside Bob Hope's Christmas specials for NBC that, from early 1965 to early 1973, included his performances for soldiers stationed in Vietnam, I examine the *FTA!*'s extensive footage of troops (as audience members, interviewees, and, in a few cases, performers) as reflective of Jacques Rancière's dismissal of the idea of the "passive" spectator. I advance the argument that "distance" (between actor and spectator) constitutes the theatrical space that is necessary for the appearance/performance of solidarity. I also consider the stark difference in how *FTA!* and the Hope specials treated the countries that "hosted" the shows. Where the latter consistently and deliberately staged an encounter with US presence abroad that figured foreign nations as backdrops and prop tables, the former devoted substantial time to interviews with local activists, performances by local artists, and footage of the towns and villages the cast visited. Reading the representation of traveling entertainment in each case, I examine the complicated ways in which the FTA sought to reference and at the same time refuse the many borders they traversed in the film. This chapter also treats the ways in which participants in the GI resistance engaged in their own form of tactical acting, made necessary by the repressive conditions soldiers faced within the military.

The book's final chapter shifts our focus to the actor, following Fonda as she travels to North Vietnam, into the films of Jean-Luc Godard and Jean-Pierre Gorin, and on to her status as "Hanoi Jane." Placing *Tout va bien* and *Letter to Jane* in conversation with the "Hanoi Jane" stories (many of them disproven) that continue to circulate about Fonda's 1972 visit to North Vietnam, I attempt to reconcile the terms according to which her involvement in the antiwar movement and her support for the GI movement have been (and are still) discussed. I consider as well the differing accounts from FTA participants of Fonda's motives and abilities, and Fonda's autobiography and personal statements concerning her status as an actor and the significance of this for her antiwar activity. From an assessment of the illegitimacy and/or inauthenticity frequently ascribed to Fonda's activism because of her status as an actress, I move to consider the way this accusation is mirrored by another accusation that is applied to individual activists and entire movements: that non-actor activists are "acting" in the way that an actor acts. Tracing the discomfort provoked by the actor in proximity to politics from Plato onward, I demonstrate that the 1960s produced a particularly explicit elision of the categories of actor and activist, one that has facilitated a disavowal of the era's radical politics. In response, I argue for refusing a discourse of legitimacy premised upon a discernible personal authenticity, raising instead the possibility that acting as an actor acts may be necessary within an activist context.

Read together, these chapters perform a historiographical and perhaps theatrical act of solidarity, recovering a forgotten radical past that we might make use of in the present, but taking it on its own terms. In a sense, this book resists, for a time, accepting the present, seeing instead the future that a past present imagined.

So as you read feel free to pretend that we haven't lost. Not yet.

1

Seeing the Antiwar Soldier

In 1964, following the commencement of US operations in Vietnam, comedian Bob Hope took his annual Christmas show for the United Service Organizations (USO) on the road, including to soldiers stationed in South Vietnam.[1] The stage shows featured, as they had in past years, movie stars, pageant queens, and popular sports figures, all awkwardly bantering with Hope.[2] The comedian's "brisk one-liners spiced with patriotic flourishes" touched on the banalities of enlisted life but settled finally on a rhetoric of necessary sacrifice.[3] At the conclusion of each of Hope's tours, footage from the performances would be compiled and edited into a ninety-minute television special, broadcast on NBC the following January or February, and watched by millions of American households. The specials offered viewers at home the image of thousands of laughing, healthy, happy young men scattered across the globe, enjoying a well-deserved break from the serious business of fighting the war.

Hope's shows would remain relatively popular throughout the war, though rising antiwar sentiment eventually meant the USO had difficulty attracting the same caliber of celebrity to participate in its programming.[4] Politics aside, and in keeping with the mission of the USO, the shows provided an understandably welcome reprieve from the boredom and danger of enlisted life. They also offered soldiers, via the televised broadcasts, an opportunity to show themselves to family back home, or at least to imagine that they might be able to do so. By the late 1960s, however, the pretense of the proud and pro-war soldier that the shows at once presumed and perpetuated was increasingly contradicted by evidence of a military in crisis. As an outspoken supporter of the war, Hope was forced to confront the fast-changing reality in person; even one of his most admiring biographers felt obligated to note that a picket greeted the "superstar" when he turned up at Long Binh Base in South Vietnam on Christmas Day, 1970.[5] Inside the stadium things were not much better. The cameras had a difficult time avoiding the antiwar placards soldiers had brought along to display, among them "Peace Not Hope," and "Where is Jane Fonda?" At the end of the show at Long Binh, writes Thompson, a group of military policemen made their way onto the stage and unrolled a banner that read "Pigs for Peace." Later in the show, a group of Black GIs "who had been giving clenched-fist salutes throughout the performance" conspicuously walked out of the venue.[6]

The unruly audience Hope faced was only the tip of the iceberg, and while it was easy to edit out evidence of dissent before footage of the shows reached audiences at home, it was internally undeniable. By the early 1970s, GI resistance to the Vietnam War had become so pervasive that even the official journal of the Armed Forces had to acknowledge the unprecedented challenges it posed to the military's ability to function. Writing in June 1971, former Marine Colonel Robert Heinl described the situation in sobering detail:

> The morale, discipline and battleworthiness of the US Armed Forces are, with a few salient exceptions, lower and worse than at any time in this century and possibly in the history of the United States. By every conceivable indicator, our army that now remains in Vietnam is in a state approaching collapse, with individual units avoiding or having refused combat, murdering their officers and noncommissioned officers, drug-ridden and dispirited where not near-mutinous.[7]

Similar assessments followed in *Foreign Affairs* and the *Marine Corps Gazette*, with the former acknowledging the military's "profound crisis in legitimacy due to the impact of Vietnam, internal racial tension, corruption, extensive drug abuse, loss of command and operational effectiveness, and widespread anti-military sentiment."[8] The latter conceded that "there are more problems today than ever before in the history of the Marine Corps, i.e., drug abuse, leadership imbalance, high [unauthorized absence] rate, lack of motivation, and unpopular war, and racial tension."[9] In 1972 Congress published the proceedings from the hearings held by the Committee of Internal Security the year prior, which discussed, in extensive detail, the nature and kind of GI resistance to the war.

In many respects, the crisis Heinl and others described reflected the cumulative impact of the countless individual, noncoordinated ways in which enlisted men expressed dissent and avoided combat, among them conscientious objection, going AWOL, desertion, mutiny, and fragging. Though largely prevented from accessing troops in the field without supervision from officers eager to hide the stark reality, some reporters did manage to publish stories on mutiny, near-mutiny, and the precarious practice of "working it out." In August 1969, the *New York Daily News* ran a story titled "Sir, My Men refuse to Go," which told of a company at Firebase Pace that had disobeyed orders to move out when they knew they were likely to draw enemy fire. In April 1970, a CBS camera crew happened to be present when another mutiny nearly took place, which the officer managed to avoid by "compromising" with his men.[10] In October, *Life* published a more thorough look at this particular phenomenon, in an article titled "You Just Can't Hand Out Orders." Cortright describes "working it out" as "battlefield democracy: commanders frequently had to conform their orders to the wishes of their men, usually by avoiding situations likely to produce casualties."[11] "Working it out" was a way to avoid mutiny, by rescinding or adapting orders such that they finally conformed to a different set of "orders" the soldiers were actually willing to obey.

"Working it out" was a tactic of survival for GIs, but it also made it easier for the military to deny or downplay the existence of such acts; if officers agreed to work it out, then they avoided the much bigger and more sensational problem of mutiny. Thus, although a few such incidents did make it into the press, these could not reflect the sheer scale of the breakdown in discipline commanders were facing in South Vietnam. Disciplining acts of resistance meant, for the military, increasing the visibility of those acts among other soldiers and potentially even drawing attention beyond the perimeter of the base; whether to punish or ignore in each case depended upon a careful assessment of the potential for any punishment to spark greater levels of insubordination or to raise civilian awareness of a crisis in the Armed Forces. For soldiers, avoiding discipline by engaging in covert acts of resistance held, on the one hand, an obvious benefit over overt forms of protest. On the other, precisely because they were "covert," the military could render such acts invisible by simply refusing to acknowledge their existence. Fred Gardner, one of the founders of the GI coffeehouse movement, which I will discuss shortly, describes the tension surrounding the relative benefits of invisible and visible acts of resistance:

> [The GI movement] was infinitely bigger than the GI coffeehouses and other visible manifestations of dissent. It was mostly invisible, in fact, because both soldiers and the ruling class wanted it that way. American GIs—showing the greatest flexibility, using a variety of subtle, brilliant tactics, going out on countless "search and avoid" missions, which were the peace marches that ultimately mattered—brought the war to an end.[12]

The diffuse and tactical invisibility of GI resistance undermined the military's ability to single out individuals for punishment. Yet, to publicize the existence of antiwar sentiment among GIs and to *organize* that sentiment, the movement required some form of visibility, and that visibility required a point of recognition beyond or outside the repressive machinery of the military, which "recognized" acts of resistance in a manner intended to obscure their existence and significance. The resistance needed an audience of civilians willing to see the antiwar soldier.

And the antiwar soldier could be hard to see. For the most part, as Gardner's quote suggests, GIs in Vietnam who were against the war followed the strategy articulated by a young private, as told to *New York Times* correspondent R. Drummond Ayers: "I just work hard at surviving so I can go home and protest all the killing."[13] Even consciously antiwar soldiers recognized and, understandably, accepted the premise that while deployed their ability to protest the war was limited. They couldn't risk visibility, not primarily because of the threat of disciplinary action but more simply because they were fighting for their lives. In some cases, this meant following orders, while in others it might mean refusing them; either way, it was the soldiers returning from Vietnam, radicalized by their experiences in combat, and with time left to serve, who would become the leaders of the GI movement, now in a position to present externally the political perspectives that had previously been largely, though not entirely, hidden.[14] "'If you look closely,'" said the same soldier, "'you'll see some beads and a peace symbol under all this ammo. I may look like Pancho Villa on the outside but on the inside

I'm nothing but a peacenik.'" That the antiwar soldier might "look like" a hardened fighter reflects another dimension of the problem visibility posed to the growth of the GI movement. Such soldiers, acting practically, are easily reframed as patriotic warriors who we can (and must) support by supporting the war. In including the soldier's reference to his beads and peace symbol, the *Times* article participates, on a small scale, in the kind of civilian spectatorship that would help support the development and growth of the GI movement by acknowledging—and validating—its existence.

From Invisible Acts to Organized Resistance

As conditions moved toward the picture painted by Heinl, it became more and more difficult for the Armed Forces to curtail the spread internally of antiwar and antimilitary sentiment (its efforts at suppression and accommodation not withstanding). While individual acts of resistance alone, writes Cortright, "would qualify the Vietnam period as the most disruptive in American history," he goes on to describe in painstaking detail how the unpopularity of the war among enlisted men ultimately gave rise to a "phenomenon of wholly different quality," "a challenge never before experienced within the armed forces: a sustained movement of organized political opposition and resistance."[15] Instances of draft-dodging and going AWOL had been documented as starting to occur almost as soon as the war began, but in the late 1960s GI antiwar sentiment rapidly transformed into a force capable of building a movement proper. By spring of 1971, the same year Heinl published his report and the HCIS conducted its hearings, officials estimated the existence of nearly 150 underground GI newspapers, in many cases circulating illegally on base. By 1972, the number had increased to 250.[16] Active-duty soldiers had begun participating in peace demonstrations by the tens and hundreds, both at home and abroad. Servicemembers also increasingly responded to policies with which they disagreed, and to punishment meted out for antiwar activity, by collectively refusing orders and organizing petitions, strikes, and pickets. Early incidents of more overt resistance were dealt with swiftly and severely, but as these increased in frequency, discipline itself prompted further acts of insubordination, which could then spread to other bases.

Key to this spreading radicalization was the development of a civilian support wing of the GI movement. Because, as Cortright notes, the Army is a daunting institution from within which to attempt to organize resistance to it, some of the initial and continuing efforts to focus antiwar sentiment within the military came from leaders of the civilian peace movement. Some were veterans of earlier wars while others had been enlisted in some capacity prior to the beginning of US involvement in Vietnam. Through targeted efforts, these civilian activists sought to direct GI sentiment into "effective, ongoing political action," and offered various forms of logistical and administrative support to this end.[17] However, and particularly in the early period of the movement's development, many civilian activists perceived their role as not simply supporting what was already happening, but as facilitating interaction between GIs and antiwar civilians. This was both in the interest of raising the former's political consciousness, and also to make GIs aware of what was happening on other bases. Many of those involved in this work were part of organizations on the far left that viewed encouraging GI resistance as part of a larger, revolutionary project. This, in the HCIS report referenced above, becomes evidence that some antiwar civilian activists were not sincerely interested in supporting the GI movement, but only in recruiting their targets to Marxism-Leninism, Maoism, Communism, or some combination of these. This premise also became the grounds for claiming that "real" soldiers were not involved in antiwar activity, and that antiwar GIs were actually radical leftists "posing" as soldiers. I will return shortly to the question of soldiers acting like radicals and civilians acting like soldiers, but for now the important point is that civilians, precisely because they could not *join* the GI movement (unless they enlisted), could validate the possibility of being an antiwar GI by establishing spaces that addressed him as such.

The first civilian-led strategy to become a force in facilitating a process of recognition and deassimilation was the coffeehouse project.[18] One of its founders, Fred Gardner, after a tour of active duty as a reservist, perceived the need for "a place independent of military influence where [soldiers] could meet and freely exchange ideas about the war and the Army."[19] Gardner and others, including those later involved in organizing the FTA show, recognized and sought to exploit the tendency of the military to be quite conservative in the entertainment it offered the troops. (During World War II, acclaimed productions of contemporary plays, including some that had been staged on Broadway and presented to high school students, would routinely be turned down because of a desire to avoid politics and even "topicality.")[20] With the help of Donna Mickelson and other activists, Gardner opened the first coffeehouse in late 1967 in Columbia, SC, near Fort Jackson. When, the following summer, in the wake of the Tet Offensive, the Army's repression of a "pray-in" organized by GIs stationed at Fort Jackson made national headlines, it drew the attention of prominent antiwar organizations to the coffeehouse project. Representatives of the National Mobilization Committee to End the War in Vietnam visited the UFO, and proposed creating a network of antiwar coffeehouses near bases around the country.[21] In fact, new coffeehouses were already underway. In June 1968, two young activists—Josh Gould, who had helped start the UFO, and Jay Lockard—tried to open a coffeehouse outside Fort Polk, in Leesville, Louisiana. Unable to get this off the ground, they headed to Killeen, Texas, having heard that Gardener had rented space there for the purposes of starting a project near Fort Hood.[22] The Oleo Strut opened in Killeen in July 1968, followed shortly thereafter by the Shelter Half in Tacoma, Washington, the Fort Dix Coffeehouse in New Jersey, the Covered Wagon in Mountain Home, Idaho, and the Haymarket Coffeehouse in Fayetteville. All told, between 1968 and 1974, over twenty coffeehouses opened near major military installations across the US.

In addition to offering a space soldiers might use to organize, the political significance of the coffeehouse lay also in the simple fact of providing an alternative to an institution that used the rhetoric of "morale" to suture the sentiment of "supporting the troops" to that of "supporting the war." The name of the "UFO," for example, referenced with no small amount of irony the nearby "cavernous, moribund" USO, whose stated aim of "supporting the troops" was suddenly forced to confront its political and cultural difference from the sort of support the coffeehouses sought to provide.[23] It was the establishment of these alternative spaces, in other words, that undermined the USO's implicit claim of objectively seeking to "boost morale." Culturally, the coffeehouses disrupted the pretense that the USO reflected the tastes of the GIs, which its conservative bent prevented it from doing. Similarly, their popularity demonstrated that troops might be interested in "support" that did not

Soldiers gather outside the Oleo Strut coffeehouse in Killeen, Texas. Photo credit: Alan Pogue. Courtesy of the artist.

presume the legitimacy or necessity of the war in Vietnam. This drew attention to the fact that the USO, in claiming to represent the interests of soldiers by offering them entertainment and respite, did so directly in the interests of maintaining the efficacy and battleworthiness of the US Armed Forces.

Sites of Recognition

At a crucial moment, then, in the development of the GI movement, as it consolidated individual acts of covert resistance into more overt and coordinated forms of protest, civilian activists offered the antiwar GI sites of recognition, and posed a direct challenge to the existing mechanisms used by the military to demand public support for the war. The forms that organized GI resistance subsequently took reflect that the movement depended for its growth and power in part upon the successful projection of an alternative to the image of the "typical" American military servicemember—obedient, clean-cut, patriotic, and proud to serve. This was an image that the USO, and Hope's tours in particular, helped to circulate among soldiers and civilians alike, ostensibly providing evidence that those fighting the war felt none of the frustration, confusion, or disagreement with foreign policy in such sharp evidence at home. The usefulness to the American military of the image of the committed and—given that Hope's shows had not changed much since he'd performed for the troops during the Korean War—culturally conservative soldier consisted in the way it could draw (while it was able) a sharp line between the American soldier and the antiwar civilian. Despite being largely of the same generation, the GI, in a clean uniform with close-cropped hair, stood in stark visual contrast to the shaggy, button-covered activist flashing a peace sign and smoking a joint (though this image is itself a reductive reimagining of the '60s activist, one largely rooted in contemporary revisions of the era's significance; I will return to this point). The more that soldiers looked like members of the same generation of young people who protested the war (among other things), the more difficult it would become to make the argument that the two groups were fundamentally counterposed. That the committed/conservative image described the majority of soldiers was no longer the reality (if it ever had been), but it was possible for the military to maintain this image, so long as those who might challenge it remained atomized and subject to disciplinary measures that effectively denied and erased the existence of dissent.

Despite growing resistance, Hope's broadcasts (and the mainstream media more generally) could continue to circulate the image of the implicitly pro-war soldier so long as there was not a viable counterimage of the American GI. To the extent that the antiwar GI's attempts at visibility happened in spaces controlled by the military, he could simply, and often quite literally, as with Hope's broadcasts, be edited out of the picture. And although major newspapers, as mentioned above, carried coverage of incidents of insubordination, the military had developed a strategy of dismissing evidence of troop disaffection in the same way it had dealt with the massacre at My Lai—by insisting that acts of resistance and the perpetration of war crimes were the exception rather than the rule, and that the men responsible constituted a tiny minority within the Armed Forces. The potential power of the antiwar GI was understood as his ability to challenge the premise that being against the war meant being against its soldiers, but this depended upon his

Members of Vietnam Veterans Against the War being arrested at the Pentagon, April, 1971. Photo credit: Maurice Simon. Courtesy of the National Office of Vietnam Veterans Against the War.

legibility *as* a GI. Veterans and servicemembers and their civilian allies recognized the importance of framing their dissent in terms that preserved, and played upon, their legibility as soldiers.[24] However, because the military consistently tried to refuse these soldiers recognition—by redefining them as not "real" soldiers—antiwar GIs depended upon the development of alternative sites of recognition, which could establish the legitimacy of the antiwar soldier *as soldier*.

This was necessarily a contradictory pursuit. Taking action in opposition to the war *as soldiers* required soldiers and veterans to "act out" their status as such, because otherwise that status might not be apparent. In the '60s, many soldiers were using the GI Bill to become college students, swelling the ranks of antiwar activists on campuses across the US, while also unintentionally giving cover to the eventual dismissal of antiwar activism as an exclusively student-led venture. College-based chapters of Vietnam Veterans Against the War (VVAW) worked with other student organizations to oppose the presence of military recruiters on campus, and the spaces and institutions of campus life provided ample opportunities to stage and publicize antiwar actions. Historian

Richard Moser notes that one of the most successful demonstrations happened during a homecoming football game at the University of Michigan. "Tens of thousands of fans stood hushed as a hundred veterans silently released black balloons and offered up a clenched fist salute to the war dead." He cites VVAW's campus campaigns as integral to the group's emergence as a national phenomenon in 1971.[25] However, as significant as the antiwar student-GI was in organizing highly visible peace demonstrations, the GI himself was easy to erase, both then and now. In *The Spitting Image*, Jerry Lembcke shows that while Hollywood films from the 1960s initially included representations of activist veterans and pro-veteran, antiwar civilians, by 1970 veterans were absent from depictions of campus antiwar organizing and already subject to "the misrepresentation of the Vietnam veteran either through his mythologization as the 'good' veteran or his 'otherization' as a person who was criminal, crippled, or crazy."[26] In the face of narratives that downplayed or rejected altogether the possibility of a politicized, activist soldier, antiwar veterans and GIs needed to maintain visibility *as* veterans and GIs. Paradoxically, then, the very line that the military attempted to maintain between the GI and the antiwar civilian was also one upon which the GI movement depended. For this reason it was important to preserve the identity of the soldier as soldier, even as many of the young men returning from Vietnam increasingly identified with the more radical movements historically associated with the 1960s. The soldier/veteran had to remain recognizable as such to put the weight of GI authority behind antiwar sentiment and actions, both to embolden civilian activists and to encourage the spread of resistance within the ranks of the Armed Forces.

Seeing the Antiwar Veteran

In confronting popular opposition to the war among American civilians, the war's supporters deployed the presumed authority of the pro-war veteran alongside the image of the active-duty soldier in need of public support. Thus, as Vietnam veterans began to organize against the war, they looked for ways to harness the legitimacy, authority, and visibility of their status as such to counter the narrative put forward by the Johnson and, to a much greater extent, Nixon administrations. In part, this was a matter of institutionalization, contesting the assumption or perception that pro-war veterans' groups spoke for all veterans. Vietnam Veterans Against the War—the first and most important of the era's antiwar Vietnam veterans' organization—started unofficially in 1967, at a peace demonstration at the United Nations in New York City. A handful of antiwar Vietnam veterans met each other after other activists (and antiwar veterans of other wars) encouraged them to go the front of the march. The six men who ended up holding a banner that read "Vietnam Veterans Against the War" became the founders of VVAW. Through advertisements, traveling speakers, and veteran-run publications, the grassroots organization quickly grew to a membership of thousands.

As the scope and scale of the antiwar movement increased, VVAW began to organize veteran-specific antiwar demonstrations. These took the form of explicitly countering the image the military projected of the pro-war soldier by proposing an alternative interpretation of patriotism.[27] In doing so, they followed a precedent set by an ad hoc group of World War II and Korean War veterans who called themselves Veterans For Peace in Vietnam. This group had run an ad in 1965 in support of an upcoming peace demonstration and organized the earliest veteran actions against the Vietnam War. In addition to participating in the construction of an antiwar veteran identity, Veterans For Peace in Vietnam "foreshadowed later VVAW activities by returning medals and discharge papers to President Johnson."[28] As the Nixon administration ramped up its efforts to diminish the existence of antiwar soldiers and veterans, such decidedly theatrical tactics depended upon a separate, civilian audience able to legitimize their theatricality as grounded in an authentic GI identity. In other words, antiwar veterans had to "act out" the military service that qualified them as veterans because to be antiwar was to call into question one's status *as* a veteran. The image of the antiwar GI was one the military, and the Nixon administration more generally, attempted to keep in check, in part by trying to define soldiers not on the basis of their enlistment status, but on the basis of the extent to which they adhered to the description of the pro-war soldier. In *The New Winter Soldiers*, Moser quotes veteran David Curry describing the way military officials transparently tried to rationalize the problem of low GI morale:

It was decided at the top that the reason our morale problem was so bad in Vietnam had to be because of outside agitators. And it had to be because of Vietnam Veterans Against the War—who were disguised as soldiers all over Vietnam at that time. So when I got back to the United States one of the first things I did was join Vietnam Veterans Against the War.[29]

This is a remarkable premise: Vietnam Veterans Against the War, an organization whose members are veterans, sends its members into Vietnam "disguised" as soldiers. The operating logic appears to be that, if a soldier stationed in Vietnam is against the war, he is not a soldier, but someone disguised as a soldier. His disguise, however, covers up the fact that he is a veteran; but because he is a Veteran Against the War, he is not really a veteran, because he was never really a soldier. Antiwar soldiers, in turn, who are not yet veterans, will never become veterans because they are merely disguised as soldiers, and as such they cannot become "real" veterans, only Veterans Against the War. Clearly members would have had to struggle to insist that being antiwar did not automatically render their status as veterans inadmissible in the court of public opinion. They did so, as we will see, through a series of theatrical acts that troubled the premise of a singular, "authentic" veteran identity, by featuring veterans "acting like" veterans.

In *The Spitting Image*, Lembcke gives a bit more of a sense of just what the antiwar GI was up against. He examines the development of what he demonstrates (quite persuasively) is the myth of the spat-upon Vietnam veteran and describes the way the Nixon administration supplemented its broad attacks on the antiwar movement's loyalty with a coordinated "grassroots" effort to draw a distinction between "good" and "bad" veterans. Declaring the second week in November 1969 "Honor America Week," the administration explicitly asked National Guardsmen to fly American flags at their homes and to drive with their lights on. Conservative veterans groups took up the call, providing a "veteran's voice speaking from the pro-war side." Lembcke continues:

> That it was not a voice in any way representative of the Vietnam generation of veterans was not a detail the public was likely to notice. It would be the voice of veterans carrying the imprimatur of established organizations with high visibility throughout the nation. [. . .] The ultimate effect

was to displace the Vietnam veteran in the public's mind's eye with the mythological "good" Vietnam veteran modeled after the conservative veterans from previous wars.[30]

In chapter 5, I will look more closely at the use of acting rhetoric to discredit activists. For now, I want to note how this authenticity-based delegitimization and erasure of antiwar GIs demonstrated the need for civilian sites of recognition, and for the GI movement to establish an organization or organizations comparable to the VFW, and its "imprimatur." As the profile of the VVAW rose, it began to function in this regard, but to decidedly different ends.

Between 1970 and 1971, Vietnam Veterans Against the War planned a series of events that emphasized the connection between GI resistance and key aspects of military and US history, and which drew upon recognizable forms of military engagement in the interest of drawing attention to the legitimacy and urgency of dissent. In September 1970, Operation Rapid American Withdrawal saw 120 veterans retrace the route used by the Continental Army through New Jersey and Pennsylvania to Valley Forge.[31] Over the course of three days, the soldiers marched through small towns en route to the site at which "America's first citizen-soldiers endured the worst days of the Revolution." Thomas Paine had called these men the war's "winter soldiers," and the term was one the movement would adopt as its own. Moser describes the scene:

> Dressed in fatigues and carrying toy weapons, the marchers trailed through small towns receiving support from some and condemnation from others. Whistling "Yankee Doodle Dandy," the new winter soldiers delivered the war to America's doorstep. As they passed through quiet villages they reenacted violent scenes from search-and-destroy missions."[32]

Civilian antiwar activists participated in these staged maneuvers as detainees, and footage of the action shows men and women with

---

(*Facing page*) During Operation Rapid American Withdrawal, antiwar veterans marched from Morristown, New Jersey, to Valley Forge in Pennsylvania. Along the way, and with the help of civilians playing the role of detainees, they conducted mock raids on the local population. At the end of the march the veterans were met by an audience of civilian supporters, who watched as they performed an "arms breaking" ceremony.
Photo credit: Sheldon Ramsell. Courtesy of the National Office of Vietnam Veterans Against the War.

their wrists bound, usually blindfolded, dragged along or strung up in a tree. Though the interactions between the veteran-soldiers and civilian-detainees are clearly controlled and agreed upon in advance, the encounters feel dangerous, as they are certainly meant to. Critically, then, even as these civilian supporters become performers alongside the veterans, they retain their legibility as *not*-veterans. This is a line they will not and cannot cross. They are not equal participants in the action, and not all roles are made available to all actors. The civilians occupy a position that is doubly disidentified with power relative to the US soldier, as they represent both the Vietnamese victims of the war and also themselves—the antiwar civilian participating in a veteran-led protest. As such, they direct our attention toward the quite specific power of the active-duty soldier, and assist in asserting the authority of the antiwar veteran by facilitating his (re)performance of military service.

At one point, in an incident that highlights the time-warping intersection of the activist "disguised" as a soldier and/or disguised as a veteran and the mobilization of the image of the "good" veteran of earlier wars, the marchers came upon a counterdemonstration organized by members of the Veterans of Foreign Wars. "One man called out, 'Why don't you go to Hanoi? They need boys like you.'"[33] Of course, the men marching were doing so in their capacity *as veterans*, as boys who had been to Hanoi. The heckler attempts to categorize the protesters as not-veterans—a categorization that may or may not be able to take hold, depending upon the movement's ability to challenge the traditional image of the good, patriotic, pro-war veteran.

When the soldiers reached Valley Forge, they were met by some fifteen hundred supporters. As the crowd chanted "Peace now!" the marchers "smartly presented their mock weapons for public review." The drill climaxed with the final orders called out in military cadence, "Company present arms—break arms!" The soldiers obeyed, "breaking and smashing their plastic guns in a wishful parody of American withdrawal."[34] Without the presence of a civilian audience that did not participate in the activities meant to echo those involved in military service, the staged display would not necessarily have been able to register as built upon the authority of its participants' identity as GIs. To gain validity and visibility, the GIs had to put on a show, occupying a space otherwise affiliated with the fake or the not-real and soliciting an audience that would, in its ability to *see* the antiwar GI *as GI*, challenge the established image recognized by the state.

Five months later, VVAW held the Winter Soldier Investigation in Detroit, Michigan, which featured over one hundred veterans testifying to the war crimes carried out by American forces in Vietnam, which they had witnessed or perpetrated. The three-day event was directed in part at claims by the US military that the recently uncovered My Lai massacre was not the result of US policy but rather the sole responsibility of the individual, low-level soldiers who had committed the atrocities. The Winter Soldier hearings were intended instead to "allow veterans to testify in a context that would link these atrocities to military policies," that is, to provide a space for that which was repressed from the military's official, mediated accounts of progress in Vietnam.[35] As with the breaking of the toy weapons, the hearings "acted out" an alternative version of an established process, while deploying the authenticity of the "actors" as the basis for the legitimacy of these theatrical acts.[36]

A final example comes in April 1971, when VVAW organized a series of actions in Washington, DC, where, Moser writes, "With the steps of government buildings as their stages, the veterans orchestrated antiwar theatre."[37] Much of what the soldiers performed disrupted any stable differentiation between symbolic and "real" actions. Over one thousand soldiers camped out on the Mall. A candlelight vigil ended with a group of veterans raising the flag, striking many present as a new Iwo Jima. Later, two thousand veterans lined up, in fatigues, to participate in a medal-returning ceremony. Moser writes, "One by one the citizen soldiers approached a microphone. Pronouncing declarations of anger and peace, of rage and repentance, the veterans hurled their honorable discharges, medals, and ribbons onto the Capital steps." Some had been given medals to throw by fellow soldiers who couldn't make the trip.

For the veterans present, the events felt as though they might spontaneously, radically transform the situation:

Right at that instant . . . we wouldn't have been surprised if somebody said, "Hey Nixon just announced that all the troops will be out of Nam and back home by supper." We would have believed it at that instant . . . We thought we'd finally done it.

As evidence of the precarious nature of what the GIs perceived to be both symbolic and impactful, "real" actions, Moser notes the reaction of some GIs when they discovered that reporters were picking up the medals they had thrown: "Listen, you newsmen, we're not giving you the medals. We're turning them in to the country . . . don't touch them!"[38] The way in which the theatricality of this moment feels, to those enacting it, as if it might produce a new reality is punctured by its own precarious dependence upon the theatrical frame: the reporters reduce the medals to props, which of course they always already were, from their ceremonial presentation in the first place, to their dramatic and differently ceremonial return to the steps of the capitol. Their capacity to signify one way or the other (or at all) hinges upon the perception of the spectators present. It is really quite remarkable to consider the layered meaning of these medals in this moment, through the phenomenological lens of the prop. They have to be the medals that were originally presented in order to carry the weight and significance of that presentation; at the same time, this status is overthrown, so to speak, by the act of "returning" them, which refuses to allow the medal to mean in the way it is intended and turns it into a symbol of betrayal. And yet, the act of symbolically—and also *really*—returning that symbol feels, in this moment, to the GI participants, as if it might trigger some non-symbolic change. When the reporters pick up the medals, they may be mistaking the real for a prop, or a prop for the real, but in any case they provoke a collapse in the significatory possibilities of the theatrical act.

As these examples make clear (and there were others), to challenge and ultimately replace the monolithic image of the pro-war soldier, GIs had to develop tactics of circumventing the military's highly effective and totalizing means of representation. Because this depended upon reclaiming the figure of the GI, they deployed their tactics always and necessarily under threat. On the one hand, this was the threat of repression in the most literal sense, as those undertaking acts of organized resistance—attending protests, circulating petitions or underground newspapers—were swiftly subjected to disciplinary measures, ranging from dishonorable discharge to jail time. But by threat I also mean to refer to the ever-present possibility that the alternative identity proposed by the antiwar GI movement would fail to register or be recognized as legitimate, and so render invisible those who rejected the military's projected image of the pro-war soldier. That such a threat existed, and in fact was realized, is made clear by the absence of the GI movement from the popular perception of the Vietnam era. More immediately, we see the reality of this threat in the media blackout that attended the Winter Soldier Investigation in 1971, leaving largely untouched the military's claims that My Lai was an isolated incident, carried out by individual soldiers working against official orders. Yet despite the ultimate erasure of the GI movement, at the time organized antiwar GI sentiment posed a real and present threat to the project of the war in Vietnam. Cortright's analysis makes this exceptionally clear, and it is difficult here to overstate the scale and seriousness of the GI movement.

The War "Winds Down" While the Movement Heats Up

The movement continued to grow in size and scope even as the Nixon administration, ushered into office in 1968 in part on the basis of promises to deescalate US involvement in Vietnam, drew down ground troops and shifted its focus skyward. However, the movement kept pace with this change in strategy, and soon rates of desertion and organized insubordination at Air Force bases rivaled those that had rattled Army bases earlier in the war.[39] This change in foreign policy took place at the same time as a change in military structure, as the administration began to develop plans to eliminate the draft and shift to an all-volunteer force. Both changes were, at least in part, a response to the impact of the GI movement, on the war and on discipline, and both were limited in their immediate success. However, in the longevity of their impact, both shifts ultimately produced the desired effect, of reasserting military discipline and excising the GI movement from popular perceptions of the Vietnam War. This was achieved in part by appropriating and incorporating, albeit selectively, some of the visual signifiers of the countercultural GI while evacuating his political content. By declaring, for example, that long hair no longer constituted an act of resistance or defiance, and therefore was not evidence of antiwar or radical sentiment, the military could more easily claim that such sentiment did not exist.

The next chapter will treat at greater length how civilian efforts to support the GI movement, among them the FTA, adapted to the fact that radicalization was spreading to the Air Force and Navy. For now, I want to focus on the effects of "liberalization" policies intended to depoliticize changes soldiers were already forcing in military structure, discipline, and image. As commanding officers increasingly found it next to impossible to enforce regulations governing personal appearance, it became apparent that it was preferable to change the rules up to a point rather than acknowledge how readily soldiers were breaking them. After assuming office, Nixon appointed a commission on the "All-Volunteer Force," under the chairmanship of Thomas Gates (the Gates Commission), with the intention of moving toward eliminating the draft by determining what changes it would be necessary to make in order to persuade sufficient numbers of young people to enlist and those already enlisted to remain. Its report, rendered quickly, resulted in immediate adjustments, including the revision of "appearance regulations," to "allow slightly longer hair." Additional measures included "relaxed uniform regulations, beer in the barracks, the opening of hard rock clubs, [and] allowance of beards and longer hair," as well as "eliminating morning reveille, easing pass restrictions, and introducing beer in the mess hall."[40] In *Dangerous Grounds*, Parsons notes that among the efforts associated with the program was the establishment by the military of "psychedelic—but not antiwar" coffeehouses, including the Right Side at Fort Hood in Killeen, Texas, and the Inscape at Fort Carson in Colorado Springs.[41] As I mentioned previously, by the late 1960s, soldiers were engaged in countless but still largely isolated and so invisible acts of resistance. Among troops deployed in Vietnam, the reality of "working it out" with commanding officers indicates that one of the military's unofficial strategies in dealing with disaffection in the ranks was to accommodate dissent in such a way that it would not appear *as* dissent. The same basic premise applied to the policies developed in response to the Gates Commission, though these were not, of course, presented in such terms. By making official changes in policy where there were already unofficial changes in practice, the military went some distance toward correcting the appearance that they no longer had control of their troops.

While, as Cortright writes, "beer in the barracks and an extra inch of hair could not erase opposition to Vietnam, nor halt the growing GI resistance," these efforts demonstrated a need for the GI movement to grapple with the visibility and legibility of the antiwar GI, and in particular to navigate the precarious terrain of performance with ever more creativity and agility.[42] If theatrical tactics were necessary to establishing the legitimacy and legibility of the antiwar GI, and indeed they were, these also continually posed a threat to that same legitimacy, to the extent that the theatrical or self-signaling was (and is) easily dismissed, rendered not-real, and could even be, paradoxically, enlisted in recuperating the very image it sought to contest. The movement struggled to achieve recognition from soldiers and civilians alike, doing combat with the overwhelming circulation, ramped up during the Nixon years, of a narrative that sutured antiwar activism to anti-soldier sentiment. To be an antiwar soldier was to be not a soldier at all—but rather something like an actor, or an infiltrator—an activist undercover, who looks like a soldier, and occupies the position of a soldier, but who has intentions other than those a soldier properly has. This connects, too, to the way in which GI dissent during the Vietnam era is represented now as largely the product of the draft, when in fact, as Cortright demonstrates, this was not the case. A 1972 study found that "volunteer soldiers were more prone to go AWOL than draftees."[43] The VOLAR program, however, aside from the policies it ultimately established, served an important function in its very premise, insofar as it validated the idea that the military's problems could be traced to soldiers who, in their unwillingness to volunteer, weren't really soldiers at all. An all-volunteer force solves this problem, not in fact but simply in appearance, so long as the military successfully downplays the largely economic factors that lead to enlistment today (and the overwhelming concentration of recruitment offices in lower income areas, particularly within Black and Latinx communities), while pretending to present the public with soldiers politically committed to US foreign policy, because they signed up. Insidiously, this logic folds back on the soldiers themselves, offering little ground for internal criticism or dissent by insisting that signing up was a simple matter of choice.

In the face of VOLAR and policies that might let GIs look a bit more like civilians, the movement would need sites of recognition and modes of performance that could facilitate the development of a broader political analysis capable of countering the military's efforts at obscuring the image and existence of the antiwar GI. In part, developing these sites would come from asserting the interconnectedness of the war with other forms of oppression—racism, sexism, imperialism—and rejecting military efforts to appeal to the GI as a figure set, somehow, apart from these concerns. Yet the legibility of the antiwar GI *as* GI would remain a critical and complicated necessity for the movement's growth, and the debates that arose over whether this legibility could be retained in the face of an expanded perception of the US soldier's identities and political interests impacted the organizing efforts of soldiers and civilians alike.

In addition, then, to the extensive logistical support civilians could provide the movement, antiwar civilians who recognized the critical nature of GI resistance to the project of ending the war also offered a site of recognition. Civilian supporters held a mirror up to the movement by building alternatives to the institutions that claimed to serve the interests of the troops. As a result, the cultivation of the image of the "soldier in revolt" as a legitimate one with which to identify depended upon the participation of non-soldiers. While this may seem, on some level, paradoxical, it reflects the way in which the image of the patriotic soldier was (and is) itself primarily constructed and circulated by groups and individuals outside of, though working in close connection with, the military establishment. As one among a number of strategic civilian interventions, the FTA would become a critical counter to the institutionalized image of the pro-war GI offered by the USO and broadcast to the public via Hope's annual Christmas specials. Ultimately, contesting the narrative that supporting the troops meant supporting the war depended upon a *dual* visibility, of both the antiwar soldier or veteran and, simultaneously, the civilian audience capable of "seeing" him as such. A self-consciously theatrical situation was needed to displace the entirely staged but officially not-at-all-staged spectacle of the soldier happy to serve. Though we will turn next to the FTA—which was, literally, a theatrical situation—we should keep in mind that its civilian actors were nevertheless spectators, engaged in the work of seeing the antiwar soldier.

2

Staging the Movement

In the fall of 1970, ex-Army doctor Howard Levy asked Jane Fonda to meet with him to discuss an idea. At the time of their meeting Levy was, as Fonda puts it, himself a "celebrity" within the GI movement.[1] In March 1966, he had been court-martialed for refusing to train Green Beret medics at Fort Jackson "on the grounds that Special Forces units were responsible for war crimes in Vietnam." The case became high profile when the judge agreed to allow Levy's lawyer to pursue a Nuremburg defense, which granted Levy permission to accuse the US of violating international law. "Thus," as a New York Times reporter wrote in the run-up to the trial, "for the first time in US history, a domestic court may hear evidence that elite American troops commit atrocious acts on the battlefield as a matter of policy."[2] While, in the end, Levy lost and served twenty-six months of a three-year sentence doing hard labor at Fort Leavenworth, his case positioned him to become an important figure within the GI movement.[3] After his release he moved to New York and began working as an organizer with the United States Servicemen's Fund (USSF). The USSF had evolved out of the coffeehouse movement and quickly became "the most important agency for providing material aid to GI papers and coffeehouses around the world."[4] Notably, its activities extended well beyond these two central areas of work and included providing entertainment. As a result, the USSF was well positioned to organize and sponsor a national tour of the sort Levy had in mind: "something like a Bob Hope type show, you know touring the bases and giving the troops some really first-class entertainment—sort of an alternative Bob Hope show."[5]

Levy's choice of Fonda was no accident: in addition to being a *bona fide* star, she was already well known within the GI movement. The previous year, she'd met Fred Gardner at a screening of Antonioni's *Zabriskie Point* (Gardner had been one of the screenwriters) and mentioned she was planning a trip across the country to visit American Indian reservations. At the time, as she put it, she "didn't even know what a coffeehouse was."⁶ According to Gardner, by the spring of 1970, he was already disillusioned by what he considered the political opportunism of the civilian activists involved in running the coffeehouses. He explained to Fonda that he was "going in the other direction, away from the movement, but that [he] would send her a map of the coffeehouses, which she could visit if she was so inclined."⁷ Fonda was indeed inclined. Though unfamiliar with the coffeehouse movement, she'd met American deserters while living in Paris, and this encounter had radically changed her perspective on the war. In a statement from 1972 provided to the House Committee on Internal Security, she describes how, immediately following her conversation with Gardner, she sought out information on the GI movement, meeting nightly with "different people, young lawyers involved with military law, some of the organizers of the movement."⁸

Over the course of that summer, Fonda visited GI coffeehouses from California to Colorado to DC, including some that would host performances of the FTA the following year. She went on the road again in the fall of the same year, this time specifically to raise money for the upcoming Winter Soldier Investigation by speaking at dozens of colleges, churches, coffeehouses, and public rallies. When Fonda appeared on campuses, it was often alongside a member of the VVAW, with the intent of encouraging student veterans to start a local chapter. At the time, noted a vet interviewed by Richard Stacewicz, "The colleges were filled with thousands of vets coming back."⁹

Along with John Kerry, she spoke during Operation Rapid American Withdrawal in 1970, at the rally following the veterans' destruction of their toy weapons. Fonda's experiences speaking to and with veterans and GIs in coffeehouses across the country in the year preceding the FTA's formation made her an exceptionally well-informed and credible celebrity advocate for the movement. She also possessed sufficient star power to attract the desired level of publicity and a broad GI audience, and to get other celebrities involved. At the time of her meeting with Levy, she was in New York filming *Klute*, for which she would win an Oscar the following year, and it was in the process of fundraising for the Winter Soldier hearings that Fonda drew together well-known singers and actors into a program she called "Acting in Concert for Peace." Many of these performers would later join her in the FTA, including Dick Gregory and Donald Sutherland. Fonda, for her part, loved Levy's proposal, particularly the opportunity to combine her work and her politics beyond the uninspiring but fruitful task of asking for money from rich acquaintances. She quickly went to work enlisting friends and colleagues to perform.

In identifying a practical point of intervention at the intersection of celebrity and politics, Levy, and others in the USSF, were recognizing that the GI movement could benefit from stepping outside a generally countercultural approach to recruitment and legibility, thereby making it more difficult for the military to down-play the unpopularity of the war among enlisted men and women. While Fonda was connected to antiwar activism, she was also decidedly mainstream in the nature of her celebrity. The tour would ultimately overlap with *Klute*'s release in theaters, and just two years prior she'd starred in the hyper-sexualized sci-fi film *Barbarella*. In many respects, and due in large part to the similarity she bore, in appearance and profession, to the kinds of celebrity guests Hope's tours featured, Fonda's participation could be counted on to draw multiple kinds of attention, from those already aware of her activism to those familiar only with her work as an actress. Attention gained via the latter could easily give way to a new awareness of the former, and so make the GI movement visible to soldiers via evidence of its visibility among (celebrity) civilians. Her star status provided "cover" to the group's political intentions, but this premise also ultimately provoked conflict over what precisely those intentions were or should be. Moreover, in its dependence upon celebrity and its emphasis on entertainment (even as these were at the center of debates over efficacy and political meaning), the FTA complicates two key narratives related to performance and politics, and highlights the ways in which they intersect: a narrative of the era's political theater that emphasizes experimentation and "authenticity," and a narrative of the era's activism that positions 1960s activists as having been merely playing at revolutionary politics. Against these, the FTA offers a way of examining the necessarily performative and theatrical dimensions of revolutionary politics and activism through the debates, tactics, and discourse that marked its brief existence.

Mixing Celebrity and Politics

The FTA at its beginning was consciously premised upon the participation primarily of well-known celebrities within the entertainment industry. In addition to meeting the needs of the movement, this was also a reflection of an established wish on Fonda's part to mobilize Hollywood's substantial left wing in support of the antiwar movement more generally. Alongside making plans for the first FTA show at Fort Bragg in Fayetteville, North Carolina, Fonda helped to found the Entertainment Industry for Peace and Justice (EIPJ). The organization was intended to—and did—serve as a fundraising vehicle for the FTA. Coverage of an organizing meeting for EIPJ in the *Philadelphia Inquirer* features Fonda and Sutherland explicitly acknowledging a strategy of leveraging the influence wielded by celebrities among the broader population: "Miss Fonda declared, to applause: 'We in this town can do more than any other constituency in the country to mobilize the people. I think it's our joyful obligation to make these things a reality.'"[10] Ultimately, as the tour progressed, Fonda and Sutherland would both shift to a discourse that attempted to downplay the star-status of its celebrity performers. At its outset, however, celebrity was a relatively uncomplicated part of the way the actors conceived of their role in protesting the war. It was also very much the way Gardner, among others, understood the project of presenting the FTA, as made clear by the fact that when the show shifted away from this conception, he would express frustration with its insistence upon an expanded and interconnected political perspective.

While the Entertainment Industry for Peace and Justice sought to organize and so make apparent Hollywood opposition to the war generally, the FTA show specifically targeted that area of Hollywood involvement in foreign policy that remained decidedly hawkish and conservative: entertaining the troops. Bob Hope's tours for the USO had long presumed to speak at once to and for the men and women of the Armed Services; Hope and the war's supporters used the positive response to Hope's annual performances as evidence of a patriotic desire among the troops to continue fighting; or at the very least, as evidence of the untenability of being against the war yet in support of the troops. I will return to the Hope specials in chapter 4, but it is important to note here how explicitly the specials sutured support for the soldiers to support for the war:

at the conclusion of the 1971 broadcast, for example, Hope's voiceover insists that "the least we can do is work together [because] our greatest strength is unity." The men we've just seen on our screens "deserve the full support" of the American people.[11] Hope made this dynamic just as clear in a comment to reporters about the formation of the FTA, when he stated that "it's obvious from a jury of 80,000,000 who watched our TV show of this year's trip that those kids over there weren't from Central Casting."[12] Indirectly, Hope's remark evokes the figure of the antiwar activist "disguised" as a soldier, even as it betrays an awareness of just how carefully the image of the pro-war, patriotic GI was being built and deployed. In fact, in comparison to the FTA's spectators, who might risk official or unofficial discipline for attending an antiwar show, Hope's performances were officially sanctioned and sometimes compulsory. Units were flown in, and a dress code enforced—the soldiers needed to look like soldiers. While a far cry from central casting, the footage of Hope's audiences that appeared on TV screens at home was undoubtedly edited with an eye to producing a particular "type."

In many respects, the Hope show was political precisely to the extent that it largely avoided an explicitly political message, presuming a political position as opposed to taking one. The war was not up for debate—it had to be fought, and all that remained was to entertain the young men obligated to fight it. (Significantly, Hope took a different tone with his broadcast audience, as the war became increasingly unpopular at home. While the footage taken from the live performances remained relatively neutral politically, his voiceover directly charged domestic viewers with supporting the troops by recognizing the legitimacy and necessity of the war.) The *New York Times* described the shows as "generally confined to traditional gibes at military foibles," and Paul Berg of the *St. Louis Post-Dispatch* noted that

> "GI humor was once concerned primarily with soldiers' gripes about such matters as chow, latrine and KP duty, hurry-up-and-wait routines, officers. It was barracks humor, and tension could be released by saying "Blow it out your barracks bag" or "Tell it to the chaplain."[13]

The Hope shows permitted a degree of irreverence while reinforcing and reifying the hierarchical structure and purpose of the Armed Forces.

Although Hope might crack jokes about "the brass," he could do so only because his routine was officially, visibly sanctioned *by* the brass: at every stop, a local commander would introduce the comedian, and in some cases, high-ranking officers would fly in to a particular location for the express purpose of appearing with Hope. The FTA show, then, clarified the political content of Hope's shows, betraying the "apolitical" character of the USO's particular "brand" of entertainment by talking about precisely that which Hope determinedly avoided—the possibility that irreverence and antiauthoritarianism might not recede into the background, but instead congeal into a challenge to the continuation of the war.

In a consideration of the FTA's purpose and significance, it is important to recognize that "entertaining the troops" was not a novel idea within the segment of the civilian antiwar movement that had been organizing support for the GI resistance for several years. The coffeehouses in which the FTA would play the majority of its shows were intended from the beginning to facilitate the presentation of musical and stage acts, as part of the general effort to provide soldiers with a place to relax, rap, and (the organizers hoped) self-organize. While military police would sometimes check out the coffeehouses undercover, as media coverage of the FTA's shows makes clear, organizing could proceed away from the overt, heavy surveillance GIs were subjected to on base. Gardner had consulted Alan Myerson of San Francisco's improvisational comedy troupe The Committee when developing the layout for the UFO. The Committee was a San Francisco–based improv theater company, formed in 1963, that had bicoastal connections. Its membership was politically active, and some of its performers were involved in experimental theater work; several members, including Myerson, would later become central to the first iteration of the FTA. Myerson, no doubt drawing on the considerable experience of any low-budget performance troupe, advised Gardner to put the lightboard right next to the cash register, so the same person could run both.[14] This was primarily to serve the needs of music groups that might perform, but the USSF would also sponsor coffeehouse appearances by theater groups, such as the San Francisco Mime Troupe, and individual entertainers. Michael Alaimo, a comedic actor who would join the FTA for the first time in Tacoma, Washington, had performed independently at the Oleo Strut coffeehouse located in

Killeen, Texas,[15] and, in *The Radical Theatre Notebook*, Arthur Sainer refers to a performance by the Pageant Players at the GI coffeehouse near Fort Dix in New Jersey.[16]

However, what was new about the FTA as entertainment was the broader audience it could attract among GIs, and the way it could, through ready media coverage, draw outside attention to the simmering discontent of many enlisted men and women. This depended upon emphasizing the FTA as entertainment, as opposed to political (or experimental) theater. To the extent that any tension existed among the FTA's many organizers and performers concerning this emphasis, it centered not upon differing investments in political efficacy versus aesthetic experimentation. No one, according to those with whom I have spoken, disagreed with utilizing the popular forms of the variety show and the comedy sketch. Rather, disagreements emerged over the kind of political content the show should include. "Political" was often taken to mean "politically correct," a term used at the time in a manner not terribly different from the way it is used today. For many, entertainment that argued a political line or called on its audience to take action appeared to conflict with the primary project of providing hip diversion, as opposed to didactic, outdated messaging, to a growing movement. Gardner was already dismissive of the coffeehouse movement by the time he helped organize the FTA, in part because he perceived it as being taken over by "politically correct" activists and their "incredibly boring" taste in entertainment.[17]

In some respects, this seems to have been an argument about scale—"overpoliticizing" GI entertainment was perceived by some as working against the GI movement's growth, by unnecessarily alienating the average audience member before someone could convince him to get involved. The more the FTA show looked like a hip version of the Bob Hope show, the bigger the audience it could attract. While the FTA show would ultimately end up at the Haymarket Square coffeehouse for its inaugural performances, the original plan was to perform in a much larger venue, either on base or in a local auditorium. This was in recognition—and anticipation—of the GI audience stars like Fonda, Sutherland, and Boyle (as opposed to less well-known groups like the Mime Troupe) could be expected to draw. In this way, too, the FTA departed from other theater groups that had reached out to the GI movement. Though the show was intended to highlight local GI organizing, making the coffeehouses an obvious choice of venue, the impact of the show as entertainment depended upon being able to at least propose the possibility of a large audience.

At the heart of defining what counted as "entertainment" lay precisely the kinds of debates over the image and identity of the antiwar GI that the movement had been confronting since its beginning, as discussed in chapter 1. Which signifiers and political sentiments would render him visible, and which threatened to submerge him in the general category of the antiwar activist, or alienate him from the movement altogether? Confusion or perhaps disingenuousness on this point manifested quickly, producing what appears to be a contradiction in the FTA's initial publicity, with coverage often featuring the performers saying the show is "not political" even as the decision to put on the show is acknowledged as politically motivated. In a New York press conference on February 16, 1971, announcing the group's plan to stage its first antiwar revue at Fort Bragg in March, Fonda remarked, on the one hand, that:

> It's been very disconcerting for many of us in Hollywood to see that Bob Hope, Martha Raye, and other companies of their ilk have cornered the market and are the only entertainers allowed to speak to soldiers in this country and Vietnam. A lot of us who have different points of view about the war and what's happening to this country have decided that the time has come to speak to the forgotten soldiers. They are the majority of soldiers. They want peace and freedom, but they are isolated in the military world and they need our support.[18]

During the same press conference, however, Fonda would insist that the show was "not an inflammatory far-left show—basically it's just entertainment."[19] More generally, coverage emphasized the show as a response, reply, or alternative to "military-sponsored entertainments," acknowledging that the performers were antiwar but that the show was "like Hope's."[20] Sutherland remarked that the show was "not trying to lay some heavy political line on anybody." Fonda framed the show as not so much providing different content, but different performers, conveying that "if the government could support Bob Hope's annual trips to Vietnam to entertain the troops, it should also support entertainers whose political beliefs differ from Hope." She explained that "the point of all this [. . .] is to show the soldiers there are those of us who understand." By leaving open and ambiguous the question of what, precisely, a civilian supporter could claim to "understand," Fonda proposed an updated version of the basic concept of supporting the troops. When a reporter wondered during the press conference whether "it were not audacious to ask the Army to underwrite a show which would be anti-Army," Fonda replied, "'I don't think so. If the Army is democratic, then they would be providing the kind of entertainment the soldiers want to see. Bob Hope is not entertainment for them, he's entertainment for the brass.'"[21] Leaving aside the fact that the Army is not "democratic," in referencing "the brass" (meaning the officer class), Fonda reflects what was, by this point, a sharp division within the military, not only along political lines, but generational ones as well. Overwhelmingly, young men were being sent to die by older men—men Hope's age, and men with whom Hope had longstanding friendships. Reporting from Saigon in 1970, Ian Wright, a correspondent for the *Guardian*, noted that Hope's routines were of little comfort to soldiers with no goal other than to survive their deployment and go home.[22] A significant part of the FTA's success would come from the fact that it targeted not the foibles of enlisted life, but the officers (and their wives) whose lives, as one of the songs put it, were "the same in peacetime as in war."[23]

Referring to the show as "not political" both posits the FTA as unthreatening entertainment that should be allowed on base, and also reassures (perhaps disingenuously) soldiers that they are not going to be treated to a lesson in antiwar activism by a group of civilians. At the same time, it is likely that this emphasis on the show being "nonpolitical" was not considered only or even primarily a tactic by some of the show's organizers—that is, it was not a pretense, but in fact an accurate reflection of the function the show should serve. For those like Gardner, whose distaste for "politically correct" entertainment was and is evident, the show's primary function was to attract an audience by not being "lame," as Country Joe McDonald put it when I interviewed him in 2012. A popular, antiestablishment musician, who would join the FTA beginning with its show in Tacoma, McDonald was expressing his belief that this was and should have been the sole purpose of the FTA.[24] As I will discuss further in subsequent chapters, "political correctness," or overt declarations of political commitment, effectively became a marker of an activist's inauthenticity and non-belonging.

The *Inquirer*'s coverage of the February 16 press conference emphasized the scale of celebrity involved, asserting that "[s]ome of the biggest names in the New Hollywood have banded together to form a kind of counter-culture USO troupe to take their antiwar message directly to 20 U.S. Army bases."[25] Besides Fonda and Sutherland, the slate of intended performers included actors Peter Boyle and Elliot Gould and comedian and activist Dick Gregory. Mike Nichols, of 1967's *The Graduate*, was tapped to direct, though scheduling conflicts ultimately prevented him from doing so. All were, at the time (as now), nationally recognized figures. Jules Feiffer and Herb Gardner, both known as cartoonists, playwrights, and screenwriters, were identified in press coverage as the show's writers, along with Boyle. Feiffer's 1967 play *Little Murders* was adapted into a film starring Gould in 1971, and his *Carnal Knowledge* was directed by Nichols the same year. Gardner's play *One Thousand Clowns* (1962) had been adapted into a successful film in 1965. A relative newcomer to Hollywood, Boyle had starred as the title character in the low-budget hit *Joe*, a film from 1970 featuring a final act of gleeful, reactionary mass murder. In *Joe*, Boyle's "gun-loving, beer-swilling, tough-talking tool-and-die maker from Queens" joins a disgruntled advertising executive in a shooting spree at a hippie commune.[26] Despite his initial feeling, after the film's release, that its message was essentially antiwar (and satirical), Boyle's character was received so positively by fans that the actor ultimately refused, for a time, to accept roles in films that he felt glorified violence.[27] Boyle had also studied at Second City in Chicago in 1968, an experience that positioned him to contribute to the show as a writer as well as a performer, and a setting that resulted in his political radicalization.[28] Gould's announced inclusion in the cast, though he did not ultimately perform, likewise would have been a significant draw—he'd appeared on the cover of *Time* magazine in September 1970, following his role in Robert Altman's *M*.A*.S*.H.*, in which Sutherland had also starred.

The only non-white member of the inaugural troupe, Dick Gregory was an increasingly controversial and popular voice on the left. Having shifted his focus from stand-up comedy to antiwar and civil rights work, Gregory's support for the Black Panther Party for Self-Defense had prompted William Buckley, Jr., to publish a brief piece of commentary on the comedian in the *Boston Globe* in late 1970. Despite being impressively patronizing, Buckley's "A talk with Dick Gregory" nevertheless gives a useful sense of how prominent a figure Gregory had become. Buckley writes: "Gregory is a force in America. Particularly on college campuses, where he comes on very strong, very strong indeed. He has spoken at 300 campuses during the last 10 months."[29] Gregory's involvement in the FTA likely stemmed from his having worked with Fonda the previous year, in a political-celebrity capacity. An announcement in the *Sun Reporter* lists the two as "keynote speakers at a rally-benefit sponsored by the Committee United for Political Prisoners (CUPP) to help raise funds for the legal defense of Huey P. Newton, Bobby Seale and other political prisoners."[30] While Gregory would have signaled, to a broader public, the group's political orientation likely more than Boyle, Gould, or even Fonda at the time, he was nevertheless identifiable as an entertainer, due to his background in stand-up and his popularity as a speaker on the college campus circuit. However, his political perspectives led him, at first, to be skeptical about doing a show for servicemembers. On the flight to Fayetteville, he admitted to a reporter that, while he didn't mind performing for prisoners, he didn't like "entertaining before a convention of bank robbers."[31] In referring to "bank robbers," it seems likely that Gregory was among those who did not see a significant difference between cops and soldiers, considering them all criminals. Ultimately, however, the audience's enthusiastic response to his highly political routine would change his perspective.

Opening Night

Because the show's organizers had drawn a parallel between the Hope show and the FTA, and because the show promised stars of a caliber comparable to that of Hope and his guests, the announcement of the intended tour in mid-February opened avenues for additional publicity. Specifically, reporters followed the group's attempts to secure access to their intended audience. By the time of the press conference, the USSF had formally submitted to Lieutenant General John J. Tolson, the commander at Fort Bragg, a request to stage the show on base and an accompanying request that they be extended the courtesies routinely offered Hope and his guests (namely, that the Pentagon would cover lodging and travel expenses). The USSF had chosen Bragg deliberately, as Tolson was considered to be at the forefront of instituting "progressive" measures, among them tacitly allowing the use of "soft" drugs.[32] Fonda and Levy attempted to use Tolson's reputation as leverage, and failing that, as evidence of hypocrisy: "Levy said if Tolson 'is really serious about the Army's so-called liberalization policy . . . then he will let the show on base . . . If not, he will ban it and let the public know it's the same old oppressive Army.'"[33] By modeling the show on Hope's and emphasizing its function as entertainment, Fonda and Levy could frame the request in terms of the resources granted to the Hope show by the military, insisting that it was only fair the military equally support other performers with other viewpoints, so long as they "just" wanted to provide entertainment for the troops.

Unsurprisingly, the group was denied access to the base, as they would be at all subsequent bases (Fonda herself had been banned previously from Fort Bragg for passing out leaflets), and so they sought another venue. In fact, not one but two contingency plans had been in place from the beginning, for the inaugural performances in Fayetteville: the Cumberland County Memorial Auditorium and, failing that, the Haymarket Square coffeehouse. In its determination to avoid sponsoring the show, the Pentagon ultimately contributed to the group's goal of politicizing that which was already political—entertainers' access to the troops—but which had maintained a pretense of neutrality via the USO's formal independence from the Department of Defense. Following Tolson's rejection, a second media surge surrounded the group's attempt to use the municipal auditorium. They were denied this as well, based on the various arguments that they would destroy the space, as audiences at rock shows had done previously, or that they were presenting a view "contrary to existing local sentiment."[34] The former would prove a recurrent concern over the course of the group's existence, despite the fact that, as articles covering shows in Killeen, Monterey, and Japan note, the audiences for the FTA performances were generally less disruptive than the audiences that attended other events at the same venues.

Reacting to the possibility that the show might not find a suitable space, 1,770 soldiers signed a petition asking Congress to reverse the decision refusing the show permission to perform on base. Soldiers

Philip Friedrich and John Berk presented the petition to Representative Bella Abzug of New York, who argued on its behalf before Congress just days before the show was to open.[35] Likely containing not only the signatures of committed antiwar activists but also of those simply interested in getting a glimpse of Fonda, the petition demonstrated already the threat posed by the show—to draw soldiers, via celebrity, to an explicitly antiwar event. The publicity generated by the military and the city government effectively banning the show contributed to its popularity, and also put the military in the position of opposing the presence of celebrities ostensibly only there to entertain the troops. Members of the USSF continued to insist that the show "is entertainment . . . and is not a political rally," even as other of the show's representatives made slightly different claims about its content. In a press conference at the Haymarket Square coffeehouse on March 9, USSF member Gary Horvitz stated that the script was "being reworked to take 'a lot of inflammatory remarks out.'"[36] In a separate article, Barbara Garson (who was not yet but would soon be listed among the show's writers, and who was known at the time for her 1966 play *MacBird!*) is quoted at a press conference in DC saying that the writers, along with the cast and the director, were in the process of "sharpening the script—not diluting it."[37] While it is unclear whether either statement is made in good faith—particularly given the fact that the former both denies and confirms the existence of "inflammatory material" in the first place—Horvitz underlines the strategy of emphasizing entertainment and downplaying political content in an effort to draw a parallel between the FTA show and the Hope shows. Garson's comment suggests, in turn, that doing so wasn't necessarily a point of complete agreement. In downplaying "the political" and emphasizing entertainment, the show's organizers tactically framed the show as "only a show" in order to ask, with the appearance of all seriousness, for the same courtesies extended to Hope. And yet, this is tactical precisely to the extent that it is difficult to discern with any certainty whether or not the troupe's advocates believed in the legitimacy of their request: they really *were* celebrities who just wanted to entertain the troops, but as they were also equally invested in encouraging GI resistance, they couldn't honestly expect the military to welcome them onto the base—could they?

Front page of the Fort Bragg–based GI newspaper *Bragg Briefs*, announcing that the FTA show would be held at the Haymarket Coffeehouse.
Courtesy of Wisconsin Historical Society, GI Press Collection.

Two days prior to the scheduled March 13 performance, the USSF requested an injunction against the ruling that had upheld the decision to refuse the group access to the Cumberland County Memorial Auditorium. The injunction was granted, but the town then demanded $150,000 in insurance, which the USSF could not secure. Finally, instead of a 2,500-seat auditorium, the FTA performed in the Haymarket Square coffeehouse, playing three shows to packed houses of over 500, in a space meant to hold 450. Attendees paid "$2.50 each for a hard wooden seat or standing room along the black, poster-covered walls."[38] This not insignificant sum (nearly $20 by today's standards, adjusted for inflation) went toward the coffeehouse's expenses, and some of it went to the USSF. (All of the performers donated their time, and those who were able covered their own travel and accommodations.) Attendance was high in spite of ongoing and varied attempts to discourage it. Coverage in the *Washington Post* described the scene on base the day of the show:

> If the Army was keeping its cool, it was by no means at ease. A tour of the base uncovered the fact that some 50 jeeps and trucks had been removed from the 503d Military Police Unit's motor pool and placed on alert behind the barracks. [. . .] [M]ore than the usual number of GIs seemed to be on weekend duty.[39]

On the subject of more informal attempts to lower attendance, *The Evening Outlook* remarked that the soldiers were "indeterred [sic] by telephoned bomb threats."[40] Apparently, having been unable to stop the show from playing in Fayetteville, and well aware of the problems that might arise if troops were openly prevented from leaving base, the military went so far as to send badly disguised military police (MPs) to join the FTA's audience. These were "easily recognized in wigs and hippie garb," further evidence of the military's inability to accurately gauge or reflect the cultural shift exacerbating GI discontent.[41] Alternatively, they may have been "badly disguised" precisely so that they might be recognized as present. Both scenarios are possible. At any rate, the military's efforts belied a claim made by Major Jimmie Wilson that, "There won't be any spooks down there taking names." Wilson also gave what amounts to perhaps the most half-hearted and laughable attempt to discourage attendance and downplay the show's significance, when he told a reporter that General Tolson "had found [the script] not so much antiwar as poorly done and he felt he couldn't allow it." Tolson was not there to speak to the press himself, as he "was out determinedly playing golf."[42]

It was not until the night before they left for Fayetteville that the full cast had been able to assemble for a run-through.[43] The lineup referenced in early press coverage would not quite come to pass, it seems because the logistics of collecting some of Hollywood's biggest figures in one place proved too great to overcome. Although Boyle and Gregory would perform with the FTA several times during its domestic tour, Gould never appeared in the FTA, at Fort Bragg or elsewhere, reportedly due to "near collapse from overwork."[44] Both Gould and Nichols were replaced by members of The Committee, Gould by Gary Goodrow and Nichols by Alan Myerson, suggesting Fred Gardner played a significant role in shaping the final cast. As a result of the last-minute changes, it seems that what began as an explicitly Hollywood venture built around national celebrities almost immediately and somewhat unintentionally acquired a set of countercultural credentials. The change underlined the FTA's dependence upon ensemble work of a decidedly different sort than any on display in Hope's shows, and the challenges this posed, both logistically and interpersonally. Speaking with Leticia Kent of the *New York Times* just before the first show in Fayetteville, Fonda explained the intended working relationship: "It's a company made up of many talented people and we all are together—and we all are equally important."[45] Despite a statement Fonda would make several months later in response to Country Joe McDonald's split with the group, that the FTA was *not* a collective, she in fact uses this term in her conversation with Kent: "One of the things we're doing in supporting the GI movement is developing an alternative lifestyle, another way to look at things, at entertainment as well as at the war. We're a collective. Everyone is of equal importance. And so we decided that no one of us would speak individually to the press." It seems as if the emphasis here is less upon the way the performance itself is developed and directed, but rather with how the group represents itself to the press, and also to the GI movement. It is likely that Fonda's move away from this conception, at least rhetorically, was the result of several factors, including her adoption of feminist politics, the logistical difficulties involved in organizing the show's tour, and the mutual frustration she and McDonald appear to have felt with one another.

Far from a single, central comedian introducing celebrity guests and their "acts," then, the FTA featured its film stars committing to a series of comedic scenes alongside talented stage performers. The sketches followed extended sets of overtly political music as well as dramatic readings of texts by antiwar writers Daniel Berrigan and Dalton Trumbo. Dick Gregory's stand-up routine echoed Hope's, but without the former taking on the role of MC. Though less consistently included in the show's preliminary publicity until the week prior to its debut, the inaugural performance also featured singer and songwriter Barbara Dane and rock band Swamp Dogg. Dane was a figure already well known among antiwar activists and especially among antiwar GIs. By mid-1970, Dane had "performed at just about every base where a coffee house or some other organizing project has been initiated."[46] She'd begun her musical career in the late 1940s, and during the 1950s she became something of a sensation as a white woman who sang the blues.[47] By the 1970s, however, her work almost exclusively revolved around the peace movement. This would be the only time she played with the FTA, in part due to a very busy schedule touring to coffeehouses in the US and abroad. It seems this separation may also have reflected political differences with some of the FTA's organizers, and in particular Gardner, for whom Dane represented the kind of politically correct acts crowding out the relaxed atmosphere of the coffeehouse.

In the end, the group of performers and musicians that appeared onstage at the Haymarket Square coffeehouse was a remarkable mix of star power and counterculture, producing an equally remarkable mix of earnest, sardonic, satirical, and light-hearted approaches to political commentary. Apparently, it was a potent mix, as it is difficult to overstate the success of the Fort Bragg performances. Every published account acknowledges in no uncertain terms how enthusiastically the audience received the three-hour performance. Headlines included "Soldiers Roar Approval" and "Jane Fonda's Antiwar Show a Hit with GIs" (*Los Angeles Times*), "500 Cheer Antiwar Performance" (*Evening Outlook*), "Antiwar Acts a Hit" (*San Francisco Chronicle*), and "Antiwar Revue Box Office Smash" (*Fayetteville Observer*). In addition to the popularity of the sportscaster sketch featuring Sutherland and Boyle (written

The cast of the FTA show when it appeared at the Haymarket Coffeehouse near Fort Bragg in Fayetteville, North Carolina. From left: Gary Goodrow, Jane Fonda, Donald Sutherland, Peter Boyle, Dick Gregory, and Barbara Dane. Courtesy of Displaced Films.

by The Committee and described at the beginning of this book's introduction), many media accounts of the show included excerpts from Gregory's half-hour long routine, such as his suggestion that the draft age be raised to seventy-five and all the "old cats" be sent to Vietnam, his assertion that, despite its efforts at surveillance "the Army ain't got no intelligence," and his final, moving expression of how much the audience's presence at the show meant to him.[48] David Gelber of the *Village Voice* called Swamp Dogg "the surprise hit" of the evening: "Whoever plays music for the Bob Hope show will never turn on an audience the way Swamp Dogg [. . .] did."[49] Instead of Les Brown's Band of Renown backing Hope's hokey "Thanks for the Memory," Swamp Dogg and his ten-piece ensemble played Dogg's antiwar anthem "God Bless America for What?" The show concluded with a series of "blackouts," the segues between them underscored by "The Lifer's Song." During the first and final rehearsal with the cast fully assembled, Myerson had asked Gardner, a songwriter, to compose a few clever verses that could cover transitions between the scenes. What he wrote became the group's signature number, with its refrain featuring the group's name.[50]

Kenneth Reich, reporter for the *Los Angeles Times* noted that "the general tone of the show was not bitter. Laughs dominated the performance, but when the audience was given a chance to voice its feeling, its views were clear." He continues:

> In one skit, Boyle [. . .] played President Nixon and announced he was going to take a poll. First, he asked who was for America leaving Vietnam immediately. There came a tremendous roar from the crowd. Then he asked who was for staying. One person off to the side said, "Baaa, baaa." "A victory for the silent majority," Boyle announced in tones used by Mr. Nixon. "We stay."[51]

Other comedic sketches included Sutherland presenting the war as a magic act, a metaphorical sleight of hand. Another, a parody of basic training, depicted a soldier being whipped into a "mindless frenzy" by a drill sergeant. Finally, the GI, ordered to kill, turns on the sergeant and chases him offstage. A parody of a press conference about the war played on the general absence of information that the military provided to reporters:

> REPORTER: How are we doing in Vietnam?
> SECRETARY LAIRD: We're winning.
> REPORTER: How about all the Americans who are dying?
> SECRETARY LAIRD: They're losing.[52]

In another scene, Nixon received "image advice" intended to "brighten up his presentation with the gnong-gnong gesture, the wa wa necktie, the rubber chicken, and other vaudeville paraphernalia."[53] The finale featured the entire cast, save Sutherland, singing the National Anthem, hands placed over hearts. Unhappy with Sutherland's unwillingness to stand and participate, the others grow more aggressive in their attempts to force him to his feet. Finally, they "stomp him into a frazzled corpse with staring blue eyes, then regroup in time to finish the song."[54]

Folksinger Dane performed the overtly militant song "Insubordination," with the troops joining in (despite Gardner's feeling that Dane was unappealing to young GIs), as well as a soft and solemn "Vietcong morale song."[55] Michael Kernan, for the *Washington Post*, summed up the show's remarkable range:

It would be hard to say which individual line drew the loudest laugh. Perhaps more to the point was the silence somehow created by Sutherland in that crowded place with the makeshift lighting and the squealing sound system and the heavy spring rain whispering on the roof, as he read the trial statement of draft resister Daniel Berrigan offering his liberty and if necessary his life if that will help to end the bloodshed and madness.[56]

In addition to expressing the overwhelming success of the show, the particular angle taken by the news coverage of the inaugural performance must also be understood as one of the show's key successes. Although preshow coverage highlighted celebrity involvement and the FTA's stated intent of "just" offering entertainment, articles on the inaugural performance emphasized the show's explicitly antiwar content, as the headlines above make clear. While the premise of "just entertainment" had worked in the interest of preliminary publicity, the shift to an explicit recognition of the political content of the show publicized not so much the show itself, but the fact of GI sentiment against the war. This is supported by the way in which the show's coverage does not, by and large, reduce attendance at the coffeehouse performances to the presence of celebrities, even as secondary headlines often referred to "Jane Fonda's GI show" or "Jane Fonda Revue."[57] Michael Kernan's article for the *Washington Post*, an abbreviated version of which also ran in the *New York Post*, went so far as to frame the show as the work of the GIs themselves, running under the headlines "GI Movement: A Show to Call Its Own" and "GIs Were the Stars of Jane & Co." Both articles opened with the following:

> In the end it was the GIs who pulled it all together, who gave dignity and unity and burning purpose to the passionate but scatter-brained USO show put on here over the weekend by Jane Fonda.[58]

The coverage that expressed this sentiment—that the GIs came through where the performers did not or could not—facilitated the shift of the site of legitimacy and authority off of the celebrity and onto the GI. While the press conferences and the appeal to be permitted on base necessarily depended upon emphasizing the celebrity status of the performers, the show itself was intended to provide an opportunity for the emergence and visibility of a GI spectator distinct from the patriotic and de facto pro-war image produced and circulated by the Bob Hope specials.

Nothing They Don't Already Know

From the beginning, members of the FTA consistently and explicitly expressed the show's inability to tell the soldiers anything they didn't already know: "They know that the war is insane. They know what GIs have to contend with better than we do. We're simply saying 'We know what you're up against and we support you.'"[59] Soldiers speaking of the tour readily identified this as part of the intention of the performance—to speak to, and not for, those whose power relative to the project of ending the war came in speaking for themselves. In an interview reproduced in Stacewicz's *Winter Soldiers*, Vietnam Veteran Joe Urgo expressed his perception of Fonda's activities relative to the resistance: "Fonda's contributions were good overall. She wanted to join up with us. We were the vets. We're the ones who have the right to speak."[60] Since the show's beginning, organizers had emphasized to the press that much of the material for the show, while scripted by Feiffer and Gardner (and in some cases lifted directly from The Committee's preexisting repertoire), came from the GIs themselves. Specifically, the blackout sketches interspersed throughout the "Lifer's Song" were derived largely from comic strips popularly reprinted in GI newspapers. In one based on a Beetle Bailey cartoon, an officer (played in *FTA!* by Donald Sutherland) tells a soldier, "I think I'm gonna get me a watchdog." "What do you need a watchdog for, Sarge?" replies the GI, "You're surrounded by two hundred armed men." "That's why I'm gonna get me a watchdog."[61]

In addition to positioning GIs as responsible for the show's existence, the performances provided a pretense for soldiers to speak to the mainstream press about myriad aspects of enlisted life, however tangentially related to the specific material presented by the show. The articles by Gelber (*Village Voice*) and Kernan (*Washington Post* and *New York Post*) in particular included extended commentary from attendees. Gelber's piece features GIs chatting after the show, discussing "stories of how to fuck the army in everyday life," while Kernan's includes a series of quotes, each expressing a profound sense of alienation, and to varying degrees, frustration and anger toward the military. One says that 90 percent of the guys he knows are against the war; another remarks that "Vietnam is a very good radicalizer," and that he was "super-straight" until he entered the service. We are confronted likewise with the extreme violence of the war, seen through the eyes of a "boy" who shows Kernan a horrific photograph of a Vietnamese woman. Her side is "gored and half her head blown off and her shirt spread and her trousers yanked down to expose her genitals." He tells Kernan:

> I took this picture. I've seen a lot worse than this. They told me the woman was just running across a field. You think I should show this to Jane? I think she should see it, she's a woman, she should know about this.[62]

The young man's comments reflect the complicated role of the show in at once drawing its legitimacy from the existence of antiwar servicemembers, while also validating and highlighting that existence. The soldier shows the photograph to a member of the press, but his feeling is that he ought to show it Jane, because "she should know about it." Here, it seems that Fonda becomes a surrogate for the American public more generally—who "ought to know" what's going on—even as she is also the means by which that information might be transmitted. At this point Fonda had not yet begun to speak publicly on the question of feminism, though she would soon begin to do so.[63] The soldier's impulse to show the photograph to Jane suggests what was very much the case—that radicalization during this period often proceeded along many paths at once. It is also worth noting that Gelber's article describes the seeming sense of abandon and fearlessness with which the GIs spoke to news cameras after the show. Perhaps there is a kind of contagiousness to celebrity here, such that the apparent impunity with which Fonda and other cast members could denounce the war might have been experienced temporarily and vicariously by their spectators. Gelber suggests something like this reading when he refers to the GIs "one after the other, looking like the captain of the high school wrestling team," as they stood in front of the cameras. I will return to this same image in chapter 4, when I consider the soldier-spectator on film.

During press conferences prior to the Fort Bragg appearance, the USSF had announced plans for an ambitious twenty-stop tour of the

FTA.[64] Ultimately, the troupe toured to only five additional domestic military installations, in California, Washington, Idaho, Texas, and New Jersey, before kicking off its Pacific Rim tour with a benefit performance at Lincoln Center in New York. Financially and logistically, organizing the tour was a significant drain on resources that were necessarily limited within the GI movement. Even as Fonda was heavily underwriting the cost of transportation and housing, the problem of money still played a role in determining the feasibility of planning a visit to a given base; moreover, issues of money were not limited to whether the money existed, but also concerned whose it was and how it was spent. Between filming for *Steelyard Blues* (a project in which much of the cast was involved), preparing for the Asia tour, and growing disagreements about the purpose, direction, and leadership of the show, it is not particularly surprising that only one quarter of the twenty-stop tour came to pass.

However, the shows that did happen were unqualified successes, reflecting the fact that in mid-1971 the domestic GI movement reached its peak. As the Nixon administration shifted away from the use of ground troops and toward an air war, higher numbers of GIs began returning from Vietnam, bolstering the ranks of frustrated and disillusioned soldiers and veterans involved in domestic antiwar activity.[65] The FTA's tour traces (and participates in) key developments and events during this period, particularly as its trajectory and enthusiastic reception reflected the military's increasing dependency upon pilots, sailors, and Marines. The popularity of the show across the different branches of the Armed Forces highlights the military's miscalculation, as described by Cortright, that the Navy and the Air Force would see lower levels of dissent. Resistance was not expected "from the servicemen involved, who, it was assumed had willingly volunteered for their jobs and, sheltered behind radar scopes and in repair shops, would function as obedient professionals."[66] As it turned out, these, too, would respond to the US's ongoing engagement in Vietnam with militant, organized resistance, and the FTA would be a part of giving expression and visibility to this newly central branch of the GI movement.

The FTA's second engagement took place on May 8 and 9 near Fort Ord, at the Monterey County Fairgrounds. As would increasingly be the case, the FTA identified its purpose in coming to a specific location not only as directed toward building the GI movement in general, but also as tied to supporting an impending event or responding to an incident of repression (though it also seems that engagements on the West Coast were easier to work into some of the performers' schedules). In the case of Monterey, the soldier-activists at Fort Ord were trying to encourage participation in a march planned for the upcoming Armed Forces Day—which troops had renamed Armed Farces Day. It would turn out to be one of the most significant GI movement activities of the year. Al Mason, a Fort Ord soldier and spokesperson for the United Servicemen's Union, called on soldiers to join USU and participate in the march, stating: "If we get together we can do any damn thing we want."[67] The FTA had gathered three audiences of over nine hundred each, with most of the attendees coming from among Fort Ord's twenty-five thousand personnel, and effectively delivered them to Mason and his message of organized resistance.

As with Fort Bragg, the USSF had requested permission (in April) to stage the show on base, but no invitation was extended. The cast included Goodrow, along with Fonda and Sutherland, and the Saturday night performance featured an appearance by Johnny Rivers, a popular musician.[68] *Rolling Stone* coverage of the Monterey performances notes an additional cast member, Don Sturdy, actually the stage name of Howard Hesseman, also a member of The Committee.[69] It was also with the Monterey shows that folksinger Len Chandler first joined the group. Chandler would perform with the FTA for the rest of its domestic tour, at Lincoln Center, and abroad. Peter Boyle did not perform this time around, prompting Sutherland, at a press conference, to explain that the cast "varies from show to show . . . it's a very malleable flow, different performers come and go when they can."[70]

Local sponsors of the three performances in Monterey included the United Servicemen's Union, a group based at Fort Ord and affiliated with Ord's underground GI newspaper, *P.O.W.*[71] Highlighting the FTA's ability to attract a broader audience than might have been immediately available to activists interested in encouraging soldier involvement in the movement, many of the GIs said they were attending an antiwar event for the first time.[72] In a change from Fort Bragg, the FTA and the USSF instituted a policy of charging admission (three dollars in this case) only to civilians; GIs got in free. A lengthy article in the *Watsonville Register Pajaronian* notes the inclusion of the band Big Brother and

A poster advertising the FTA's second stop, in Monterey, California, near Fort Ord. Courtesy of the People's Oral History Project—Monterey, CA.

the Holding Company. A variety of "local" talent provided additional opening acts, among them Cat Mother and the All Night Newsboys and the CIA (Comedy in Action). According to "About Face!," the USSF's newsletter, CIA played the "usual USO circuit, until they were booted off for their antiwar material." Coverage also mentioned "nine Women's Libbers from the area," foreshadowing the eventual introduction of feminist content into the show itself, though at this point in the FTA's existence its sketches remained focused upon the experiences most common among and familiar to its predominantly male (and predominantly white) audience.[73]

A week following the stop in Monterey, the show appeared in San Diego, and coincided with "Armed Farces Day" events there, on May 15. This time, the group had requested to perform not on a base but, as Hope had done many times before, on the deck of an aircraft carrier, the USS *Constellation*. The request had been denied and so the FTA appeared at the Russ Auditorium to capacity crowds of twenty-four hundred GIs. However, as had been the case at Fort Bragg, the decision by military authorities to deny soldiers officially sanctioned access to the show "coincided with and helped spur a pioneering organizing effort":

Several weeks before the scheduled May 15 performances, Concerned Military circulated a petition requesting that the show be presented on the deck of the carrier USS *Constellation* (a courtesy routinely extended to the Bob Hope show). Although nearly fifteen hundred members of the crew signed the appeal, Captain Harry Gerhard flatly rejected it. Nonetheless, the show's performances in San Diego were a huge success, attracting over four thousand people, a majority of them servicepeople.[74]

The ongoing politicization of access to entertainment reinforced a key strategic purpose of the FTA: to facilitate opportunities for GIs to express discontent via the pretense of an uncontroversial request based on the precedent set by Hope. Entertainers, so the logic goes, who wish to perform for the troops, and by whom the troops wish to be entertained, ought to be allowed to do so. At the same time, the FTA's measurable impact within the GI movement, and so within the antiwar movement more broadly, serves as a reminder of the significance of its exclusion from the accepted history of the period's political theater.

Reconfigurations

Following the Armed Forces/Farces Day performances, the next FTA appearance would not occur for approximately two months, and during that time two major and interrelated shifts in its content would occur. Over the summer, between the shows in San Diego and Tacoma, Fonda spent time in Oakland and Berkeley, outside of San Francisco. *Steelyard Blues*, directed by Myerson and starring Fonda, Sutherland, Boyle, and others, was in the works (filming in Oakland) and Fonda's daughter Vanessa (with Roger Vadim) was enrolled at Blue Fairyland, a left-wing cooperative kindergarten in Berkeley. It was the same school that Seven, the child of Woodstock star Country Joe McDonald and his wife, Robin Menken, attended. As a result of the connections Fonda would make during this period, and the negative experience working with some of the actors involved in *Steelyard Blues*, the FTA would undergo a significant transformation that played out for the remainder of the domestic tour. McDonald, an exceptionally popular figure among GIs, agreed to appear with the group at its upcoming engagements in Washington, Idaho, and Texas, while Menken became one of the show's writers and actors. Menken played a critical role in shaping the direction of the show, as she pushed to include more politicized content and to move away from The Committee's "static" material, which she felt "[superimposed] a political satire on a situation that had gone past that spectator level." Soldiers, she contends, were making a "dangerous commitment" to see the show, risking a file or the stockade, and she felt the show should do more to reflect and respond to this reality. She describes writing and rewriting material prior to each stop on the tour in order to incorporate issues specific to a given base, which she'd learn about through the publications run out of the local coffeehouse.[75] In Killeen, Texas, for example, where GIs had recently organized a successful boycott of Tyrell's Jewelry Store (for offering soldiers deploying overseas a "deal" that involved buying something on credit and then having the debt forgiven if they didn't make it back), the show included a sketch based on that effort.[76]

It was also around this time that Francine Parker, an LA-based television producer and member of Entertainment Industry for Peace and Justice, joined the FTA. By all accounts, Parker was a force to be reckoned with and would quickly alter the working dynamic of the group. Through McDonald and Menken, Fonda also met Nina Serrano, an activist and poet living in Oakland who served as co-director of the show with Parker. Serrano, McDonald, and Menken had recently made a film together about Chile, titled ¡Qué Hacer! (1970), and McDonald and Serrano had worked together in 1965 on *The Changeover*, a play by Fred Hayden. The cast also added songwriter and singer Rita Martinson, who was active in the Black liberation and anti–Vietnam War movements. Perhaps unsurprisingly given these changes and the context of the rise of the women's movement during this period, the FTA began to address issues of sexism and to look for ways to incorporate feminist material and themes into the show. Menken helped to develop this new content, along with Parker, Serrano, and Fonda. The attention to issues of sexism was not restricted to the show's content, however, and Country Joe recalled, in a recent interview and not without a degree of dismissiveness, consciousness-raising sessions Menken would host at their shared home, which other female members of the cast would attend. While the shift would see a marked diversification of the group's cast and material, it would also ultimately lead to the departure of several of the troupe's male performers, most notably Boyle, Country Joe, and the members of The Committee.

The definitive split would not occur until after most of the domestic tour was concluded, but cracks had formed and would continue to grow during the last few stateside performances. Internal tensions did not, however, impact the popularity of the show. Both of the FTA's two shows in Tacoma, Washington, on August 7 and 8 filled the three-thousand-seat Tacoma Sports Arena with audiences drawn from nearby Fort Lewis and McChord Air Force Base.[77] This stop saw the addition of performers Menken, Michael Alaimo, Ben Vereen, Darryl Henriques, and pianist Yale Zimmerman. A Broadway actor and dancer, Vereen had starred as "Hud" in the 1968–69 productions of *Hair* in New York, San Francisco, and Los Angeles; it seems likely that his involvement with the FTA came through the EIPJ. Henriques, an actor and acrobat who had performed with the San Francisco Mime Troupe in 1967, was brought into the show by Nina Serrano.[78] Zimmerman was brought on by Len Chandler, who found him playing piano in an LA restaurant. Alaimo had also worked with the Mime Troupe, though more recently he'd been in New York, performing with a Harlem-based Puerto Rican street theater group. Alaimo and Zimmerman would stay with the show through the Asia tour, while Vereen and Henriques would not participate beyond the next stop in Idaho. Following the shows in Idaho, Vereen began rehearsals for the Broadway production of *Jesus Christ Superstar*, precluding him from appearing in Texas, though there may have been other reasons he chose to part ways with the show. Serrano recalls being disappointed that Henriques was not invited to participate in subsequent performances, though it is not clear what the terms of his departure were.[79]

At the Covered Wagon coffeehouse in Idaho the FTA performed twice, after shows in Boise the day prior. At Boise State College's Liberal Arts Auditorium, two capacity crowds of four hundred each had turned out to pack the place, and the Covered Wagon sold out as well.[80] According to Jeff Schutts, who has written a detailed and compelling history of the Covered Wagon, Vereen was particularly well received by the Idaho audiences. He also reflected the introduction into the FTA cast of more radical political perspectives around race and racism. Interestingly, however, Vereen's comments to activists at the Covered Wagon intersect with concerns expressed by Gardner about the direction of the coffeehouses and the FTA. At the same time, Vereen seems to push back against the idea that entertainment becomes less effective politically when it explicitly advocates for political action:

> What we got to do is get our shit together at home. I mean even this revolution is being exploited. We sell records, and where does the money go? I mean, our leaders are in jail and we are selling posters. Now in Boise there were a thousand people at those shows. If those people put their consciences to work, they could do it. They could accomplish something... if they really care... I think they just wanted to be entertained.[81]

The terms in which Vereen expresses his concern are productively ambivalent; as a Broadway performer, his apparent dismissiveness toward entertainment seems as if it could either reflect a frustration with his own involvement in *Hair*, or instead a frustration with mainstream performance that isn't sufficiently political, as perhaps he considered *Hair* to have been. Alternatively, we could understand his critique as targeted at an audience of civilians and students (in Boise), considered in comparison with the predominantly GI audience at the coffeehouse. Either way, Vereen's remarks reflect a dynamic that is not typically highlighted within historical discussions of 1960s radical and experimental theater—that where theater was intended explicitly and tactically as an intervention into a movement, the answer to the question of whether or not theater or entertainment was an appropriate use of resources was not necessarily always given as a "yes."

That the FTA took this question seriously is reflected in the fact of its dissolution, following the end of its tour overseas (discussed in the next chapter). When theater ceased to be a useful mode of participation in the project of building the GI movement, the group ceased to exist. It is not at all clear (no one seems really to remember) to what extent the end of the FTA was planned or discussed, or whether it just happened. What is clear is that the FTA was developed with a specific purpose, and its participants, organizers, and spectators were regularly engaged in discussions about the extent to which the money and time devoted to the FTA might be better directed elsewhere. While a number of organizers I have spoken with expressed frustration with the way the FTA was run, and particularly how much it cost, all conceded that the show had been a remarkable success, and that the GIs "loved it." Moreover, as this and the next chapter reflect, the FTA had a measurable, documented impact on the militancy of the movement at specific bases, in a manner that is tied directly to the specificity of its form. It was as theater *and* as popular entertainment that the show could offer sites of recognition that not only validated but amplified and legitimized the figure of the antiwar GI: by politicizing spectatorship through its requests to perform on base, drawing its material from underground GI newspapers, and centering the spectator in mainstream coverage of the show.

The FTA could use theater tactically, recognizing its advantages and limitations, because its commitment was to a political project, not an artistic one. Rather than operating as its motivation, or its raison d'être, theatrical practice offered a specific mode of political intervention that facilitated the possibility of recognition while undermining the stability of fixed identities. At every turn, a central concern was the relationship between the politics of the performers and those of its spectators, and the possibility that the former might, in some way, exert undue and invalidating influence over the latter. These were not merely tactical disagreements but reflected underlying political fissures, and indexed distinctly different perspectives on the formation of solidarity and its role in movement building. In its shift, explored at greater length in the next chapter, from an emphasis on entertainment to an explicit expression of a politics that extended well beyond the plight of the white, male GI, the FTA navigated this terrain in ways that offer an opportunity to reexamine how the figure of the activist was constructed, on the right and the left alike, during the 1960s, and in the decades following. The fluidity offered by the interplay between reality and fiction, spectator and performer, object and subject, form and content, is revealed as at once the absolutely necessary condition of revolutionary change and as the basis for rewriting its possibility out of historical existence.

3

Say It! Solidarity Without Guarantees

As it turned out, most of the sketches, the part that I was playing was the feminist or the one that was making fun of the woman who wasn't the feminist. I mean, it was kind of—Those were the parts I got. So, in saying the lines, I was reading the script of a feminist, and that's how I became one. And talking to the women in the military and talking to the women in the Philippines—the Filipinas, the Hawaiian women, the Japanese women, the Okinawan women—they made me a feminist. So I came into feminism through a global door, and when I got home from that, I just had to rethink everything in my life.
—Holly Near

On the Monday before Thanksgiving, 1971, the FTA played New York City's Philharmonic Hall to a capacity crowd of two thousand. It was, as Dick Brukenfeld wrote in an article for the *Village Voice*, "an unusual evening at Lincoln Center." As if to make his point, his review of the event begins not with the blackout sketches or the show's signature song, nor even with Fonda or Sutherland, but with an extended description of Nina Simone performing "My Sweet Lord," by George Harrison:

> "I really want to see you," wails the high priestess of soul. Weaving like a benign cobra, Nina is shifting the rock rhythm from knees and hips to shoulders and arms, taking us through 100 changes, now expanding, now modulating, now listening, stretching out a phrase like taffy. Cool and controlled, she works an excitement . . . like sex on velvet.
> "I really want to see you."
> "Ha-le-lu-lia," answers the Bethany Baptist Choir, 20 draft-age singers clapping and tambourining their counterpoint behind her.

Like William Blake finding the world in a grain of sand, Nina's exploring every facet of that song, approaching it from every direction before taking us in to land. She's bringing us to an ecstasy that's close to religion.[1]

If Brukenfeld's opening manages to communicate little about the reason for the evening's performance (besides, perhaps, his reference to "draft-age singers"), it does reflect the fact that it was also an "unusual evening" for the FTA: for the first time, most of its spectators were civilians, attending as a kind of surrogate audience to support the show's ability to tour to those for whom it was actually intended. The "basic FTA show," some version of which had been playing to troops stationed across the country for several months, occupied only two of the benefit's five hours, and, in a description that contrasts sharply with his initial rapture, Brukenfeld finds that while the show "not surprisingly, attacks military and political establishments," the evening was "happily free of heavy anti-war propaganda." In his estimation, the effect of the show on soldiers "must be . . . to sing Miss Simone's song, to tell them someone they already know, like Mr. Sutherland and Miss Fonda, really wants to see them." Besides Simone's opening number, a "Broadway salute to the GI movement" featuring Dick Gregory, Ossie Davis, Faye Dunaway, and Eli Wallach preceded the presentation of the FTA show itself, and offered again an awareness of the evening's displaced spectator, at once invoked and largely absent. Proceeds went to support the United States Servicemen's Fund in general and the FTA in particular, as the latter would depart shortly for a tour of the Pacific Rim. Stops were slated for Hawaii, the Philippines, Japan, and Okinawa.

Beyond the unique features of an event that asked, as Brukenfeld writes, civilians to put themselves in the place of servicemembers, and besides the ecstatic contributions of Simone and other celebrity guests, the version of the FTA that arrived in Manhattan was representative of what the group would present during its time overseas.[2] However, in comparison with the show that had debuted months earlier at the Haymarket Coffeehouse near Fort Bragg, both cast and content had changed to reflect a broader set of questions connected to the US's involvement in Vietnam. There had been new additions to the troupe that rebalanced its composition in terms of race and gender, including Bay Area Black poet and activist Pamela Donegan, the young white actress and singer Holly Near, and Black comedian Paul Mooney. (Mooney was actually a last-minute replacement for James Watson, Jr., a Black actor who was listed as one of the upcoming tour's performers on the October 11 press release. Mooney indicates in his autobiography that Watson put him in touch with Fonda.) New sketches addressed sexism, racism, and imperialism, connecting these issues with those that had been central to the show from the beginning: the war's unpopularity among GIs, the rising death toll, the military's repressive policies and exploitative hierarchies. The *Daily World*'s coverage of the Manhattan fundraiser reflected the new, more expansive scope of the show's message, referring to it as a "double-barreled attack on the racist-male supremacist military system and the war in Indochina."³

Yet that these were shifts in tone and focus would not have been readily apparent to the Lincoln Center audience, as few would have had the basis for making such a comparison. Indeed, even many of those involved, as performers or organizers, were, when I spoke to them, not aware of what the show had been before they joined, or of what it became after they departed. Thus while Brukenfeld's opening description of Simone's performance leads *me* to note, for example, the significance of a Black woman effectively replacing a white man (Country Joe) as the benefit's high-profile musical act, this is likely a reading particular to my own distanced, scholarly perspective, and its bird's-eye view of the path the FTA forged both geographically and politically over the course of its brief existence. And at any rate, much about the show remained the same, from the central roles of Fonda and Sutherland, to the mix of slapstick humor and solemnity, to the explicit emphasis on drawing its material from underground newspapers and other GI sources, to its remarkable popularity with its intended audience. Following its performances in Idaho, the FTA had played its September shows in Killeen (two each on the 18th and 19th) and San Antonio (one on the 20th), as usual, to packed houses and enthusiastic crowds. As had happened in Fayetteville, the Killeen city government tried to prevent the group from securing public venues; and as had happened in Fayetteville, they ended up in the local coffeehouse, with lots of grudging small-town coverage. The *Killeen Daily Herald*, which had carried a number of articles covering (and editorials supporting) the city council's decision to deny access to a local hall, ran its cover story the day after the first performance under a title seemingly intended to downplay the show's warm reception by its audience: "Show Features Antiwar Skits."[4] San Antonio posed no problems. The show filled a downtown club with over 2,300 spectators, "military, front to back[. . . .] Less than 50 tickets were sold to civilians," according to the *San Antonio Light*.[5]

That the FTA show could remain popular and recognizable despite significant changes to its cast and content helps to highlight the tactical nature of the FTA, its rootedness in political practice and movement building, and its disinterest in much of what has been preserved of radical or political theater history from the era. As importantly, it signals the way in which an alternative political narrative appears if we read against the grain of political (theater) history, attending to that which left little to no trace because, as an evolving activist practice, it took on a new form when the old one ceased to serve. In its erasure and recovery, the FTA offers a new perspective on the kinds of tensions and disagreements that prompted its reconfiguration prior to its Lincoln Center performance and Pacific Rim tour, as these were by no means unique to the GI-oriented performance project. Similar challenges faced any organization or group that sought to raise political consciousness around a particular form of oppression while failing to recognize other, intersecting forms of discrimination and marginalization. Black women activists fought for representation and equality within the movement for Black liberation as well as within the feminist movement. Gay and lesbian activists fought for representation and equality within movements that presumed the straightness of antiwar activists, feminists, and Black, Indigenous, or Chicano radicals. In each case, multiply marginalized groups had to fight against the premise that their visibility threatened the "coherence" of the larger movement. In its dependence upon the "legibility" of the antiwar GI *as GI*, and so, seemingly, upon whiteness and maleness as the terms of representation, the GI movement constantly contended with the ways in which an expanded image of the antiwar servicemember was at once imperative—to connect to and reflect the diverse experiences of enlisted people—and also potentially a threat to the basis upon which that movement made its claims of legitimacy. Like other movements, it would have to challenge the existing terms of representation even as it was required to build its legibility upon them.

The new cast of the FTA show. From left to right: Rita Martinson, Jane Fonda, Michael Alaimo, Donald Sutherland, Len Chandler. Not pictured: Pamela Donegan, Holly Near, and Paul Mooney.
Courtesy of Displaced Films.

A different but related version of this contradiction confronted most if not all of the radical or political theater groups working during the 1960s and '70s, in the form of a growing recognition that the political goals or commitments of a company were not automatically reflected in its internal structure, its chosen content, the diversity of its membership, or the demographics of its audience. This was true, to varying degrees in varying ways, of the Free Southern Theater, the Open Theater, the Living Theatre, Bread and Puppet, the San Francisco Mime Troupe, At the Foot of the Mountain, The Performance Group, and El Teatro Campesino. Deliberate efforts had to be made to challenge the inherited biases and structural inequality informing artistic practice. However, in comparison with the FTA, most of these groups were not tied quite so existentially to a predetermined audience, and so the political and artistic choices they might make could attract (or alienate) new categories of spectators without this automatically posing a threat to the group's project. Indeed, in some cases a shift in the composition of the audience was precisely part of the point. The political stakes of inclusion, where they were in conflict with a group or leader's established artistic vision, provoked debates over the relationship between the two, and a tack toward inclusion and equality in a group's structure and process typically impacted the form and content of its work as well.

While, in many cases, a newfound attention to the politics of process provoked a group's reassessment of its practice and product, most of these groups did not make work according to the needs of a specific movement, nor, as noted above, did they remain obligated to the same audience regardless of what else they might change. The FTA, in contrast, as first and foremost a political project, experienced a transformation motivated primarily by differing perspectives on how to serve the GI movement by performing for enlisted men and women. Because its political intervention was simultaneously an artistic one, political disagreements were often articulated as creative differences, and as a result, it is difficult to describe the fissures that led to the group's reconfiguration as only one or the other. The FTA's performances in San Antonio—the final stop on its domestic tour excepting its performance at Fort Dix just prior to the Lincoln Center benefit—were the last to include members of The Committee or Country Joe McDonald. At some point (those involved whom I interviewed only vaguely recollect the event), the female members of the troupe confronted members of The Committee over accusations of sexism; this solidified a split that had been developing since Parker took over directorial control from Myerson, and which was exacerbated by Fonda's experiences during the filming of *Steelyard Blues*. As she explained in a *New York Times* articles published just weeks before the Pacific Rim tour, she wasn't the film's star and so was not treated like a star; she describes realizing, as a result, that men often don't listen to women and that she'd been protected from this awareness by a relative level of privilege, due to her wealth and fame.[6]

Though McDonald's name appears on the October 11 press release detailing the plans for the FTA's Pacific Rim tour, and while his manager, Bill Belmont, made many of the initial arrangements for the tour, in the final week before the Lincoln Center performance McDonald gave a press conference at which he announced he was quitting the group. He counted among his reasons for leaving Fonda's elitism and the fact that the group didn't operate as a "collective." Fonda shot back: "Well, it's not a collective. And I disagree with him that it should have been. We're a group of people from different backgrounds and we're united simply in supporting the soldiers."[7] McDonald recollects a phone call with Fonda in which she hung up on him after he told her he wouldn't be heading overseas.[8] Though Robin Menken had been a key driver of the feminist turn the FTA was taking, she too parted ways with the show, for reasons that are similarly a mix of political and artistic disagreement. Since first joining the FTA for its August performances in Tacoma, Menken had advocated for the inclusion of material in the show that more explicitly addressed issues faced by Black and women servicemembers. While the show had always been built around content that came from GI newspapers, Menken sharpened its intervention with sketches that addressed issues specific to the bases the show would visit. She ultimately felt sidelined as a writer and for this reason did not tour with the group abroad.[9]

Thus, when the FTA took the stage of the Philharmonic with a cast in equal numbers men and women, Black and white, without Menken but also without The Committee, its appearance reflected a set of conflicts and struggles familiar within the narrative of political history, and political theater history, of the 1960s and early '70s. However, the FTA, with its singular goal of supporting the GI movement, faced a unique set of circumstances, one obscured by the civilian audience it happened to have that night: whatever changes it might make to its cast, leadership, or content, its audience of mostly young, white, working-class men would remain the same. From its outset, the FTA had performed the possibility and necessity of civilian-soldier solidarity by drawing its content and legitimacy directly and explicitly from its audience. As discussed in the previous chapter, Fonda and others publicly stated that they could tell their audience nothing the GIs didn't already know, and they took their material from underground GI newspapers. They also performed that material in such a way as to stage evidence of a common purpose while emphasizing a critical difference in immediate circumstances. To this end, and without explicitly identifying its target audience as white and male, the show at first implicitly centered this figure, as it sought to challenge the assumption that the "American soldier" was necessarily pro-war. Any specific grievances portrayed initially belonged to a generalized image of the antiwar GI. As a result, the show expressed civilian support for the GI movement while failing to address any of the complexities either category—civilian or servicemember—necessarily contained. When the FTA began to explore the ways in which the exploitation of white GIs intersected with other forms of exploitation, inside and outside of the military, a number of challenges presented themselves. In particular, new tensions developed around the already fraught question of entertainment, and the extent to which its political impact depended upon avoiding or downplaying, rather than introducing, issues beyond those common to most members of the audience. The concern was not only that the show might alienate some spectators by taking a position on issues other than the war, but that *associating* antiwar soldiers with such positions might threaten the antiwar soldier's critical legibility *as* soldier. If, as chapter 1 claims, the political efficacy (and growth) of the GI movement depended upon the visibility of the antiwar GI *as* GI, then the FTA show needed to avoid obscuring his specificity as a very particular kind of activist—not a hippie, not a college student, not a communist pretending to be a veteran. Sketches about imperialism, for example, or immigrants' rights might invalidate the soldier-spectator's antiwar position by rendering him too-radical by association.

The fact that, despite such concerns, the FTA *did* significantly expand its content over the course of its brief existence forms the basis for this chapter's central argument: that at the intersection of the FTA's successes and its failures lies a remarkable illustration of solidarity as a practice, one engaged in the "negotiation and renegotiation of forms of political identification."[10] In *Solidarity: Hidden Histories and Geographies of Internationalism*, human geographer David Featherstone poses an alternative to a traditional understanding of solidarity as a "given" relation based upon similarity. Featherstone argues instead that

> solidarities are usefully thought of as transformative political relations. There are no guarantees about the kinds of transformations wrought by solidarities. They can entrench as well as challenge privilege and can close down as well as open up political possibilities and alliances.[11]

His book presents numerous case studies, examining the intersecting, international movements that developed in response to colonialism, the

Cold War, and climate change, among others. Each study is directed differently toward the same project of discovering erased connections and analyzing their construction, and he approaches his task by "positioning sources such as texts, political songs, and activist testimonies as part of, not separate from, the conduct of political activity."[12] What makes Featherstone, relative to other academic treatments of solidarity, especially useful for my purposes, is that he foregrounds the ways in which activists "tell themselves about themselves," but positions this telling as a site of transformation. His model recognizes expressions of common interest or purpose as improvisational constructions that pursue solidarity on necessarily precarious ground, because that which is "told" is subject to change in the act of telling. Featherstone argues for defining solidarity as a relation that is built or constructed, rather than "something which just binds already formed communities together."[13]

Moreover, in his attention to "hidden histories," Featherstone emphasizes a point central to my own historiographical project: the ease with which the *process* of movement building, and its dependence on the changing consciousness of its participants, can be forgotten in the telling of political history. That is, it is *because* solidarity proposes the possibility, as Jodi Dean puts it, that "anyone" can be a comrade that its existence is so readily subjected to historical erasure.[14] Dean, writing about the figure of the comrade in her book of the same name, depicts the relation that "comrade" names as one that "cuts through determinations given by the present."[15] The comrade is "generic" in a critical sense; its sameness with other comrades is the sameness of "being on the same side." This is why, for Dean, anyone "but not everyone" can be a comrade—*someone* must be on the other side and not, therefore, a comrade. For Dean, the designation of comrade does not accept that solidarity can be built only among and between those who already identify with each other in some way. Rather, it situates solidarity as a radical reordering of the perception of common interests across difference.

I should note that my use of the word "solidarity" is informed by my sense that the term has been "reclaimed" somewhat over the past ten or fifteen years, particularly as a result of the Occupy movement and its reopening of class politics as both discourse and practice. Which is to say, by using solidarity to discuss the GI movement and the FTA, I mean deliberately to invoke not only the relation it describes, but also the way in which it is often used to declare that relation *and* the significance of the context within which the declaration is made. One can say "solidarity!" in a way one cannot say "allyship!" or "support!" "Solidarity!" is a uniquely self-contained expression. Driving by a protest but unable to stop and join, you can yell "solidarity!" and your meaning will be instantly understood. Somehow, it means more than "I support you!" or "I agree!" It means, as I hear it, "I am not the same as you but I am with you, I perceive your struggle as connected to my own." A critical difference is expressed, but it is a difference that binds and connects. At the same time, however, this declaration, like "comrade," is always at risk of seeming like a performance—an invocation and occupation of a past political discourse that no longer pertains. It is still a bit dusty, even if, over the past decade or so, it has become less so. Using it here, I mean to invoke all of these facets: its performative quality, its historical connection with leftist discourse and Marxist politics, and its ambivalent relationship to the present. While Featherstone's book is an academic study in a way that Dean's is not, his emphasis on "the invisible" helps to explain why the expressions "solidarity" and "comrade" feel at once so relevant in our contemporary moment, and also anachronistic or, perhaps, theatrical—the politics of solidarity have to fight against the inexorable pull, under capitalism, to erase the perception of common (class) interest across difference. Absent this perception, sincere invocations of "comrade" or "solidarity" become the words of actors, rooting performances in a past that they ought to recognize has been left behind. This is why, particularly for younger activists in the US, being called "comrade" can make even an avowed socialist "cringe or laugh (or both)." This is the experience described by one of Dean's reviewers, who goes on to explain that "it's hard to hear the word *comrade* without simultaneously hearing a lot of other inherited cultural baggage."[16]

Dean illustrates precisely this point when she opens *Comrade* with Obama's speech at the 2016 White House Press Correspondents Dinner. As part of his routine, Obama jokes about Bernie Sanders being a comrade. Dean walks us through the multiple ways in which the joke "works"—on the one hand, Obama was referencing the accusations, from the right, that he (Obama) is a socialist, and so the sort of person who would call someone "comrade"; Sanders, on the other hand, is *ac-*

tually a socialist, and therefore someone you might actually call a comrade, but who, some would argue, was *not* Obama's comrade because he didn't sufficiently support Obama's political agenda. Whichever way you read it, though, undoubtedly part of the joke is that no one seriously calls each other comrade anymore, regardless of whether they might, on some level, identify as a socialist, or even a communist. A comrade exists only in the past—or as someone merely playing at revolutionary politics in the present.

What all this suggests is that performance—and more specifically theater, as I will argue—might be a useful way to think about how activists navigate the problem of establishing an awareness of common interest where none is presumed to be. This chapter uses an analysis of the FTA to explore the particular challenges and advantages (and perhaps even inevitabilities) of expressing or building solidarity through performance, and argues that theatricality plays a central role in shaping activist discourse and practice. I first examine the shift described briefly toward the end of the previous chapter, when Fonda and other members of the cast became more politicized around the issue of women's oppression, and consider the significance, in relation to solidarity, of the position of those who disagreed with the direction of the FTA. Then, I look broadly at the way in which the FTA deliberately constructed the appearance of solidarity between soldiers and civilians, in part by emphasizing the distance and difference separating actor from spectator. Building on this, I examine how the introduction of anti-sexist material into the show itself successfully navigated the intersection of multiple political concerns, in comparison with the rupture produced by the development of interpersonal conflict. I argue that the distance and displacement facilitated by the staged representation of anti-sexist politics—which derived from the group's performance of soldier-civilian solidarity—allowed for a recognition of the relationship between sexism and militarism. Finally, I examine the contours of the Pacific Rim tour, noting the many ways in which the FTA's organizers understood the show as an opportunity to trace and highlight interconnected relations of power and common points of grievance. Drawing in particular upon the "maps of grievance" Featherstone offers in *Solidarity*, I propose that the tour itself constitutes a tactical performance of solidarity, made at once precarious and possible by the necessity of following in Hope's wake.

Militancy and Authenticity

In considering the question of how the FTA navigated the terms of solidarity within the framework of live performance, it is important to examine how debates concerning the politicization of the GI movement were already playing out, and the extent to which these were dependent upon a shared or contested understanding of the political significance or function of entertainment. As discussed in the previous two chapters, the development of the GI movement depended upon establishing the legitimacy and legibility of an antiwar GI identity. To raise the visibility of this identity, civilian activists collaborated with veterans and active-duty soldiers to provide sites of recognition, in the form of coffeehouses, solidarity committees, and entertainment. In keeping with the militancy of the period, participants in and supporters of the GI movement in many cases sought to connect struggles waged by soldiers against military policies to broader struggles against racism and sexism. Many of the activists involved in the latter understood these struggles as part of a revolutionary project, and they brought their political perspectives and goals with them into the work they did in collaboration with and in support of resisting GIs and antiwar veterans.

Though debates over the FTA's political orientation did not significantly impede its operation until several months into the tour, these were not new disagreements within the GI movement and its civilian support network more generally. They centered particularly around the extent to which the services or spaces that civilian supporters offered GIs should overtly encourage organization and politicization or should instead simply reflect the recreational interests of the current generation of enlisted men. For Fred Gardner, one of the founders of the coffeehouse movement and writer for the FTA, the question was one of opportunism. According to the retrospective narrative he provides in "Hollywood Confidential," radical activists like Tom Hayden were initially dismissive of the prospects for GI resistance. He recalls Hayden insisting that "soldiers were no better than cops," and "that [Gardner's] plans for getting in touch with them provided no 'blueprint for converting them.'"[17] With the success of the coffeehouse movement, however, Hayden and others recognized the potential for GI radicalization and began almost instantly to get involved. This broader participation of activists on the left distorted, as Gardner saw it, his "original concept of the coffeehouses as places for GIs to take it easy (as opposed to bases for proselytizing)." Gardner writes that after he left Columbia for Waynesville, Missouri, to set up another coffeehouse there, he heard from GIs at Fort Jackson that the new "movement people" running the UFO were making the place decidedly less "groovy."[18]

Some of Gardner's comments on this point suggest his concern centered upon questions of organizational strategy. During its first months, the coffeehouse had been a "magnet" for dissident GIs, and in February 1968, a group of soldiers planned the first group antiwar action at Fort Jackson. As with other forms of GI resistance, the modest protest leveraged its participants' identity as soldiers to protect against—but also draw attention to—any disciplinary action that might follow from the act of protest. The men decided to protest by publicly praying for peace. David Cortright describes how the thirty-five "uncertain but determined soldiers gathered in front of the main post chapel for what had been advertised as a silent protest service for the war." When the group was stopped by military police, most of the men left quickly; two, Robert Tater and Stephen Kline, were detained. According to Cortright, news of the protest "created a sensation within the peace movement" and prompted its leaders to "view soldier dissent with great optimism."[19]

Based on this event, Gardner, rightly, perceived that GIs were capable of self-organization—that given the space and the resources to do so, they would find ways of making their antiwar views known, and these would likely be more powerful than anything civilians might think up on their behalf. However, in his concern that the activists now running the UFO were "over-fertilizing" GI newspapers with political content, for example, or pushing soldiers to engage in open acts of resistance, "which resulted in the soldiers getting busted or given punitive reassignments, while the civilian lefty organizers gained status within the movement for being involved in a 'struggle,'" Gardner risks erasing the militant, activist GI who might, of his own volition, "over-fertilize" the newspaper or advocate open acts of resistance.[20] David Zeiger, the filmmaker whose *Sir! No Sir!* documents the rise of the GI movement, contends that "there was tremendous concern among civilian activists for the safety of GIs who took political action, and it was the GIs themselves who quite willingly faced those risks and took the consequences, even going beyond what civilian organizers were advocating. Gypsy Peterson, who founded the *Fatigue Press* [and smuggled hundreds of copies of it onto Fort Hood while stationed there], is a prime example, and there are hundreds, even thousands more."[21]

In this light, Gardner's complaints betray what seems to have been a more general distaste for the introduction into the coffeehouses—and by extension, into the space of the GI movement more broadly—of political issues and questions beyond those he perceived as directly and immediately pertinent to GIs. For Gardner, there was not so great a distance separating the local authorities' evident prudishness in requiring the UFO to take down a "Young Aphrodites" poster and the new staff members' decision to replace Marilyn Monroe with Eldridge Cleaver. Despite the fact that the latter reflected, at least in part, growing anti-sexist and anti-racist sentiment among the civilian supporters of the GI movement, Gardner seems to find little difference in practice between the city inspector—"we don't want no breasts around here"—and those most likely interested in raising the level of politics inside the coffeehouses and, perhaps, making space for women servicemembers to get involved. Tellingly, he equates the political "opportunism" of figures like Hayden with the "political correctness" of performers like folksinger Barbara Dane, a term he uses to refer, derogatorily, to those who insisted upon infusing the coffeehouses with the anti-sexist, internationalist, and/or revolutionary politics that some civilian activists brought with them into the movement.

In chapter 2, I discussed how the FTA's initial publicity downplayed its "political" function and instead focused upon its intention of entertaining. It is important to recognize that this was a tactic on two levels, and not everyone involved agreed with both of these. On the one hand, playing up the show as entertainment dealt with a practical concern regarding publicity. That this was calculated and continued to serve an important purpose in advertising the show during the Pacific Rim tour is made clear in the correspondence between the FTA's organizers. In one letter, Paul Lauter of the United States Servicemen's Fund explains the policy of securing a place to perform and *then* asking for permission to come on base.[22] And in fact, in some locations, the base's refusal could mean an additional layer of publicity particularly appealing to locals. In the Philippines, Louis Wolf notes, extra publicity would derive from the fact that Americans were being kept off an American base. As he wrote to USSF organizers as preparations were being made for the tour, "On this again, our analysis is: 'Great! Fine! Right on! The more the brass denies the show access to bases, the more GIs will want to see the show.' [. . .] Also, the local media would really dig on it: the show being denied (as Americans) entry to U.S. bases."²³

The show's function as entertainment was also emphasized by those within the movement (both civilians and GIs) who understood the political or politics to be opportunistic, didactic, and inorganic. If we consider the significance of the GI as such to the visibility, legitimacy, and significance of the GI movement, the logic appears to be that by overpoliticizing the GI movement, the GIs involved might become less recognizable *as* GIs. GIs who also identified as—and looked and acted like—revolutionaries might forgo a critical legibility. For people like Gardner and Country Joe McDonald, the emphasis upon the unadulterated political subjectivity of the GI echoes (albeit to different ends) the delegitimization efforts of the Nixon administration. Both attempt to downplay the existence of the extremely politicized, revolutionary GI, and do so in part by defining the GI as incompatible with a certain strain of radical politics. To be clear, I do not wish to overstate the point and attribute to Gardner and McDonald a position neither of them would recognize as their own. They were both open advocates on behalf of the GI movement. Both understood the reality of military service, as indeed they both had served. But insofar as they identified with the "old left," or at least insofar as they did *not* identify with the "new left," they tend to paint the student and youth radicals of the era with a very broad, negative brush, one that undoubtedly catches young, radical GIs in its stroke.

A vivid (and rather funny) example of the conflicting investments in entertainment versus politics appears early on. Although it does not seem to have produced any immediate fallout within the ranks of the FTA, a written exchange prior to the inaugural Fort Bragg show foreshadows the development of a similar tension among the group's members. In a letter to Jules Feiffer (one of the FTA show's writers), three women staff members at the Haymarket Coffeehouse explain that "since this is a counter USO show, we think that the script should have none of the sexist scenes in it that Bob-Hope-Specials have—dancing girls or any portrayal of women being inferior to men (which they aren't). please! no moquery [sic] of women!" They continue:

> [. . .] if it turns out that there are parts in it which we (women on staff) think are sexist, we hope you would take them out after the first show. If you don't we will a) pull the plug; b) hang you and mike nichols in effigy; c) hang you and mike nichols; d) scream like shit; e) cry.

Feiffer jots down, on the letter itself, what appears to be his intended and slightly exasperated reply. After expressing mild annoyance that his name is misspelled and remarking upon another spelling error, he responds to their request/threat:

> There is a scene, a Bob Hope parody, in which Jane comes on as one of those girls Hope always takes with him to Vietnam. If Jane thinks its sexist she doesn't have to do it; if you think its sexist Jane doesn't have to do it; I myself think it's a satire on sexism but look, I only wrote it.[24]

It's easy enough to imagine that Fonda appearing onstage dressed anything like "one of those girls," regardless of authorial intent, would not necessarily have been enjoyed by its audience only or even primarily as satire. Indeed, it may well have resolved a problem—albeit problematically—that dogged the show throughout its existence. In her autobiography, Fonda recalls the disappointment some GIs expressed when they realized the famous actress they'd come to see was going to remain fully clothed: "One soldier told Holly Near that they'd torn down my *Barbarella* poster in anger."[25]

Under the premise of satire, a sketch like the one described here would have had the benefit of reinforcing the civilian-soldier distinction, by, on the one hand, making a clear reference to Hope's program, and, on the other, by giving the troops what many of them likely wanted—Fonda wearing not a lot of clothing.[26] I am not suggesting that Feiffer's response is disingenuous, but rather I want to point out the way in which the emphasis on entertainment missed or disavowed the other political questions raised by staging representations of women. So long as the FTA's political impact was understood as existing solely in relation to its value as entertainment, the inclusion of Fonda as "one of those girls" appears as a completely legitimate proposal, made more so by its contextualization as satire. The sketch was never performed, deferring for a time the question of to what extent the FTA might sustain political discourse beyond those issues directly and visibly relevant to the antiwar GI. Once the question was raised again, later in the tour, it played out along similar lines, but now with troupe members holding differing opinions on the entertainment value and relevance, or lack thereof, of sympathetic female characters within a show targeted at a GI audience.

The rift between Country Joe McDonald and Fonda reflected a similar frustration on the part of the former with the introduction of "politics" or political correctness into the troupe's organization and content. McDonald, like Gardner, understood his own political contribution to the movement as consisting in providing entertainment that reflected the feelings and interests of an antiwar GI audience. Related to this, and complicating the already significant tension around anti-sexism and feminism, were accusations of elitism, directed primarily at Fonda but sometimes also at the cast as a whole. Generally speaking, however, these were not charges made by GI spectators, but by civilian activists working in support of the GI movement, and also by McDonald. In fact, McDonald frames his departure from the group as a response to Fonda's elitist treatment of the GIs. The press release announcing his split explained that he was leaving the show "because Miss Fonda is an amateur in the peace movement who wants to run everything and is harmful to the peace movement."[27] Interestingly, his press release also claims that the show "has racist, sexist and elitist elements." He does not elaborate upon these, emphasizing instead the fact that Fonda exercised significant control over the direction of the show, and that she raised or provided most of the money needed to cover its expenses (which was true). The statement concludes with a reference to his press conference at the Stanhope Hotel, during which he said "that if an anti-war show is going to travel, its aims and content should be decided after discussion within the peace movement rather than reflecting one person's views."[28]

As a later section in this chapter will explore, it is quite clear that the aim and content of the Pacific Rim tour *was* decided after discussion with many individuals and groups active within the peace movement. For this reason, and based on an interview conducted with McDonald in 2013, it seems that his primary disagreement with Fonda, though couched in terms of elitism, centered upon the introduction of feminist material into the show and the complementary "feminist takeover," as Fonda described it to reporter Vivian Gornick, of the troupe's leadership.[29] To be clear, the way in which Fonda and Parker in particular pursued the problem of perceived anti-sexism within the group seems to have been, in keeping with the militant tenor of the feminist movement during this period, at times quite alienating and hostile as it manifested interpersonally. Speaking about the confrontation the FTA's women members provoked with The Committee, Nina Serrano acknowledged that she, Parker, and Fonda felt they were fighting a "battle": "we had burning issues because the feminist movement was just starting and we were into feminism and we were breaking barriers and we were warriors, bringing it into this huge anti-imperialist struggle."[30] Menken, in a 1972 interview with Alan Farley, describes it as a "purge situation" and that the four women constituted a "flying wedge": "we went back to the old cast, and said there are demands not being met, and we're going to change it."[31] Fonda remembers little about the meeting with The Committee, but in Gornick's account of her conversation with the actress during the FTA's flight to Hawaii, she quotes Fonda describing what had happened as a "heartbreaking struggle." Fonda felt that she had been the "token woman" in the FTA, until Parker had helped her to see that the feminist struggle was "[her] struggle also."[32]

While McDonald's accusation of elitism seems ultimately to stem from a disagreement over the relevance of anti-sexist sentiment to the predominantly male GI movement, the same accusation reflected a different set of concerns and tensions when it came from activists running the Shelter Half coffeehouse in Tacoma, Washington. In a lengthy "Open Letter to the FTA Show Cast," "The Tacoma People" first acknowledge that they were pleased that, during the time the FTA spent in Tacoma, "the cast was heavily involved in a struggle with sexism." They go on, however, to express frustration that the cast had not made time to sit down with the staff and discuss problems that had arisen due to the "huge class differences [that] exist between members of the cast and the Tacoma people." As the letter continues, it becomes apparent that some in the FTA had expressed concerns over a perceived lack of GI participation in the coffeehouse and in making arrangements for the show, and indeed it feels as though this criticism may have, at least in part, provoked the accusations of elitism: Who were these Hollywood actors to come in and criticize the work of local activists? The writers do, however, acknowledge that the criticism was at least in part justified, but attribute this to the fact that at the time the Shelter Half and the GI Alliance "were undergoing a serious division over the issues of sexism, racism, and classism and GI versus civilian control."[33] Here, they might evoke McDonald and Gardner's characterization of the "over-fertilizing" civilian activist, imposing his politics on the antiwar GI, even as they all seem aligned on the question of Fonda's "elitism." Overall, the letter serves as a window onto the profoundly contradictory position the show perpetually occupied: for the show to be a success, significant sums of money had to be spent. Though these came, by and large, from Fonda, Fonda's ability to pay was taken as evidence of elitism and proof that she had not sufficiently "struggled" with her class status.

The same bind appears in an account McDonald gives of one of the few meetings he attended during which changes to the show were discussed. He recalls being rebuffed when he suggested that a woman play Lyndon Johnson.[34] According to McDonald, Fonda replied that that wouldn't work, because the GIs were all working-class kids who didn't know how to spell. McDonald was offended by this, especially, as he explained to me, because he considered himself a working-class kid, and he didn't know how to spell. Both the Tacoma letter and McDonald's anecdote recall the USSF report on the FTA's first show at Fort Bragg, insofar as the report's reference to the performers' "professionalism" appears, in the context of these later accusations, like it might reflect a kind of rigidity around the form and content of the show and also concerning the logistics of its presentation. Parsing whether Fonda's dismissiveness toward McDonald was elitist, or whether the FTA didn't "sit down" with the Tacoma organizers simply due to time constraints, is basically impossible. I would suggest it is more helpful to recognize how difficult it could be to navigate critical differences in identity and experience among celebrities, soldiers, and civilian organizers as they collaborated on the shared project of staging the show. The tensions that would finally fracture the FTA and lead to its reconstitution reflect not the failure of solidarity's performative, but rather the "contested processes through which solidarities are generated."[35] Gardner and McDonald emphasized the necessity of standing in solidarity with the antiwar GI on his own terms, but did so without considering that the antiwar GI identity might not be fixed but instead continuously constructed and performed. In contrast, the FTA undertook precarious performances of solidarity, based on the possibility that any given GI might accept an expression of solidarity premised not only upon his own interests, but upon the different yet connected interests of someone else.

Solidarity on Stage

Though I draw upon Featherstone's understanding of solidarity, I propose to alter his premise slightly, supplementing his use of the word "transformative" with both "theatrical" and "performative." I do so to identify more precisely the precarious dimensions of solidarity and its dependence upon both the "pretense" of theatrical performance *and* the world-changing power of the performative. To express solidarity, or to call someone a comrade, is to claim a relationship that challenges established categories of identity and interest. As a result, solidarity's expression has the strange and difficult task of referencing a relationship, or constellation of relationships, that only appears, and so, in a sense, only comes into being, in the instance of solidarity's expression. In the manner described by J. L. Austin, then, solidarity is performative; one declares it into being. Yet, in making appear that which is not meant to appear, solidarity is also predicated upon that kind of performance that Austin claims invalidates the performative utterance: that which is framed infelicitously, and threateningly, by the stage. Like actors, those who express solidarity must act "as if" relations exist that do not yet (appear to) exist. This becomes the basis upon which solidarity may be enacted or made to appear, but it is also deeply precarious. Should such expressions be spoken in such a way—which is to say, by such a person or people—that they can be rendered illegitimate, then they cannot produce evidence of the relation they intended to make visible. Instead, their failure to make visible a solidarity relation reinforces the premise that the basis for such a relation does not and could not exist. If, however, that performance is already self-identified as a performance, the "as if" escapes the threat posed by accusations of inauthenticity. Already contained within a framework that presumes infelicity and inauthenticity, the "as if" can work at once with and against attempts to categorize activity that is "real" away from that which is not. The FTA leveraged this precarity, presenting as harmless—which is to say, meaningless or infelicitous—expressions of solidarity that, if responded to as real, could take on the force of the performative. If refused or erased, they could fall instead under the protection of the pretense of theater's infelicity.

This dynamic played out in the performance itself, in ways that used and exceeded the written content. Critically, by offering expressions of solidarity, the show would reveal the preexistence, within the ranks of its spectators, of the antiwar sentiment it expressed from the stage. This reinforced the idea, discussed in chapter 2, that the show couldn't tell the soldiers anything they didn't already know. I mentioned in the first chapter that the group's name takes its significance from its operation of reworking the Army slogan "Fun, Travel, and Adventure!," by which it references this same operation as performed by the GIs but without automatically appropriating their results.[36] In the same spirit, "Free the Army" was, technically, the refrain of the show's signature tune, and it is in the process of singing this refrain that, in footage from the group's Pacific tour, we can see the performers acting out their own secondary status relative to the soldiers, as the "ones who have the right to speak." They do so, however, in such a way as to allow temporary, albeit limited, inclusion:

> I went down to that base
> They took one look at my face
> And sent out an order to bar me
> I said Foxtrot, Tango, Alpha
> .... Free the Army![37]

The first word in the final line is preceded both times by the singers exaggeratedly trying to contain themselves—it seems the singers want the audience to understand that they really want to say "*Fuck* the Army," but they perform the pretense that they can't quite or won't, for whatever reason, bring themselves to do it the first time through. The second time, as they are making the long, drawn-out beginning of the word, Len Chandler turns and says quietly (but the mic picks it up) "say it!"—and they do. Instead of "Free the Army," they shout "Fuck the Army." Chandler shouts an extended version: "Fuck the Army, and the Navy, and the Marines!" as roars of applause continue. The effect of the technically unscripted "say it" allows the performers to participate in a particular ritual normally reserved for members of the community, which is also the audience. The difference between the two groups is not covered over in this performance of spontaneity, but is framed desirably as necessary and efficacious. When the performers draw out the first letter of "Free," implying that it might also turn out to be "Fuck," they signal the distance between the civilian and the soldier; if we imagine the first letter of the word spoken by the former reaching through space toward the latter, requesting permission to speak its conclusion, we can recognize the unpredictability or instability of this operation. Will the audience grant the letter a landing, and accept the offer of solidarity? It seems they usually did. An article from the *San Antonio Light* reviewing a September 21 performance notes that soldiers would "correct" the group's "syntax" during the signature song.[38] This is almost certainly a reference to the spontaneous transformation of "free" into "fuck."

Instances of carefully delimited audience participation played out in a similar manner, leveraging the unpredictability of the punchline to make appear the already ongoing infiltration of antiwar sentiment into the ranks of those tasked with fighting the war. In a sketch featuring Fonda as Mrs. Nixon, the president's wife, in flowered hat, tells the president that dissidents are storming the White House demanding an end to the war:

"You'd better call in the 82nd Airborne," he replies.
"But you don't understand, Richard. This IS the 82nd Airborne."

The article from which I took this description continues, "The cheer that followed was more than a cheer. It was a roar, a visceral reflex that burst from 450 throats in the same instant."[39] Missing from the article's description, however, is something that can be found in the documentary footage taken of this moment. Fonda, as Pat Nixon, gestures toward the troops in front of her as she says the final line of the sketch; the specific detachment supposedly storming the walls in the scene (e.g., the 82nd Airborne) changed from performance to performance and was always a reference to the specific troops, part or all of them, attending that particular evening. Moments such as this perform the identity of the audience as distinct from the identity of the performers, while proposing the possibility of shared interests.[40]

A further example appears in the film, in a scene from the series of blackout sketches referred to collectively as "Insubordination." The setting for the sketch, as announced by a printed sign, is Firebase Pace, where the men of Company B had recently refused to go out on night patrol.[41] A number of actors playing GIs (among them Fonda and Sutherland) sit killing time on base; Fonda reads a newspaper, Pamela Donegan and Donald Sutherland play cards. Michael Alaimo enters as an officer. His first problem is that none of the soldiers salute—he takes off his hat and shows it to his men, asking in a whine for "just a little ten-hut, eh guys?" When this fails, and they ask him what he wants, he triumphantly announces that he is looking for "volunteers" to go out and bring back a half-track (an armored personnel carrier that looks like a cross between a tank and a truck). They continue to ignore him, even after he tells them that he'll let them take their weapons along this time, referencing the trepidation with which officers sometimes viewed their own armed men. Sutherland asks his fellow "soldiers" if there are any volunteers, but also turns this question out toward the audience, halfheartedly pointing and looking past the lights into the auditorium.[42] The spectator-soldiers laugh; no one volunteers. Though brief, this moment nevertheless draws upon the audience's presence in establishing the legitimacy of the scene the actors are performing, but without disrupting the line dividing civilian from soldier. In a way, it is an inversion of the common starting point of many forms of audience participation: asking for a volunteer, and hoping to get one. At the same time, however, it echoes the premise of Augusto Boal's Theatre of the Oppressed, to the extent that it simulates a moment of conflict that any given member of the audience might face the next time he finds himself in Vietnam. Along these lines, it is possible to argue that by asking for volunteers, Sutherland provides an opportunity for the GIs to "rehearse" the act of not volunteering. Yet the act to be performed is an act that cannot be performed by joining the performance. By offering participation on terms that require refusal, the offer ultimately reinforces the distinction between actor and spectator, keeping each in his or her proper, legible place. In performing solidarity, members of the FTA carefully delineated their own participation in the circuit of mimetic action. The parts they took did not give them license to take part in the GI resistance; their gestures of participation were meant to reinforce difference, rather than erase it.

We Are All Prisoners of War

What is perhaps most remarkable about the FTA show is that even as it confronted the same tensions and political disagreements that surfaced in almost every left organization of the period (including radical theater groups), it successfully expanded its content to address the very issues it had been unable to resolve internally without prompting the departure of some of its performers. I want to suggest that this, perhaps even more so than the examples given in the previous section, reflects the performative dimension of solidarity—that the outcome of its expression is not guaranteed. Though this dimension exists regardless of whether or not solidarity is expressed through, literally, a staged performance, its theatrical presentation in the form of the FTA shows offers an opportunity to see solidarity's performative at work, alongside the threat of its misfire.

In particular, solidarity in performance foregrounds Featherstone's emphasis on solidarity as not "given." Between the intent to express solidarity and its recognition and acceptance on the part of its intended audience exists the possibility that that expression will instead appear infelicitous, hollow, and parasitic. While the show was consistently able to draw its audience into an expression of political understanding and agreement concerning the war, much more precarious were its efforts to explore related but potentially less familiar political content—solidarity in the first instance made possible but *did not guarantee* that their spectators would recognize the connection between the war and the other issues the show portrayed. This dynamic is sharply in evidence in a reporter's description of the "sisters from Monterey," who performed an opening act for the FTA's show in Monterey, California:

> [the women] presented a skit comparing the role and treatment of a private by his superiors to that of a woman's treatment by men. The women's lib group dressed in jeans, army gear, or dresses according to their roles didn't seem to mind the catcalls and wolf whistles they received when they came on stage. The men in the audience laughed loudly and seemed to sympathize with the portrayal of the downtrodden GI but there were moans as the girls pleaded for equal pay and an end to being stuck in the

kitchen. Nevertheless they cheered loudly when the "sisters" concluded their act saying "the brass and the system they support are our common enemies."[43]

Here we can see quite clearly the precarity of performing solidarity. When the women come onstage, they are confronted with an immediate misrecognition—they are treated in precisely the manner that they, through their performance, hope to discourage. However, because of the duration of the performance, and the fact that it continues within its own fictional world, the GIs are neither directly challenged in response to their catcalls, nor are they successful in disrupting the sketch. The scene continues, introducing a GI (played by a woman) into the space of the performance and drawing on the audience's familiarity with the experiences being represented. The fact that the spectators move between sexist behavior and positive responsiveness draws our attention to the way in which a staged performance facilitates a *recognition of recognition*. If the "sisters" were offering a site of recognition to the GIs, as I discussed in chapter 1, then we see here the significance not only of being recognized but of discerning in that recognition an expression of solidarity that proposes the possibility of common interest across difference. While it is impossible to say whether any GI in attendance at the Monterey performance left with his views on women transformed, we can say that the "sisters from Monterey" produced experiential evidence of a contradiction where one had not previously appeared to exist.

The FTA approached the problem of integrating anti-sexist material in part by expanding the show's content. When Menken joined the group, she developed a series of sketches featuring a character named Kitty Mitty. A small-town girl, Kitty joins the Armed Forces to escape the uninspiring prospects she faces at home: marriage to Frank (or Hank) and a job at the "tire burning factory." She wants to "do something helpful," and so she joins the Women's Army Corps and finds herself . . . washing dishes. As she navigates her new world, she acts as witness to the treatment of ordinary GIs. The scenes are brief and comedic, but also decidedly dark. As Kitty sits in the hospital's waiting room, she watches the doctor treat each patient based on rank. A soldier enters, missing one of his arms:

SOLDIER: Help me, help me.
DOCTOR: I expect a salute soldier.
SOLDIER: I can't, my arm.
DOCTOR: A couple of APC [aspirin-phenacetin-caffeine tablets], soldier.
SOLDIER: My arm, my arms [sic] just got cut off.
DOCTOR: So have a buddy unscrew the cap.[44]

At another point in the same sketch, the doctor tells a woman in labor to come back when her husband makes corporal, but leaps to his feet when the wife of General Strifemore (the doctor refers to her as Mrs. Sir) enters. Through the ever-present figure of Kitty, the scenes link the concerns of enlisted women to those of enlisted men. Significantly, they do so not by introducing new information, but by generalizing a set of already familiar experiences in such a way that they locate a central female character as a possible point of common identification. The premise of the sketch is not gender-exclusive, though it is gender-specific; leaving small town life for a job in the Armed Forces is a scenario undoubtedly familiar to many of the FTA's spectators, but Kitty's particular dilemma is represented in part by two interchangeable and uninspiring suitors. In her 1972 interview, Menken describes that she'd been worried about the new material at first, whether it would "work against what the show had to do." But, she found, it didn't: "the GIs understood, they could see the parallels with how she was being treated. There was no break in identification." Instead, she says, "it solidified the resistance in the army and allowed women and men to work together. It was the most wonderful thing that happened."[45]

The show, unlike attempts to change intergroup dynamics, could propose scenarios meant for reflection, not immediate action. As with the sketches that expressed civilian-soldier solidarity, those that introduced a feminist perspective into the show not only relied upon content, but also upon the particular dynamics established through the act of performing before a live audience. In a letter to Elaine Elinson, advance person for the Pacific Rim tour, on new material to be included in the show, Fonda's assistant Ellen Lustbader writes: "Added to Kitty Mitty will be a) scene in Saigon hospital b) scene with psychiatrist c) WACs in barracks d) song about sexism (not sectarian ... funny)."[46] The "song

Robin Menken and Donald Sutherland in "Kitty Mitty." Jane Fonda (dressed as Pat Nixon) and Rita Martinson hold up an American flag in the background.
Courtesy of Displaced Films.

about sexism" Lustbader references is almost certainly "Tired of Bastards Fucking Over Me," featured in the 1972 film. Written by Beverley Grant, the song's verses describe experiences of everyday sexism, with each brief narrative punctuated by a chorus:

> They whistle for me like a dog and makes noises like a hog
> Heaven knows they sure got problems I agree
> But their problems I can't solve 'cause my sanity's involved
> I'm tired of bastards fuckin' over me

Like the "Women's Libbers" in Monterey, the song appears, in the film documenting the tour, to provoke a mixed response. When Holly Near sings a line that refers to a man who is "just trying to score," members of the crowd laugh, but they also whoop or cheer. While the song overall feels, despite Lustbader's assurances, a bit sectarian—or at the very least as if it might enact a thinly veiled criticism of the gathered audience—the final line of the song in performance appears to rescue the sentiment from this fate, firmly resituating it within the framework of a GI-oriented antiwar variety show. In an enthusiastic kickline, the singers repeat the song's refrain, the final time with a slight twist:

> I'm tired of bastards fuckin' over me
> Yes, I'm tired of bastards fuckin' over me
> Oh yes, I'm TIRED of *FUCKERS* FUCKIN' OVER ME![47]

The emphasis I've included here is not taken from a script but is rather my own description of what we see happen in the film—the women's voices rise suddenly in volume, with the remarkable effect that as soon as the final word is sung, the audience instantly, almost startlingly roars with approval. I want to suggest that the repetition of the word "fuck" here works in a manner similar to the use of the same word in "The Lifer's Song," discussed earlier. The expletive serves as a kind of currency or contract. While it is used here to express anti-sexist sentiment, it serves as a link to the same performers' expression of *antiwar* sentiment, in part because it feels as if it traffics in what has been established as a GI trope. Of course, the word "fuckin'" appears throughout the song, but this final moment participates in an expression of such gleeful and powerful rage that its sentiment becomes infectious.

Though the new material introduced into the show's set script focused primarily on incorporating the issue of women's oppression, other additions addressed labor solidarity and racism. In a brief dream sequence, Kitty imagines giving an acceptance speech after receiving a "Helpfulness award":

> We say we're fighting for democracy, but I know people are starving all over the United States, and I even heard that army boys are breaking thru union pickets and actually putting people out of work.[48]

The emphasis on labor solidarity within the GI movement was not a new phenomenon, but was again a question on which civilian activists had differing opinions. Gardner was thoroughly dismissive toward a push to have GIs support a lettuce boycott, "as if GIs had any way of stopping the Pentagon from buying scab lettuce." He continues: "[the civilian organizers] justified such ludicrous tactics in the name of 'consciousness raising'—as if GIs needed to have their consciousness raised about their powerlessness."[49] Fonda, on the other hand, even during the FTA's first stop in Fayetteville, took every opportunity to connect any issue she could to the GI movement, as in this example recounted by Michael Kernan for the *Washington Post*:

> During the afternoon between staff meetings, press conferences, and a rehearsal, Miss Fonda suddenly decided to go down to Colonial Stores and join a picket line for Cesar Chavez' lettuce workers. "It was a spur of the moment thing," she said later. "But this is one of the concerns of

the GI Movement. The Army has been buying non-union lettuce in huge amounts. The guys have been picketing here for three weeks." It was typical Jane Fonda: impulsive and disconcerting, but when you thought about it, it made sense.[50]

The reporter's grudging recognition of the logic of solidarity here again reinforces the precarity of its appearance. Fonda's "impulsiveness" nearly renders the act nonsensical, and yet it is precisely her impulsiveness and his initial sense of incongruity that draws Kernan's attention to a connection that ultimately "made sense." Similarly, we might think of the FTA's expanded content as "impulsive" or "incongruous," but it "makes sense" in the event of its performance.

The show also moved in the direction of addressing racism within the military. A series of sketches collectively titled "Insubordination" included a scene in which two Black GIs get busted for giving each other a Black Power handshake. Another emphasized Black and white GI solidarity. Interestingly, neither of these appears in *FTA!* (the film of the Pacific Rim tour), nor did anyone, including Fonda, recall these sketches when I asked about them. It is possible that they were written for the "Insubordination" series, but not included in any performances. Alternatively, it is possible that they were included in the show but not in the film. On the one hand, this latter scenario might seem unlikely, as the film includes footage of Black soldiers demonstrating their militancy and discussing racism within the military. On the other, it is equally possible that that footage—of actual soldiers giving a Black Power handshake and discussing racism—may have made it seem unnecessary to include a staged representation of that same militancy. At any rate, the scenes as they are given by the scripts are striking, and unique among the FTA's material in that they depict violence, as opposed to a description of violence. While the "Insubordination" sketch referenced earlier and set at Firebase Pace represented GIs *threatening* violence against an officer, the sketch that centered upon the Black Power handshake ended with a much more explicit suggestion. This comes after the officer tells the men they're headed for a court martial. The GIs confer:

> "Motherfucker . . . well, if we're going to be charged with all that shit we might as well do some of it . . . right, blood?"

"Right on, blood."

They roll up their sleeves and start chasing the officer offstage.

Though they chase him offstage, precluding an onstage beating, the next "Insubordination" scene features a group of Black GIs shoving a military police officer around and "beating the shit out of him." A white GI joins in, and eventually "they all lift him into a Hamlet funeral lift, and carry him off, as he yells out lamely, 'You're all under arrest.' He makes pig sounds as they carry him off." This last scene evokes the militancy (and pig imagery) of Black Revolutionary Theatre and is decidedly more immediate and serious in what it proposes than the rest of the FTA's material.[51] Regardless of whether or not these sketches were performed, they demonstrate an awareness on the part of the FTA's writers and performers of the level of militancy among Black antiwar GIs. At the same time, they feel as if they might press up against the limits of the variety show format. They read not unlike short plays by Amiri Baraka and Ben Caldwell, and for this reason it is more difficult to imagine the cast pulling them off, particularly alongside the slapstick comedy of the blackout sketches.

Maps of Grievance

As the show traveled from Hawaii to the Philippines, and on to Okinawa and Japan, the FTA's performances traced what Featherstone calls a "map of grievance." The term refers to an accumulation and representation of "the dynamic practices through which political activity makes sense of and brings into contestation relations of power."[52] As the FTA sought to connect "grievances" across national border, gender identity, enlisted status, and race, it reconfigured the significance of Hope's well-worn route by attending to the specificity of the locations the USO shows treated as backdrops and to the diversity of the spectators that Hope's routines consistently rendered white and male. As Featherstone describes the "non-aligned logic" at work in solidarity activism during the Cold War, "connections and solidarities" generated by the FTA's tour "sought to change the terms on which opposition" was constructed.[53] The inclusion of an ever-growing list of grievances was not merely additive but transformative, theatrical, and performative.

The FTA's map of grievance is preserved (and re-performed) not only in *FTA!*, which documents the group's travels, but in the extensive and lively correspondence between those making the many arrangements for its tour. Plans for the Asia trip had begun as early as July 1971. A preliminary itinerary shows that the group had hoped to tour to Korea and Guam in addition to Okinawa, Japan, and the Philippines. The first reference to taking the FTA abroad comes in its first press conference, prior to Fort Bragg, when members of the cast express the desire to take the show to Vietnam. Unlike any other location, where the local government would decide whether or not the show could visit, to (even enter the country, much less) visit soldiers stationed in South Vietnam, the permission of the US government would have been necessary. Permission, of course, wasn't granted. Fonda was, however, invited by the government of North Vietnam. Though she would in fact visit the following year, in 1971 she was unwilling to visit unless the Viet Cong allowed the FTA to perform for US prisoners of war. Unsurprisingly, this request was also denied.

Much of the information about the FTA's Pacific Rim tour referenced below comes from dispatches sent to the show's organizers by advance person Elaine Elinson. Elinson joined the project in late September 1971 and left for Honolulu in mid-October. At the time, she was working with the Pacific Counseling Service and the Pacific News Service, and so was highly knowledgeable about the region. At each site—in Hawaii, the Philippines, Okinawa, and Japan—she made arrangements for performance space and housing, sent back detailed technical notes and sketches of the chosen venues, and advised on the local issues the writing committee might wish to address with additional or adapted sketches. Her extensive correspondence reflects the extent to which the show understood its Pacific Rim tour as an opportunity to link diverse struggles with those central to the GI movement. Historiographically, the archival materials available regarding the Pacific Rim tour offer at once a great deal of detail and a marked absence. While Elinson's dispatches clearly outline the many meetings that likely occurred between the cast, GIs, and local groups, the media coverage, unsurprisingly, contains only details about the shows. Thus, in many cases I am relying upon a description of a planned event that may or may not have come to pass. In doing so, I recognize that I may at times be constructing an inaccurate narrative of the FTA's activities. However, I contend that the *map* produced by these documents is legitimate regardless, to the extent that this map traces transmitted expressions of solidarity—even if they finally proved infelicitous.

In following in the footsteps of the USO tours, it was of critical importance to those involved with the FTA not to reinforce, even as it was impossible to avoid fully, the dynamic of US dominance represented by the bases the show targeted. From the beginning, plans for the international tour emphasized a range of approaches the cast and crew could take to navigate through this narrow space. Early correspondence among the tour's organizers makes clear a desire on the part of all involved to contextualize the concerns of the GI movement within the broader picture of US imperialism. In a letter dated August 5, Alan Miller of the USSF articulated this expanded vision:

> Focus of the show will be directed to G.I.'s—but attempts will also be made to relate to the general anti-imperialist struggle in Asia, i.e. through one large general audience show in a large auditorium in the central cities in addition to the base related performances. Also Jane and the other women in the show will work with women: military dependents, bar girls, etc. During these periods, the men in the show might do special gigs, visits, etc. at hospitals, etc.[54]

If they had visited US bases abroad to support GI resistance without highlighting the local impact of US presence and intervention, the FTA would have participated in erasing the other, ongoing acts of resistance against US foreign policy undertaken by local populations in de facto occupied countries. To mitigate this threat, the FTA undertook a range of strategies. Some of these corresponded to tactics used domestically, namely the inclusion of sketches specific to local concerns and the incorporation of local acts (especially musical performances) into the show. Additional measures were devoted to arranging meetings not only with GIs, but with local anti-imperialist groups and women's groups as well. The ultimate effect, as represented by the film and in Elinson's documents, is a map that reflects the challenge an interconnected and international anti-imperialist movement might pose to US global dominance. Tracing the tour's progression provides an opportunity to examine the points on this map and the efforts of members of the FTA, in collaboration with GIs and local activists, to make visible the lines between them.

The tour's first stop was Hawaii, where the cast performed at the Civic Auditorium on Thanksgiving Day. According to Elinson's assessment of the venue, it was "a funky-ass place with bleachers and folding chairs and floor sitting. It's kind of old and green but very good for audience relating."[55] The military not being an institution to break easily with its own precedent, the group was denied the right to stage the performance on any of the several bases in Hawaii. The group was, however, given a cut-rate price on the local four-thousand-seat auditorium. This was thanks to organizers from the Liberated Barracks coffeehouse in Waikiki, who pitched the show as a "Thanksgiving benefit" for the GIs. *Liberated Barracks* was also the name of the local GI newspaper, several copies of which were sent ahead, in October, to the writing committee so that local concerns could be included in the show. In particular, the organizers hoped that the show might supplement material about the GI movement with content addressing the problem of racism toward Asian Americans and Hawaiians, as well as the GI movement's "responsibility" to Hawaii, Asia, and the Pacific people. Elinson's dispatch on Hawaii describes at length the devastating impact of military presence, and also rampant development, upon the indigenous population.[56] While it is unclear to what extent these themes were incorporated into the performance, they did influence the cast's activities offstage. A schedule for the Hawaii visit indicates that the performers spent the day after the show meeting with local groups, including a Kokua Hawaii/Pacific Rim collective, which was made up of "Hawaiian liberation and third world community organizing groups," and "women's groups" ("though," the entry continues, "the Third World women relate to the Kokua group and will meet the women there").[57] This was a consistent practice throughout the Asia tour and a consideration in the planning and scheduling from the beginning. As it sought to address and highlight the concerns of local groups, however, the show retained its central focus on the GI movement. In so doing it made possible the appearance of a connection between the struggles of indigenous and anti-imperialist activists and the actions of antiwar soldiers.

In Hawaii, the FTA's visit happened to coincide with the arrival of the USS *Coral Sea*. At a press conference shortly after the cast's arrival on November 23, Fonda addressed those gathered "in a clear voice and at a machinegun clip":

> We wish to extend greetings to the 1,300 crewmen of the Coral Sea who signed a petition demanding the attack carrier, which has been responsible for much of the devastation in Vietnam, remain home.[58]

Earlier the same month, after huge civilian protests in San Francisco supporting the sailors on board, three of the ship's officers had publicly resigned and thirty-five soldiers stayed behind when the carrier departed. While the FTA was in Hawaii, "approximately 50 sailors from the ship attended a meeting with the show's cast, and several hundred crew members were among the more than four thousand people who attended the FTA Show performance." Cortright continues, "When the ship pulled out to continue its journey to East Asia, another fifty-three sailors were missing." In a particularly vivid illustration of the way in which the FTA was tracking and challenging the path of US militarism, the *Coral Sea*, due to arrive at Subic Bay in the Philippines the same day the FTA was to arrive in Manila, was "kept in waters beyond the bay."[59]

In the Philippines, the information the group had been given about the country's political history and current situation resulted in the inclusion of new material in the show, as made evident by the coverage of the several performances they gave there.[60] While Elinson's detailed notes identified in advance local concerns for each of the sites the FTA would visit, suggesting scenes that might be added, only one nationally tailored sketch appears in the photocopied scripts Elinson has held onto, and neither this one nor any other appear in the film. However, the extensive coverage of the show's visit to the Philippines consistently mentions the sketch, confirming that it was, in fact, performed. A simple narrated comedy pantomime tracing the history of US intervention in the country, this sketch not only highlighted the relationship between the GI movement and the local anti-imperialist struggle, but reflected months of political education and preparation on the part of the troupe's members. Those making arrangements for the FTA's six-day visit (primarily Louis Wolf) emphasized the need for the cast and crew to understand the severity of the political situation. This was made all the more urgent when on August 21 (and after plans for the tour were already underway) a rally of the Philippines Liberal Party was bombed at the Plaza Miranda in Manila. Grenade blasts killed nine, including a five-year old boy, and injured many more. Then-president Ferdinand Marcos took the opportunity to suspend the writ of habeas corpus and subsequently arrest hundreds of activists. Such tactics were part of an established strategy of intimidating and repressing the Communist Party, members of which were involved in organizing the FTA's visit. Kabataang Makabayan, a student organization supportive of the Communist Party, had also helped to organize the tour; they had seen their chairman, Nilo Tayag, and general secretary, Mindo David, incarcerated following the bombing.[61]

Internal correspondence makes clear that the visit to the Philippines was in part intended to lend support to the underground revolutionary movement led by the Communist Party, and particularly the youth wing represented by Kabataang Makabayan. As a result, the cast had been advised from the beginning to walk a careful line—avoiding overt criticism of the current regime (for example, by not referring to Marcos as a fascist during conversations with the press), while also familiarizing themselves as much as possible with the country's history and political context; to this end, they were advised to read *Philippine Society and Revolution* by Amado Guerrero. In particular, the FTA's American and Filipino organizers wanted to draw the attention of antiwar GIs to the impact of the US presence and influence on the people of the Philippines. Thus, even under the most precarious of circumstances, with key members of the organizations unofficially hosting the FTA in jail, it was still agreed by all involved that it was as important as ever for the show to happen as planned. In light of the bombing and the consequent slide toward martial law, even greater care was taken with the group's housing and security, all to be provided or approved by "movement people." Other preparations followed accordingly, as Wolf's letter of September 10 makes clear:

> The U.S. military plays a very important advisory and strategic role in the country, and as in all puppet-states, the local Establishment seeks to protect its puppeteer. In this context, it is conceivable that some strings

might be pulled to try to prevent the show from coming to the country, or once here, to try and limit its activities. It was due to this fear that we had thought of sponsors.⁶²

As a result of the precautions ultimately taken, from the outside, the circumstances of the group's visit appear bizarre. Among the FTA's official sponsors was the Philippine Amateur Swimming Association, an arrangement that required Fonda to hand out medals at a swim meet during the group's stay in Manila. In another effort at providing political cover, Michael Alaimo recalls that immediately after their arrival at the airport, the cast was delivered, exhausted and in need of a change of clothes, to a fancy luncheon attended by the president's brother. According to the FTA's printed itinerary, the luncheon was hosted by the Philippines Table Tennis Association (or at any rate, that is what the acronym appears to stand for, and it certainly seems within the realm of possibility given the sponsorship of the Swimming Association). The tour's underground organizers had recognized that a high-level meet and greet with the FTA's celebrities would buy some time before Marcos and his inner circle caught wind of the show's content. While aware of the necessity of the event, it seems not everyone behaved as well as they might: Alaimo remembers Donald Sutherland spilling his drink, not altogether accidentally, onto one or another of the esteemed guests.⁶³

Elinson's advance dispatches from the Philippines also indicate that, after the National Press Club declined to sponsor the show, she reached out, successfully, to the Philippine Educational Theater Association. She writes:

> The head of it is pretty much of a reactionary and puppet of Marcos— but he likes to prove how important he is. So, Mr. Dornoy Valencia, right-wing columnist of the Manila Times and producer of the third World Theater Festival to be held in Manila the month of December (click, click) has promised us that there will be no problem with the tourist visas, and that if there is, he himself will take care of it in the name of experimental theater and art.⁶⁴

Giving credence to Elinson's claim about PETA's political orientation is the fact that the 1971 Third World Theater Festival was formally endorsed by the office of the president. Presumably, the festival avoided explicitly political content, or at least proposed that it would do so. However, it is worth considering whether PETA, as an arts organization, was simply pursuing a strategy of survival similar to those employed by the more radical political groups—promise innocuous programming but deliver something decidedly less neutral. With the declaration of martial law in 1972, PETA's founder, Cecile Guidote-Alvarez, was forced into exile; despite this, the group continued to work throughout the martial law period.

While the odd sponsorships of the tour bring to light connections between and uses of front organizations by Filipino revolutionaries, the group also directly engaged with more explicit expressions of revolutionary sentiment. A day off was scheduled so that FTA members could, if they chose, attend the Bonifacio Day parade and rally. The holiday commemorates Andres Bonifacio, the leader of the 1896 Philippine Revolution, which won the country independence from Spanish colonial rule. In the film, footage of the day's events presents a fascinating complement and contrast to the FTA show and its vaudevillian comedy. As marchers move at a rapid pace along a central street, a young woman with her wrists tied is pushed along; in fact, the scene appears in the film so abruptly and with no introduction that it reads initially (at least to this viewer) as a moment of actual physical violence. It quickly becomes clear, however, that she represents the Philippines under Spanish rule. Underneath footage of the parade we hear the crowds singing the Communist "Internationale" in Tagalog, as subtitles appear on screen. The film cuts to footage of a pageant-like performance, staged by the celebrants. The young woman, her wrists now freed, poses in response to shifts in the music (no longer "The Internationale," but still clearly revolutionary). With the final verse, she creates a sharp line with her body, as she extends her arm holding a rifle into the air and tilts her head back.[65] It is a stunning and moving image. In the film, we can just make out members of the FTA in the gathered audience, sitting on the ground around the monument that is serving as a stage. As I will discuss in chapter 4, the FTA depended upon the spectator as a political subject; here, too, we see the activity of spectatorship deployed as a way of drawing our attention to struggles of which we may not be aware. The American actors "throw focus" onto their Filipino counterparts.

Upon the group's arrival in Tokyo on December 7, the show encountered the difficulties it had expected to find elsewhere; in Japan, however, these came as a surprise. The cast and crew had secured tourist visas in advance, and the Japanese consulate in Los Angeles had assured the group that these would be sufficient, given that the performers were not receiving any compensation for the shows they planned to stage in Japan. However, Japan's Immigration Office ruled otherwise, noting that regardless of whether or not they were to be compensated, the purpose of the group's visit was "apparently for theatrical performances," not tourism.[66] After being held at the airport for three hours, the group was permitted to proceed to a hotel as the office considered an appeal to its decision. While the following morning the immigration authorities agreed to allow the visitors to stay, they were still prohibited from engaging in any "theatrical activities." The Pacific Counseling Service and Beheiren (Japan Committee for Peace in Vietnam) promptly held a joint press conference at which Fonda announced that the group had filed a request with the justice minister to permit the FTA to perform as planned.

During the press conference, a representative from Beheiren claimed the government action was prompted by "fear that the entry of the FTA troupe might give impetus to antiwar activities by U.S. servicemen at U.S. military bases in Japan."[67] This seems a plausible assumption, given the strength of the Japanese peace movement (clearly articulated in Elinson's dispatches) and the impact such an explicit collaboration between US and Japanese activists might have in emboldening GI antiwar sentiment. Ultimately, however, the problem was resolved and represented as a technicality. The immigration authorities called the consulate, and the story checked out. The group was allowed to keep its engagements in Fussa City, near Yokota Air Base, and in Yokosuka, near the naval station there. To return, however, for the additional shows the FTA had planned to give after it paid its visit to Okinawa, the ministry required the cast and crew to secure specified visas—which they did. At Fussa, the show played to over 800 GIs in a hall meant to hold 520, and in Yokosuka, an audience of nearly 1,400 included some 500 GIs.

In Japan, the solidarities constructed by the tour deliberately extended beyond the immediate present and into the past, proposing the possibility of not repeating that past into the future. In what seems one of the most striking expressions of international solidarity, the FTA was slated to participate in a rally planned by Beheiren for December 8, marking the thirtieth anniversary of the bombing of Pearl Harbor. It was held under the slogan "Stop a second Greater East Asia Co-Prosperity move," in reference to the program that oversaw the infamous bombing of American ships in 1941.[68] The FTA was to offer a "solidarity greeting": the whole cast would sing "The Lifer's Song" (here referenced in Elinson's letter as "the FTA song") and then several members would deliver short statements. Organizers of the event suggested Jane, "either Rita or Pamela (a black woman)," and Nina "(as a pocha [chicana] and long int'l traveler in int'l solidarity—and all women, because the Japanese are not very strong in women's liberation and it would be a good thing for the FTA to be represented by women)."[69] While ultimately the cast members were not able to participate, due to the difficulties they had encountered with immigration, the event's complement, in a sense, makes an appearance in the film, when the performers visit the Hiroshima museum. The cast members listen to headphones and move through the exhibit as we hear excerpts of the audio tour provided by the museum. Pamela Donegan speaks almost under her breath to the others, underlining the point the scene's inclusion in the film is already making: "This is Vietnam, this is Pakistan, this is every place, every—they're where the war machine hits, this is all this . . ." Within the film, the moment feels suddenly slow and contemplative, and appropriately so, as we are presented with the fallout of imperial conflict: burned, twisted bodies, children with birth defects, bombed buildings. The framed photographs evoke images of the Vietnam War while holding them at a distance.

As had been the case in the Philippines, the FTA presented shows in major Japanese cities as well at venues located near US bases. In the case of Kyoto, the former warranted additional explanation, as very few GIs could be expected to attend; the nearest base was three hours away. Elinson explained that most of the Japanese activists working with the GI movement lived in Kyoto, including many of the people staffing the soon-to-open Iwakuni MC coffeehouse, and the show went ahead. Elinson also arranged meetings for the cast with the Sanrizuka peasants "who physically fought Japanese police for over 6 months to protect their land for [sic] being redeveloped into an airport," and with the Camp Fuji Mothers, "a group of women who have been picketing and struggling against U.S. Army use of their farmland on Mt. Fuji for over ten years."[70]

The negotiation of the terms and limits of solidarity took a variety of forms, as several examples demonstrate. While in Japan, Elinson responds in writing to the latest version of the script she's just received, explaining that while she loves the new material, she has doubts about the one with the sportscasting on the Vietnam war: "People in Asia might find it hard to deal with it in that way—as it is heavy day to day reality here that might hit their homes and families next. It might just be a little strongly lighthearted if you know what I mean."[71] She goes on to say that she will check with Japanese and Filipino friends. Though it is unclear whether they expressed their approval, the film indicates that the sketch was kept in the show.

Apart from questions of content, even seemingly simple components of the tour could cause political friction, and these had to be navigated carefully to avoid reinforcing or relying upon the dynamic established by the presence of US bases in foreign countries. One example of this problem involves the fact that the FTA traveled with a massive amount of equipment. This appeared to local activists as a waste of money, as it would be significantly cheaper to make arrangements for the necessary equipment in-country than to arrange transport for the show's cargo. "Also," explained Elinson, "people feel somewhat offended (especially in Japan) that you are not using their equipment. Remember the GI movement in these countries is very much tied in with the Asian national movements, and people do feel the show is a joint effort." Though she reassured the US organizers that she would convey to their Japanese hosts that it was easier for the tech crew to set up familiar equipment, she encouraged the FTA to "watch any tendency for cultural imperialism."[72]

Individual political convictions of members of the cast could also sometimes conflict with the wishes of local activist organizers. One such incident played out in relation to the Philippines, when a cast member (it is not indicated in the correspondence who) expressed his or her unwillingness to meet with members of the mainstream press. After the cast member was apparently unswayed by Elinson's insistence that speaking to the "pig" press was advisable and important, according to the local activists, the cast received a letter directly from Kabataang Makabayan. The letter explained that some members of the movement were also members of the mainstream press, and that speaking with the press would provide much-needed publicity and also political cover for the show. It seems, given the extensive coverage of the press conference that subsequently appeared in numerous Filipino publications, that the dissenting member acquiesced.[73]

In between its performances in Japan, the FTA visited Okinawa, which, even more so than the Philippines, reflected the reach and impact of US imperialism. Since the end of World War II, the US had "retained" Okinawa as a territory; in 1972; the island would "revert" to Japan, but the many bases and training areas would remain. The FTA sought to amplify the objections of the local population to the US's occupation, and to this end at least one of the shows included a performance by a group of Okinawan musicians. I know little about the logistics of the musicians' inclusion in the live performance, specifically whether or not the GI audience was provided with something comparable to the subtitles that appear in the film. The lyrics are sharply critical of US presence on the island. The singers stand straight at the microphones, their eyes closed for the duration of the performance, and at the song's conclusion, the audience instantly roars with applause.[74]

The FTA cast also lent their support to an ongoing strike of seventeen thousand Okinawan base workers, and footage of the All-Okinawa Military Employees Trade Union, known as Zengunro, holding pickets at entrances to most base gates features in *FTA!* As some of the union's members describe on camera in the film, the workers on the base were striking over the discrepancy in pay and treatment between Okinawan and American employees performing the same duties. An article titled "Jane Fonda Joins Dull Strike" (and subtitled "Another 'Instant Okinawa Expert'") in the *Okinawa Morning Star* describes the scene:

> Miss Fonda mingled with the Okinawan pickets at Kadena's Gate 2 in Koza, telling them that she supports their struggle. She also denounced US military authorities for their treatment of the Okinawans in general. The movie star then turned her thoughts to American servicemen standing guard inside the gate. She said they should acknowledge why the Okinawan base workers are fighting. She added that the US is ruling

Okinawa unfairly and is trying to rule the whole world the same way. Then she asked the servicemen to join in Zengunro's fight.[75]

In *FTA!* we are directly addressed by one of the strikers, who speaks to the camera about the situation faced by his fellow workers; this is intercut with footage of Michael Alaimo speaking over a bullhorn, expressing his support. A military jeep drives by, and while the two soldiers seated in the front remain expressionless, the man in the back leans toward the camera and flashes a peace sign. This basic structure is repeated throughout the film, as the performers explicitly state their support for a given struggle to its participants, while those engaged in that struggle speak directly to the film's viewers, via the camera. The map accumulates its point across these bodies and spaces, each staking its visibility upon the visibility of the other. The actors pull focus and then "throw" it, again and again.

From its summer schism, the FTA went decidedly in the direction of solidarity's performative, refusing the premise that the GI could not also be a revolutionary. The Pacific Rim tour charged onto the global scene as an ecstatic embrace of the possibilities of endless, multiplying points of connection, its organizers and performers lobbing expressions of solidarity at every identifiable target: women, people of color, migrant laborers, Filipino Communists, Japanese peasants resisting the theft of their land, Okinawan base workers on strike. Many, but not all, of these were accepted and returned. When I first spoke with Fonda in 2013, she confessed that she found herself embarrassed by the film that documents the tour, because she felt it tried to do too much, connect everything up. However, about the tour itself she had no regrets. What this suggested to me, in part, was that the live shows facilitated successful expressions of solidarity in a way that the mediated and edited form of the film could not. At the same time, I wondered whether Fonda's embarrassment—which I was surprised by, because I find the film profoundly moving, precisely because of its evident desire to *connect*—was prompted not by the film specifically, but by the inadequacy of the film relative to the memory of the experience. This made sense to me. When I watch the film, I want nothing so much as to be there then, but now.

More recently, however, with the rerelease of the film on Netflix in 2021, Fonda's perspective seems to have changed. This is perhaps, at least in part, out of necessity, as she was put in the position of promoting the film. But "necessity" seems an inadequate and ungenerous way to characterize her renewed commitment to the film. It seems more likely that the intervening decade, with its resurgent politics of solidarity, and Fonda's own renewed involvement in activism, characterized now as it was then by a willingness to see connections across diverse issues and identities, has cast the film in a new light. Its anachronism now appears as a strength, rejecting the limitations of our present progressive politics and proposing instead the necessity of a revolutionary politics that presumes the performative—and theatrical—practice of solidarity.

Audience reaction to Bob Hope show in Seoul, Korea. Oct. 23, 1950.
Photo credit: Capt. Bloomquist.

4

Enlisted Audiences and Emancipated Spectators

"I don't want to get into an argument," Hope said, "but it's obvious from a jury of 80,000,000 who watched our TV show of this year's trip that those kids over there weren't from Central Casting."

In an attempt to determine the first year Bob Hope presented his USO-sponsored Christmas show to American servicemen, I ended up on the United Service Organizations' blog. An entry from May 6, 2010, titled "Remembering Bob Hope's First USO Show" suggested the page would yield precisely what I was looking for—and it did, though not directly: "Can you believe it's been 69 years since Bob Hope performed his first USO Show, at California's March Field?" Not wanting to do the math, I checked the caption below the photograph at the top of the page, assuming its date would solve the problem. The picture, however, while clearly intended as representative of the article's content, was not from Hope's first USO show at California's March Field on May 6, 1941. In fact, the image didn't include Hope at all. Instead, the black-and-white snapshot showed a group of laughing men in matching heavy jackets and warm hats, with the caption "Audience reaction to the Bob Hope show at Seoul, Korea October 23, 1950."[1] This not-quite-right and yet entirely appropriate image neatly reflects the focus of this chapter: the spectator as the object of spectatorship. That a bit of text on Bob Hope's first USO show is accompanied by a photograph not of the show itself but of audience members from a show nearly a decade later suggests what is indeed the case: Hope's USO performances, while explicitly intended to boost morale and express support for those serving in the Armed Forces, have also always been about circulating images of soldiers among civilians. In the early years of Hope's work for the USO, the forms in which civilians could access images of soldier-spectators were restricted to photographs and to the mental image one might construct in listening to the bursts of audience laughter punctuating Hope's radio broadcasts of his performances for the troops. The 1941 show at March Field was the first remote broadcast of Hope's popular nationwide program, *The Pepsodent Show*, and also the first time he performed for—and tailored his material to—an enlisted audience. The March Field performance inaugurated a practice that would continue for the rest of Hope's career, with the mode of civilian access to these performances transitioning in 1954 from live radio broadcasts to television specials. With the transition to broadcast television, the level of the audience's access to images of soldiers became at once more and less direct, as his annual Christmas tours were not transmitted simultaneously to a civilian audience, but instead were edited into ninety-minute-long TV specials and aired early the next year.

An advertisement for the 1967 broadcast of the Bob Hope Christmas Special on NBC.

As I argued in chapter 1, the GI movement depended for its development and growth upon constructing and disseminating an alternative image of the American soldier, both among soldiers themselves, but also among the broader American public. During the Vietnam War, Hope's television broadcasts delivered documentary evidence of high-spirited, patriotic, and well-entertained troops directly into millions of living rooms across the country.[2] Thus, while the FTA's performances provided a counterpoint to the Bob Hope USO tours for tens of thousands of active-duty troops at home and abroad, they left largely untouched Hope's other, arguably more significant audience—the millions of US households that watched his Christmas specials on NBC every February. As the anti-USO show, the FTA was unlikely to gain access to airtime, nor to attract the financial support of companies like Chrysler (Hope's sponsor). So Fonda and the FTA's second director, Francine Parker, decided to present an alternative image of the American soldier in Vietnam via a feature film, using Fonda and Sutherland's celebrity to facilitate distribution and publicity. Filming took place during the group's Pacific Rim tour, adding no small amount of expense and hassle to the trip. Released within days of Fonda's infamous visit to Hanoi in July 1972—and thus contributing to an already confusing timeline of the actress's involvement in antiwar work—*FTA!* was in theaters barely a week before it was pulled from circulation by its distributor, American International Pictures. Most copies were destroyed. Bad bootlegs surfaced in subsequent years, and a few screenings were organized by activists and academics in the later 1990s and 2000s. When David Zeiger wanted to include footage from *FTA!* in his documentary on the GI movement, *Sir! No Sir!*, Parker agreed, but on the condition that Zeiger remaster and rerelease *FTA!* as well. Zeiger had suggested that, in the process, the film would benefit from additional editing. Fonda agreed, but Parker refused, and so it was rereleased in its original form in 2009 by Zeiger's company, Displaced Films.[3] Screenings were held in New York and LA and at some major festivals, but beyond that it was only accessible on DVD. In 2021, prompted in part by Fonda's renewed profile as an activist due to her participation in climate activism and her weekly arrests at "Fire Drill Fridays," the film was restored by the organization IndieCollect and made available on Netflix. This second "rerelease" garnered considerable attention from major media outlets and talk shows.

The publicity poster for the 1972 release of *FTA!*
Courtesy of Displaced Films.

Although some have claimed that Fonda was responsible for the film's original disappearance, substantial evidence exists to the contrary. It seems likely that these accusations stem from Fonda's objections to an earlier film that would have used footage from the first performances at the Haymarket Coffeehouse in Fayetteville. A GI newspaper covering the show's opening notes that a camera crew was on-site, and a *Rolling Stone* article covering the show's stop in Monterey refers to a "film of the Cabaret's Fort Bragg appearance," scheduled for release later in 1971. Additionally, USSF correspondence following the Fayetteville debut discusses plans for a film.[4] In fact, this proposed film would become the cause of several layers of controversy, first, when Paul Lauter, of the USSF, attempted to secure Fonda's permission to screen it at fundraisers for that organization. Fonda refused, apparently unhappy with the quality of the recording and insisted instead that the group would make a new film during its Asia tour. The dispute seems to have been driven, at least in part, by a disagreement over the purpose of the film: it seems that while Lauter and others in the USSF had been thinking of the film as a way for more GIs to see the show, Fonda (and likely others in the FTA, including Parker) were interested in a broader audience, of GIs *and* civilians. Though this film would indeed be made, the relationship between the USSF and the FTA had effectively dissolved by the time the performers left for Hawaii (even as the USSF had organized the Lincoln Center fundraiser immediately prior to their departure), and so the USSF was uninvolved in its production or distribution.[5] The existence of the initial film would become the source or cause of the rumors that Fonda had prevented the release of what was actually the second film.

In fact, it seems far more likely that the swift disappearance of *FTA!* was the result of government intervention. According to Parker, speaking with David Zeiger around the time of *FTA!*'s rerelease in 2010, the film disappeared after Sam Arkoff, head of AIP, received a call from the White House. Writes Zeiger:

> Sam Arkoff, the enigmatic head of American International Pictures, which was distributing the film, told her he had received a threatening phone call from the White House—and that is why he pulled the film. Is the story true? There's no proof, but I can't think of another reasonable explanation for Sam Arkoff, a man who knew how to wring every penny

out of a film, yanking one starring Jane Fonda and Donald Sutherland from theaters at a big loss (and, apparently, destroying all of the prints, since none were ever found).[6]

Watching the film today, it is not at all difficult to imagine why such a call might have been placed. As with the Hope specials, the clear purpose of the film was to display images of soldiers; in contrast to the Hope specials, *FTA!* displays soldiers as they express antiwar sentiment, roar with laughter at sketches that portray varying degrees of insubordination, and, perhaps most threateningly, discuss the prospects for organizing resistance within the military. We also witness how thoroughly military discipline has ceased to exist: speaking on camera, soldiers stationed in Japan reveal that, in spite of Nixon's claims to the contrary, they have seen nuclear weapons being transported onto US ships within Japan's territorial waters; and Black GIs discuss at length how serious they are about waging a different kind of war once they get back home. In other words, it seems likely that the order from the White House came (if it did) not because the *content* of the FTA show itself was particularly incendiary, but because the footage of the show's spectators—soldiers criticizing the war—posed an indisputable counternarrative to the premise that being against the war distanced one from, rather than connected one to, the men and women serving in the Armed Forces.

FTA! was not the first film to feature evidence of antiwar sentiment within the ranks of the Armed Forces. *Different Sons* and *Winter Soldier*, for example, offered their audiences clear evidence that the chain of command was breaking down. A critical difference, however, lay in the fact that *FTA!* could access and represent *active-duty* soldiers, while *Different Sons* and *Winter Soldier* focused on forms of veteran protest; the former follows participants in VVAW's Operation Rapid American Withdrawal, during which veterans marched from Morristown, New Jersey, to Valley Forge State Park in Pennsylvania. In towns along the way, they staged raids with the help of civilians who played the role of Vietnamese villagers subjected to abuse by American troops. *Winter Soldier* covered the Winter Soldier Investigation—a series of hearings in Washington, DC, during which veterans described war crimes in which they had participated, and built a case that these actions were a matter of military policy rather than aberrations for which individual soldiers should be held solely responsible. Also relative to these films, which were more or less ignored by the mainstream media, *FTA!* could attract (until it was pulled) considerable publicity and also a broader viewership, due to the celebrity of its performers. This is not to diminish the significance of these other films—they posed a powerful counternarrative to the military's claims that antiwar veterans were nonexistent and that war crimes were not a matter of policy.[7] It is simply to note that these films represent different tactical applications of performance and spectatorship. In *Different Sons* and *Winter Soldier*, veterans perform as soldiers, seeking an audience of civilian spectators (both at the actions themselves and, subsequently, as viewers of the film) willing to validate their oppositional representation of the war. In *FTA!*, the soldier appears in the role of the spectator, but so that we might see the powerful position he holds in relation to the project of ending the war.

What the deliberate display of the soldier-spectator in both *FTA!* and the Hope specials suggests is the need to reconsider the political significance (or potential, or valence) of the spectator as spectator, both by challenging investments in "activation" that position the spectator as inherently passive, but also by complicating a counterproposal of spectatorial emancipation that seems not to account for the possibility that the spectator as spectator might act as an actor acts. While this language suggests (as is indeed the case) that this argument is directed in part toward a discourse of passivity and activity that is particular to political theater history and performance theory, I am also arguing that this decidedly theatrical frame can help us think the significance of solidarity, authenticity, and legitimacy, as these pertain to the practice of revolutionary politics. As in the previous three chapters, my discussion focuses on the use by activists of practices (whether these are framed as performance or not) that deploy the presumed inauthenticity and illegitimacy of staged activity to enact relations of solidarity and threats of resistance from within the precarious frame of performance. By attending particularly to the spectator as an object of spectatorship, I consider how the theatrical frame can disrupt a discourse of authenticity by enlisting the spectator in the construction of its fiction, and so offering to that fiction the legitimacy of the spectator, and to the spectator the transgressive possibilities of fiction. What appears as the occasional and threatening failure of this construction in the Hope specials, insofar as the spectator's participation is tethered to the legitimacy of the war, becomes a productive collapse in the context of the FTA, as the spectator is acknowledged as uniquely positioned to end the war precisely in his refusal to act. At the same time, as I will discuss, the "inaction" of the spectator becomes the grounds for erasing what was in many respects the most radical and militant movement of the Vietnam era.

I begin with a discussion of the extent to which *FTA!* mirrors and also departs from the format of the Hope specials, considering how the different editorial choices evident in each produce different modes of cross-temporal encounter between the soldier-spectator of the original performance and the civilian audience of the eventual broadcast special or feature film. I examine the ways in which each project produces and performs for its doubled audience, constructing or deconstructing experiences of co-presence and liveness, particularly through the presence or absence of direct address. I then look specifically at the soldier-spectator on stage, comparing the ways in which *FTA!* and the Hope specials facilitate, frame, and use the soldier as a source of legitimacy and authenticity in the space of the performance. Finally, I engage with the ongoing debate over the desirability and possibility of the active spectator, first through the figure of the agent provocateur, who acts like a spectator engaged in self-activation, and then through a consideration of what I identify as the tactically theatrical modes of resistance soldiers utilized in staging violent opposition to military policy during the Vietnam War.

At Home and in the House

In 1964, as the Johnson administration began to escalate US involvement in the war, Bob Hope added South Vietnam to the list of stops on his annual USO Christmas tour of American bases overseas; and in early 1965, NBC broadcast the first installment of "Around the World with the USO," edited down to ninety minutes and presented commercial-free.[8] The specials, which continued for nine years, followed a consistent format throughout, characterized by a rhythmic shift back and forth between footage of the show and footage of audience response, and structured by a linear representation of the tour's progression from base to base.[9] At the outset of each special, a booming, disembodied voice, underscored by a drum roll, announces the military installations visited as footage of each location appears briefly on the screen (the location might be represented by footage of the audience, of the show, or of the local landscape). After declaring "It's Around the Globe with the USO," or "It's the Bob Hope Christmas Special," or both, the announcer segues into a list of the performers, again paired with footage of each celebrity, now backed by big band music. The booming voice gives way, finally, to Hope's, and the music transitions into "Wild Blue Yonder," the anthem of the US Air Force. Hope begins his voiceover (which will continue throughout the program) by cracking jokes about the press conference held prior to each tour on the tarmac of Van Nuys Airport in Los Angeles, as footage of the same appears. The cast boards and the plane departs, always with a joke from Hope about whether it'll be able to get off the ground. The special then touches down at each of the bases previously listed, and footage from the performances at each base is presented in such a way as to mirror roughly the show the troops in any one location would've seen. So, for example, we might arrive first at a base in Korea, where Hope delivers a few jokes and then introduces a juggler; after we leave Korea we head for Thailand, where we see another piece of Hope's routine before he brings out the Gold Diggers for a dance number. A viewer of the television broadcast would ultimately see a single iteration of each act from a set likely performed at all bases, intercut with footage of the soldier-spectators at a specific base watching the act recorded there in turn. Throughout, Hope's voiceover offers narrative continuity, as he remarks upon the troupe's travels and introduces performers before they appear onstage.

By far the most significant structural element of the Christmas specials is the extent to which they screen images of servicemen.[10] During the Vietnam War, the Hope broadcasts undoubtedly offered the only sustained engagement Americans were likely to have with images of groups of soldiers gathered together informally in a single space. (These gatherings, however, were not always voluntary. In a 1980 article on Hope for *Rolling Stone*, Timothy White quotes a number of servicemen saying that attending the shows was compulsory and that troops could face "confinement to quarters" if they refused to go.)[11] Roughly one-third to one-half of the shows' airtime is devoted to footage of the troops, which primarily takes the form of several-second shots of the soldier-as-spectator. Hope's jokes (almost without fail) are punctuated by a cut to the audience and by a complementary roar of laughter and applause. These shots capture soldiers laughing, clapping, and taking photographs, and they vary between close-ups of two or three audience members and wide-angle shots that show the size of the crowd. Quieter moments, such as the singing of "Silent Night" that concluded each show and each special, also feature cutaways to footage of the audience, now subdued and contemplative, with many members singing along. Regardless of the tenor of a given moment in the show, the rapid and rhythmic cuts between stage and house suggest that the images of Hope's soldier-spectators are meant to function as evidence of a desired and appropriate reaction to the material presented by the performance. In this respect, the footage, paradoxically, works not unlike the still photograph with which I began this chapter, verifying the existence and efficacy of a performance via a de- and recontextualized image of the activity of spectatorship. By de- and recontextualized, I simply mean that, presumably, the laughter we encounter when the broadcast specials cut to footage of the audience after Hope lands a punchline is almost certainly *not* footage of a response to that precise moment in Hope's routine. This is not to suggest any kind of insidious misrepresentation on the part of the specials' editors (though there are accounts of the difficulties the film crew faced avoiding antiwar posters in the later years of the war).[12] Likely, editing the footage would have been primarily a practical matter of working with multiple reels of simultaneously shot film. My point is rather that the spectator, in the context of the specials, is a floating signifier, useful to the extent that he carries no meaning of his own and so can be put in relation to other signs or images (or jokes) to produce a coherent image of model spectatorship.

At the same time, however, the images of laughter are not only evidence of an appropriate response on the part of the soldier-spectators, but also a model for the distant yet present response of the at-home audience. Thus, while the duration of these shots (however brief) is not strictly necessary to our recognition of the laughter as laughter—a photograph would work just as well—it is most certainly necessary to our experience of simultaneity, our sense, as viewers of the television special, that we are spectating *with* these soldiers, even though we are also spectating them spectate. In other words, while the Hope broadcast specials foreground the GI spectator as the reason for these performances, the show itself was edited and represented in such a way as to position the home viewer as equally its intended audience. The specials do not "document" the multiple—and necessarily at least slightly different—versions of a show that different soldiers watched in different places and at different times over the course of several weeks. Rather, *they* are watching a show meant for *us*, the meaning and impact of which (for us) depends upon their presence as a single spectatorial entity. This is taken to its remarkable and explicit conclusion when, at the closing of each special, everyone—and I mean everyone—appears singing "Silent Night." Bob Hope asks the audience at Long Binh or Da Nang in South Vietnam to join in after the first verse, but then in his voiceover, he tells us that the cast will be "joined on film by all the guys who joined us around the world."[13] As thousands of voices, presumably from a single recording, can be heard singing the words, we cut to footage of each of the audiences we've already visited, all of them singing along.

No one present in the audience of the live performance would have had access to this remarkable finale; soldiers at Da Nang could not suddenly find themselves singing along with soldiers at Long Binh. This is not to say that one could not make the argument that the Hope shows could make soldiers *feel* as though they were singing along with soldiers stationed at other bases, who'd sung or would soon sing the same song in a different place and time. But this could not be made to happen in so literal a sense as when the voices are edited together for the purposes of the special. The specials *produce* the soldiers as singing *together* for the sake of the television audience, imagining (by enacting) a future in which the soldier-spectator and the TV viewer will once again be in the same space at the same time. As soon as we begin to think about the lag or drag of the specials, the urgency of constructing a temporary future in the present becomes painfully clear, precisely because any degree of contemplation makes the impossibility of doing so apparent. Writes Ken Bell on attending Hope's show while stationed overseas, "We all longed to be home in time to see clips of the show on Bob Hope's Annual Christmas Television Special, but that wasn't even vaguely possible."[14] Moreover, there must have been at least one spectator, captured by Hope's cameras, who was dead by the time friends or family recognized his face on a screen at home. This unbearable possibility, and its potential impact on the popularity of either the specials or the war, is avoided by the premise of simultaneity that the specials propose when they let us watch and laugh *with* these soldiers.

This is not to say that part of the pleasure of watching the specials was not the possibility that one might catch a glimpse of a loved one stationed abroad, or perhaps a glimpse of his specific base, or hear Hope reference his specific detachment or company. The posters GIs would bring underline the opportunity the live shows offered to communicate—or to feel that one was communicating—with family back home. Rather, in arguing that the Hope specials produced a contiguous audience of soldier spectators, my point is that by establishing a singular "there," the specials made possible for the at-home viewer the experience of a "now." Undoubtedly, it was the ability of the special to produce this "now" that contributed to its unprecedented success, as millions of viewers tuned in in 1971 and 1972 for the Christmas specials recorded the month prior. Looking at the comments on the Amazon.com page for the DVD box set of Hope's Vietnam-era specials, it is easy to see that the experience of co-presence offered to at-home viewers during the war has been replaced by a similarly lucrative desire on the part of the buyer to see if he can seem himself in one of the specials, because he had attended one of the shows.

The rapid transitions from space to space, paired with the consistency in editing, and the final cross-temporal sing-a-long produce the effect that the troops appear as essentially the same, divided among a series of far-flung outposts. Even as individual units and detachments are regularly identified, either by Hope as a part of his routine or because he comments upon the banners and posters groups of soldiers have brought along to show Hope and his cameras (and the home audiences promised by those cameras), the effect is ultimately that of a single spectatorial subjectivity, made accessible to us as a coherent object—the American soldier over "there." Underlining the fact that difference plays out not between bases but between the occupants of all bases on the one hand and the diverse regions in which these bases are occupied on the other, is Hope's apparent preference for opening a show by walking onstage in some version of a given country's "local dress." Inevitably, his appearance in this manner draws an enthusiastic response, as it stages for the soldiers and at-home audiences the fundamental foreignness of the sites the performers visit; mocking the local culture more generally features throughout Hope's routines and narration. In transitions we often, though not always, cut to a map, which the camera pans across as if following the group's movements from one location to another. Often, though not always, we watch the performers deplane, as Hope's voiceover comments on the differences between climates. In fact, the specific locations figure prominently in Hope's routine, but, in a sense, interchangeably, staging for the at-home audience both the insignificance of the countries occupied by US bases and also the sacrifices made and difficult conditions faced by the performers making the trip.

In addition to the visual elements of the specials that constructed the image of the soldier-spectator, the structure, and in particular the way the sound of the applause of the soldiers functions as a kind of rhythmic interruption, becomes constitutive of the specials' narrative. The pacing of the editing and the near-absence of silence, combined with the careful arc of Hope's voiceover, facilitates a progression from comedy and pleasure to contemplation. The latter transitions finally into a reaffirmation of common purpose and support for the war. Hope moves from speaking to us, to speaking to the GIs, to speaking to us about the GIs, to, finally, speaking for us. Over the course of his concluding remarks for the special filmed in 1964, he subtly moves from a "we" that refers to the cast of the show to a "we" that might include us all:

> We want to thank Secretary of Defense Robert McNamara for making this Christmas trip possible [. . .] Let's face it, we're the Big Daddy of this world [. . .] I talked to a lot of our fighting men over here and even though they're putting up a great fight, against tremendous odds in this hide-and-seek war, they're not about to give up, because they know if they walk out of this bamboo obstacle course, it would be like saying to the commies, "come and get it." That's why they're laying their lives on the line everyday [. . .] And they said thank you [. . .] I don't think any of us ever had a better Christmas present.[15]

In the specials, Hope's voice exists both then and now, here and there. His opening voiceover gives way to his stage presence, and then picks up again on the other end of the routine, at which point he tells us what we already know: that the "most important show wasn't on the stage—it was out there in the audience, on the faces of the men."[16]

Theater of War on Film

As it did with the structure of the live show, the FTA's filmic iteration draws upon the established example of the Hope television special, adapting a number of its formal elements while rejecting its content. I explained in chapter 2 that this adaptation should not simply be understood as an uncritical use of a ready form, nor should it be understood as a radical reinterpretation or inversion of that form. Its appropriation appears, rather, to be the result of practical and tactical considerations—the form is familiar and accessible, and allows for the FTA to reference the Bob Hope show while escaping the limitations of functioning as parody. That is, the FTA at once draws on the popularity of the Hope show while making clear that its primary critique is leveled not at the show itself (as would be the case with a parody), but at military and foreign policy more generally. During a press conference in Japan, Fonda described this dynamic: "We consider ourselves more serious than a mere alternative of [Hope's] shows, although he is not our enemy."[17] The distinction also reflects the disagreement that developed between organizers of the show around the question of entertainment, discussed in chapters 2 and 3. At the same time, the FTA show's explicitly political orientation, paired with the striking footage of soldiers raising clenched fists and peace signs, highlights the already deeply political project of performing for and screening the soldier-spectator in Hope's supposedly more "neutral" shows and broadcasts. At every turn, the FTA film contradicts the logic of the Christmas specials by disrupting the seeming seamlessness between its form and content. By replacing Hope as narrator, for example, with the images and voices of soldiers, or by at once offering and troubling the sense that the film is tracing the linear progression of the tour, *FTA!* draws our attention to the work the image of the soldier-spectator is always, in either case, being made to do.

FTA! follows its namesake troupe, now newly diverse, during its month-long tour to US military bases in Hawaii, the Philippines, Okinawa, and Japan. Original plans for the tour had proposed additional sites along Hope's usual route, including Korea, Guam, and Hong Kong, as well as South Vietnam, but for various logistical and political reasons, these were all dropped from the itinerary. As with the Hope's broadcasts, footage of the performances is intercut with footage of the soldier-spectators. From its outset, however, the FTA film follows a much less rhythmic structure, and in fact, it took me several viewings before I recognized that a linear progression loosely organizes it. As with the Hope specials, we eventually track the travels of the troupe through the use of a map graphic and footage of planes landing and the cast emerging, but because we spend substantially more time in each location, the map's reappearance does not reinforce a linear progression so much as it reminds us how nonlinear the film—and by extension, the tour itself—feels. No line is drawn from place to place. (In fact, the film's representation of the tour is not linear at all, as it suggests the troupe went from Hawaii, to Okinawa, to the Philippines, and then Japan. The tour actually went from Hawaii to the Philippines, then to Japan, then Okinawa, and then back to Japan.)

Visually, the map graphic in *FTA!* is similar to Hope's, but in place of his self-deprecating commentary and the opening notes of "Wild Blue Yonder" is a contemplative (if slightly orientalist) instrumental underscore. The absence of spoken text is significant, as it signals what will be the case throughout: the FTA film is without any consistent narrative voiceover, whereas Hope's commentary stitches together each phase of the USO tours. Instead of a familiar voice, the first thing we encounter in *FTA!* is silence and text, as white words appear against a black screen:

> This film was made in association with the servicewomen and men stationed on the United States bases of the Pacific Rim, together with their friends whose lands they presently occupy.[18]

Following this text, we encounter a form of introduction that differs sharply from Hope's. Instead of a generalized direct address, situating us as a participating audience, we cut to the first voice we are given by the film—a white Marine, clearly unrehearsed, explaining to someone standing next to the camera that he is against the war:

> I mean, how can you write your mother and tell her you know that her her her handsome young darling marine, you know her hero is, you know, is anti-military you know, but I sat down and wrote her a letter and told her exactly how I felt and my mother wrote wrote back and she said that she fully understood and she was happy that I felt that way and that I was anti-military.[19]

He is followed by a Black GI ("The way this war is we are really in a pinch [at home], so why should we go over there and put our lives down?"), a second white GI ("it was jail or the service"), and a white WAF, who explains how she ended up enlisting after high school: with no job, no money . . . "the Air Force came along and there I was."[20] Then, in what may or may not be a direct reference to the footage of a plane taking off that marked the performers' departure in the Hope specials, we watch a plane take off. Over this image, the FTA film feints in the direction of a voiceover, as Sutherland intones, "Thinking of going places?" It turns out, however, that this seductive possible direct address is part of a sketch, in which Sutherland, as a pilot, and Fonda, as a WAF, bond over their vision of "democracy"—which Sutherland's character clarifies means protecting the free market from unfair competition.[21] The sketch transitions into the FTA's signature musical number, "The Lifer's Song," and for several minutes, we watch the series of blackout sketches in its entirety.[22] While we hear the laughter of the soldiers, we do not cut to footage of the audience for visual evidence. The song's conclusion introduces the meaning of the film's title—"Fuck the Army! And the Navy! And the Marines!"—and then we return to footage of another soldier speaking about his position on the war, explaining how he became injured and began to question the purpose of the military's presence in Vietnam.

It's important to note that the footage of soldiers that appears at the beginning of the film is recorded outside, in indeterminate locations. The soldiers do not look at the camera, and they appear to be responding to a general prompt, along the lines of "Why are you against the war?" or "How did you come to be against the war?" We are not in a formal interview situation, and we do not see the interviewer. It is, in fact, one of the more striking aspects of the film, these unframed comments, that surface, confront us, and then disappear. We meet soldiers in each location, though again it is not always easy to remember where, exactly, we are, as the film does not emphasize the inclusion of visual clues. This is especially true when, later on, in Japan, we meet in passing two soldiers who have both been injured and discharged; one of the men, who has lost an arm, says he has been wandering around Japan for two years. They appear to be traveling on foot (despite the fact that the other of the men uses crutches), backpacking through the city of

Iwakuni, though we do not know where they have come from or where they are going. The moment stands in contrast to the footage included in the Hope specials of the comedian and his celebrity guests visiting wounded men recovering in military hospitals. Where the latter is an image of sacrifice made meaningful, via its integration into a collective celebration of patriotism, the former passes through the space of *FTA!* but remains unincorporated—the men seem uninterested in the show, or the GI movement generally, and no one presses them on this point.

After the opening "interviews," we return to the show and observe an extended sing-along with Len Chandler. Here we do have footage of the soldiers, sitting in civilian clothing in the bullring in Okinawa (though there would be no way for most viewers to identify the location at this point in the film). However, though we are given visual access to the troops, it is immediately clear that this will be an entirely different kind of display than what we find in the Hope specials. The camera pans across the audience, avoiding the rhythmic shot-countershot characteristic of "Around the World with the USO." The camera seems to allow our gaze to roam. We watch not only Chandler and his spectators, but we also look briefly at children playing on a wooden fence, or at Sutherland offstage, distractedly clapping along. We take in the whole scene.

The song is quite long, long enough for the lengthy opening credits to finish rolling across the screen before Chandler sings his final, enthusiastic round of "They can kiss my ass!" Up to this point in the film, we have had no direct explanation of what, precisely, we are watching or where we are. We know that the film involves soldiers, that it stars Jane Fonda and Donald Sutherland (among others), is explicitly antiwar, anti-imperialist, and is perhaps even mildly revolutionary. Finally, following the conclusion of Chandler's song in the bullring, and over a map graphic decidedly more detailed than the one that appears in Hope's 1972 special, a bit of text explains that in 1971 the FTA toured bases along the Pacific Rim "in response to the growing movement of American GIs to end the war, U.S. militarism and military injustice."[23]

Despite the suggestions made by the introductory text and the maps that we will be given a linear representation of the tour's progression, the sketches presented in the film are edited in a manner markedly different than Hope's specials. In a move that functions perhaps intentionally as the inverse of one of the specials' conventions, the sportscaster sketch known as "Red and Red" (performed by Alaimo and Sutherland) is represented in its entirety, but via footage compiled from multiple performances.[24] Subtle differences in lighting and costume signal that we are watching an edited performance, the timing of which is perhaps made even more virtuosic by the editing process. Though we hear the audience's response, we see it only twice, and briefly; the sketch is presented from beginning to end, interrupted only by shifts between its different performances. The combination of the almost absent audience and the presence of multiple different performances effectively refuses the coherent "there" produced by the Hope specials. We cannot easily locate ourselves in relation to the FTA's present, unseen audience: we are not "there," and we cannot even be sure, exactly, where "there" is. This is important in two respects; first, the refusal of a "there" underscores the FTA's investment in strengthening connections between antiwar GIs and local anti-imperialist groups and movements. Hope's specials depended upon a careful and selective recognition of the specificity of the countries he visited. This usually involved incorporating elements of local culture into his routines as a nonthreatening and superficial backdrop, or an opportunity for prop comedy. In contrast, *FTA!* disrupts our sense of easily accessing diverse locations by drawing our attention to a multiplicity of performances.

Second, the absence of a coherent "there" proposes a relationship between the spectator of the live show and the spectator of the film that is not one of support, but of solidarity, with its precarious proposal of a mutually constructed relation. Hope's easy transition between a "we" that speaks for civilians and a "we" that speaks for all Americans is precisely the construction of a relationship of support, dependent upon the absence of an alternative to this "we." Additionally, insofar as Hope's shows were often described as bringing "home" to troops stationed abroad, they create a closed circuit of US geographical dominance when they deliver "home" back into the home. There is no "outside" that might allow either soldiers or civilians to propose an alternative relationship to the established interests upon the basis of which the war is being fought. In contrast, *FTA!* constantly challenges any sense we might have of our unproblematic incorporation into the live show's audience by emphasizing not only the limits of our access to the stage show, but also the diverse and overlapping interests of different segments of its enlisted audience. While the linear structure of the Hope specials allows us to feel as though we are watching what the troops are watching, *FTA!* instead positions us as at a remove from the action taking place. This makes it possible to recognize that the stage show we witness via *FTA!* is not meant for us and is not what we are here to see, and that for this reason, we will not be given the same degree of access to the experience of its performance. Relations between spectator and actor, civilian and soldier, here and there, then and now, exist not as given but as to-be-constructed on the basis of diverse material realities and shared interests.

The *FTA!*, as a theatrical release, could not presume to speak to its audience in quite the same way as Hope's television broadcast. Nor, I would argue, did it want to. The show is not narrated—we are not spoken to directly, except, perhaps, to the extent that we can understand the film as an attempt to give us direct access to the thoughts and feelings of enlisted men and women. The interviews with servicemembers rarely find them looking directly into the camera. Likewise, the performers never appear to acknowledge the presence of the cameras, whether they are rolling while the show is happening or afterward, during conversations with GIs. In fact, eye contact with the camera is so rare on the part of the GIs or performers that, when it does occur, it stands out. Early on in the film, Fonda comes onstage to announce that the troupe is "trying to figure out what to do about the fact that there are a couple thousand more GIs outside who can't come in." The film cuts to a shot from, we can assume, the doorway of the performance venue; a crowd of faces peers in, and the young man closest to us, smoking a cigarette, is staring straight at us, as we look back at those who did not see what we've just seen. His stare feels almost accusatory, and the look is not a particularly friendly one.[25] Apart from this moment, we watch communication take place, between GIs and the performers, in the rap sessions that would follow or precede most shows. We see Fonda and the others in sustained engagement, listening (an activity for which Fonda would soon face grave charges) and, we might say, modeling listening—"throwing focus." The Hope specials, in contrast, offer us relatively consistent "eye contact," and in fact, the spectator sitting at home might imagine herself to be meeting Hope's gaze likely more than any soldier could have, in the vast arenas where the shows were typically performed. No doubt this is due in part to Hope's use of cue cards, positioned, one assumes, near a central camera; nevertheless, the effect is to feel included, despite the fact that we are not present.

Consider a moment that is, if not unique, at least exceptionally pronounced. During a show at Da Nang Air Base in 1966, singer and conservative activist Anita Bryant introduces a song she is about to sing by speaking—as would make sense during a performance before a live audience—to the soldiers seated in front of her. She tells them, gravely, that they will understand this song "better than a lot of folks back home."[26] She then delivers a deep, resonant performance of "Battle Hymn of the Republic." She is in practice, if not in fact, saying to us in the tongue-in-cheek manner of one who wishes to make clear the target of a critical statement, "I'm looking at you, buddy." Disconcertingly, however, she sings nearly the entire song *with her eyes closed*. There are two brief exceptions, when she casts her glance, smiling, to each side of the camera, making eye contact, we can assume, with soldiers in the audience; but the vast majority of the song's duration involves the home viewer looking at someone who appears to be refusing our gaze. In a way, this performs the contradiction inherent in Bryant's claim, that the song she will sing for the soldiers really ought to be sung for the home audience. She sings it for them, because we need to hear it. It seems the point here is not that the soldiers will "understand it better," but that we, the future-yet-present audience are to understand that they understand it better. The camera tells us we are Bryant's audience, even as she withholds, in a sense, her presence.

In this moment, we can read a dynamic that positions the at-home viewer as the intended audience not only of the broadcast special but of the live show as well. This is something the FTA consistently attempts to avoid. In a scene memorable primarily for its composition, we are given a profile view of Fonda speaking at a press conference. For not a terribly short amount of time, we watch her talk without meeting her gaze. She is discussing the soldiers and what they are doing.[27] We are not invoked by Fonda, as we are by Bryant, nor are we directly addressed. While Bryant stares us down with her eyes closed, compelling our support for her "live" audience, Fonda's profile can neither shame us nor presume our agreement. We are invited to listen and to decide where we stand. In this moment, she is not speaking to soldiers but to the press, and so in this way too we are separated from the show's intended audience; we are not asked to support the soldiers in some general sense, but to occupy a position in relation to them based on what we can come to understand about the war—we are asked to stand in solidarity with antiwar servicemembers. Bryant and the special script us into and onto what is presented as the only possible position: supporting the troops by supporting the war. The "we" Bryant's performance instantiates is a "we" that we cannot choose because it has already been chosen for us—identification with this "we" is compulsory, and we will not co-construct its meaning. *FTA!*, in contrast, acknowledges a choice, the possibility of refusing the "hail" or of being hailed differently, of constituting a different "we." This is a choice that, of course, the film encourages us to make in a particular way, and its argument is carefully constructed to this end.

Soldiers on Stage

I turn now to the soldier-spectator onstage, and the extent to which his presence there in *FTA!* and in the Christmas specials mirrors or departs from the practices of audience inclusion and participation that became common currency among many politically committed theater groups working during the 1960s. Audience participation was a regular feature of Hope's live performances, and footage of the same was often included in the specials. From watching the specials, it's apparent that these moments were typically thoroughly scripted, and usually deeply awkward. A representative example occurs during the 1970 special, as part of a bit between Hope and Gloria Loring.[28] After making some remarks about Loring's recent marriage, Hope brings a young soldier up on stage to meet the singer. The rest of the audience laughs, boos, and applauds as the GI takes his place at the microphone. Hope asks the soldier's name, and at first he doesn't reply, as he is apparently distracted by Loring's presence (he is staring at her from the neck down and scratching his chin). It is unclear whether the soldier's initial failure to reply is part of the routine. Finally Hope gets an answer—"Samson"—and quips, "What do you hear from Delilah?" They cycle through a couple more punchlines, and each time the soldier takes longer than strictly necessary to answer the question and provide the setup. It is possible to read this either as an overenthusiastic response to direction he may have received, to "act nervous," or he may in fact *be* so nervous that he is having trouble remembering his lines. A third possibility is that the soldier is drunk. Regardless of the actual circumstances, the scene is profoundly awkward. And yet this strikingly inept interaction seems to have been in keeping with the overall style of Hope's shows, which reporter Margy Rochlin describes as a "non-style really. It was supposed to be like watching famous people getting together for an hour to have a good time in front of the camera."[29] A regular dependence upon amateur soldier-performers was both a reliable way to get a laugh and an effective means of reinforcing the show's pretense of political neutrality and simple support.

In contrast, the FTA's spectator, as presented by the film, appears on stage only three times. In every case the presence is clearly bracketed away from the actors' performance and involves text that, while in two cases written in advance, has not been scripted by the FTA's members. The first of these happens in Okinawa, and involves a single soldier performing a song he has written for the gathered audience. In one respect, he is reminiscent of Hope's soldier, beckoned onto the stage—he seems at once excited and absolutely terrified. He's brought along with him the lyrics to his song—he comments with a grin into the mic that he was afraid he'd flub the words, then realizes and remarks that he hasn't written down the chords. His face is bright red. He sings well, and doesn't miss a beat. The song's message is simple, and delivered with a smattering of musical clichés, prefaced with "this is kind of about tonight and what it's all about":

> Let me tell you what this night is for
> They're gonna try and stop the war
> They're gonna sing their songs and then
> They'll go to Tokyo and try again
> So let us listen, hear what they say
> Tomorrow's gonna be a brand new day[30]

Even as Len Chandler kneels in front of him, holding up the sheet with his lyrics, this soldier-performer reinforces his identification with the audience as a group distinct from the FTA's members.[31] Chandler seems to know precisely how to bring this moment to a dramatic conclusion. As the soldier sings the final chorus ("la la la la la la la-da-da-a"), Chandler stands up and harmonizes, and then joins in (still harmonizing) on the final line: "Tomorrow's gonna be a brand new day." Significantly, Chandler does not sing the lines that refer to "us" (the soldiers) and "they" (the performers), instead contributing an almost comically high-pitched countermelody. As it plays out the relationship between the soldier and the civilian, the song also produces a compelling resonance with another solo performance, Rita Martinson's "Soldier, We Love You":

> I heard today you took a stand / and refused to fight in Vietnam [. . .]
> Soldier we love you / Standing strong / 'Cause it's hard to do /
> What you know you must do / 'Cause it's true /
> Yes, it's true. / They locked you up in their stockades /
> Yeah, they locked you up 'cause they're afraid /
> That you would rap and spread the word /
> But you can't jail truth, it will be heard . . .[32]

Martinson's use of the "we" and "you" is reinforced and even answered by the singing soldier's "they" and "us." Additionally, in a departure from the format of the Hope specials, the film does not intercut images of the soldier-spectators with footage of the soldier-performer, though it does during Martinson's performance. The soldier's song is presented to us by a single camera. The absence of images of the audience for the duration of this moment suggests, perhaps, a way of negotiating the doubled audience that prevents the soldier-performer from being (con)scripted into a show on terms other than his own. In the Hope specials, soldiers appear on stage in order to be incorporated into the performance, and these moments work not unlike an episode of "The Price Is Right": one lucky member of the audience is given the chance to join the celebrities. Of course, this is a reward or gift that only a tiny handful of servicemembers will get to experience, but nonetheless the show holds out the possibility of being among those chosen to participate.

The "gift" of audience participation in the specials also functions as a way of linking the soldiers to the viewers at home, to the extent that these gifts are inherently structured and perceived as being in exchange for the gift the soldiers are giving civilians by fighting for their freedom or way of life (according to such rhetoric). In perhaps the most explicit demonstration of this dynamic, the 1967 special features an extended section during which Hope brings a series of soldiers up onto the stage.[33] One of these is a soldier whose fiancée has written to Hope. Hope explains that in the letter he received, the fiancée asked that the GI to whom she was engaged get to kiss the "prettiest girl" in the show. From backstage appears a makeup girl, indeed quite pretty, who then, indeed, kisses the soldier. Hope sends them both off with the remark that the kiss with the makeup girl was a reminder to the soldier of what he was fighting for. The gift of the makeup girl, facilitated by Hope, is in fact "given" by the fiancée, suggesting that, in exchange for his service, infidelity (albeit of a very minor sort) is permissible and even desirable, insofar as it reinforces the relationship between patriotic duty and traditional family values.

The soldier on stage in the Hope specials makes explicit the operating logic of the specials overall, which positions watching—which is to say witnessing—as a form of support. Support, here, appears as a predetermined and fixed relationship, as opposed to a position one could choose (or refuse) to occupy; it differs in this way from solidarity, which depends upon choosing that which one could also refuse. The act of watching the Hope specials automatically scripts one into its rhetoric of support, producing entertainment as a political imperative to which one has already responded, by watching. In this way, the specials offer us as a political position the idea that the most important thing we can do is watch. As I've discussed in chapter 1, the Hope shows largely avoided commentary on the war itself. In fact, when I first began watching the Hope shows, I was surprised to discover just how apolitical they seemed to be. His stand-up is restricted to jokes about military life, racist remarks about the enemy and, consistently, the country or region in which he is performing, and sexual (and usually sexist) innuendo. The guests he brings on stage perform, with few exceptions, in a manner completely devoid of overt political content. Jugglers juggle, beauty queens list their measurements. It is largely only in his concluding remarks—which have been prepared for the broadcast and are not part of the routine we see him present to his soldier-spectators—that Hope explicitly states his support for the war. Even as this comes in increasingly vague and ambivalent terms as the war drags on, the "we're all in this together" instated by Hope's floating "we" suggests we all (soldiers and civilians alike) collectively have a passive relationship to the war—it is being fought, and we either fight it or watch those fighting it. Those of us at home are its spectators; but soldiers are also, in some respect, its spectators. This, perhaps, is the political nature of their appearance in the Hope specials as such: we see them as spectators, as inactive, such that we can conceive of their activity elsewhere—fighting the war—as a collective undertaking in which we are included. Decisions have been made; now all that remains is to carry out the orders, and some of us have been chosen to do the dirty work while others have not. The latter must, then, offer support to the former. This dynamic bypasses the space that might exist in which to question why the war is being fought, and whether it ought to be.

It is not necessary to argue that the GIs enlisted as performers are ventriloquized by Hope's show—framing it in this way denies the important effect of the participants' difficulty participating. Which is to say, the embarrassment and awkwardness of the GIs who appear on stage seems at times to disrupt the intent of the writers who have provided them with lines. At the same time, I would argue that it is entirely appropriate to refer to the "use" of the soldiers by the show, rather than their inclusion or participation in it. One moment in particular stands out in this regard: as the final bit in the same section of the 1967 special referenced above, an older soldier is brought onstage, and Hope makes cracks about his age.[34] After some awkward back and forth, the soldier, forgetting the final line he's meant to deliver, leaves the stage before the routine has concluded, which produces the effect of making Hope seem mean-spirited toward and derisive of a long-enlisted GI. Even as the band begins to play transitional music, the man is hustled back up onto the stage and essentially required to say his final line, which turns the joke back around on Hope, referring now to the *performer's* age. What had seemed, in the absence of its successful conclusion, to be a series of jokes made at the expense of a GI is finally revealed as really being about Hope. In this particular exchange, the revelation of the strict scriptedness of the stage(d) appearance of the soldier undermines the function of that appearance as a kind of reward or gift. When the GI refuses, or perhaps simply misunderstands his role in the gift giving, he is drafted into the performance anyway. The soldier has taken over (however unintentionally) the performance, exceeded its limits, and transformed Hope into its spectator. The show is not supposed to be watching anything. We encounter, suddenly, the manipulation involved in sustaining our recognition of the soldier on stage as a spectator, even as he is asked to act like an actor. If the spectator can choose to do something different, he disrupts the carefully constructed common purpose into which both audiences are supposed to be invisibly scripted: soldiers fight and civilians support.

If the Hope shows "used" the soldier-performer, it is reasonable to ask whether this should be a way of describing what the FTA did as well. Perhaps unsurprisingly, I would argue that the show went to considerable lengths to avoid "using" the soldier in any manner similar to Hope's. While, undoubtedly, the very fact of screening images of the antiwar soldier in service of a set of political goals constitutes "use," I would suggest that the conception of the show overall, and the careful organization of its tour, were rooted in a deeply held conviction that soldiers were the ones who had the right to speak, and that they already knew, on one level or another, everything the show had to tell them. If the show "used" soldiers—their images and voices—it was to amplify ideas and messages that had come from the GI movement or been forged by civilian activists in conversation and collaboration with GI organizers. Even the issues that the show seemed to impose upon a basic antiwar politics, such as the base workers' strike in Okinawa, or the exploitation of sex workers in the Philippines, were already being explored in GI newspapers and coffeehouses. Interestingly, this material does not appear in *FTA!* in the form of sketches but is instead referenced by the cast in conversation with GIs. This suggests that, in editing the film, Parker and Fonda and the others involved were careful to portray the soldiers on their own terms. When, as I mentioned earlier, some soldiers they interview seem uninterested in the GI movement, they do not press the point, nor do they edit their existence away. They let them, quite literally, speak for themselves.

The second instance of soldiers on stage in *FTA!* happens during one of the shows in Yokosuka, Japan.[35] From what I have been told by several of the show's cast members, it is the only time such an incident took place on the Pacific tour. We see a couple of young men—they look like GIs, but more on this shortly—perched on the edge of the stage; in the background we hear Donald Sutherland, wrapping up his reading from Dalton Trumbo's *Johnny Got His Gun*. One of the men starts heckling him—booing, gesturing with thumbs down, yelling for the spot operator to get the light out of his eyes: "Turn it out or I'll break it out." Another of the men gets to his feet and calls after Sutherland (whom we cannot see, but who presumably is leaving the stage), "You want to fight them here, or you want to fight them at home?" Members of the audience immediately begin to heckle the hecklers, prompting the seemingly slightly inebriated speaker to direct his question toward his fellow sailors—"Here or there?" As Holly Near takes the stage to sing the show's next number, Sutherland and his castmates—Fonda among them—gather backstage and discuss how to proceed. Moments later, after Near's song concludes, Sutherland walks back out onto the stage and tells his adversaries that they're "gonna have to split," or else the show can't go on. A couple of audience members second the sentiment, prompting Sutherland to look out at the auditorium and ask, "If you want them to leave, would you tell them?" The audience erupts in noisy agreement. A few of them—a man in a colorful poncho, another in a collared shirt and jeans—make their way up to confront the hecklers, and for a moment, it seems a fight might break out on the stage, now seemingly clear of actors. But it doesn't, and the show's supporters slowly but surely, confidently but peacefully, escort its detractors from the auditorium. As they do, musician Len Chandler leads the crowd in shouting "Out! Out! Out!," pumping his fist in the air, while Sutherland and the rest of the cast burst into song: "Move on over or we'll move on over you, 'cause the movement's moving on," to the tune of the "Battle Hymn of the Republic." No one, in this moment, has their eyes closed. The audience roars its approval and sings along.[36]

The appearance of soldiers on stage in this capacity is, strikingly, an appearance that reinforces their relationship to the performance as spectators. The FTA's spectators quite literally come to the defense of the performance and performers. When Sutherland asks the audience to act, in the sense of taking action, they do so. They take the stage, in order to clear the stage of spectators (or "spectators," as I'll discuss shortly) who attempted to intervene in the show. We might here think of how welcome or at least appropriate the form of intervention attempted by the hecklers might have been in the context of a show that seeks to provoke confrontation and intervention—in the Living Theatre's *Paradise Now*, for example, or The Performance Group's *Dionysus in '69*. In the case of the FTA, it is an intervention against this kind of participation in which the spectator is asked to participate.

Watching the soldiers take the stage in defense of the show, it is certainly the case that a different kind of performance is taking place. One soldier, dressed in jeans and a white sweater, seems (but there is no way to know for sure) aware of the frame into which he has stepped. He cycles quickly through a series of subtly different postures, as he tries on possible modes of confrontation or engagement with one of the hecklers. When I speak with Len Chandler about this moment, he confirms my sense of its significance. "That moment shows everything," he says and then silently rises to his feet, showing me how these men shook out their arms, like boxers getting ready for a fight: they were saying, "We will kick your ass here tonight." Chandler continues: it was "the greatest demonstration of their support of what we're doing. 'I will fight you here in this moment to let them continue to do what they're doing.'"[37] We can see this act of protection and facilitation as one taken on behalf of the *film's* eventual spectators as well. Watching the film, a year or decades after the fact, the civilian audience sitting in front of a screen has no recourse to join the soldiers in their defense of the show. Instead, we watch those with power in a given situation take action, with which we can identify and from which we may benefit, but in which we cannot participate. This directly mirrors the more general dynamic of solidarity at the heart of the FTA's project—to reinforce the particular power of GIs in relation to the project of ending the war.

The film ends with the third appearance of soldiers on stage. We cut from footage of the cast at the Hiroshima museum to the interior of an auditorium. Four or five GIs are on stage, reading from a prepared statement, which includes a list of demands. The FTA's performers stand behind them, only sometimes visible, depending on the camera's angle. The GIs take turns reading the demands, and after each point, the audience roars. Via the camera's lens, we roam through the house, coming in close contact with raised fists. At first, to a cynical viewer, it might seem that these close-ups are compensating for a small audience; but then, shooting from behind the soldiers on stage, the camera captures the sheer size of the space and the fact that it is *packed*. The spectators recede into the darkness at the back of the hall. When we return to the stage, we see Fonda in the background, as one of the GIs lists the bases that the statement demands be closed—it is, of course, a list of all US bases abroad. As the young man continues reading off the names of the bases, the length of the list causes more and more audience response, and in a visual reflection of this, Fonda, nods her head more and more vigorously, a smile widening on her face, until the list concludes and applause erupts.[38]

Though I do not wish to overanalyze the visual setup of this moment, it seems significant that the performers of the FTA do not clear the stage—rather, they step back, ceding the downstage area to GIs who face the audience and turn their backs to Fonda and company. The soldiers do not so much join the performers on stage as they momentarily and partially displace them. By remaining on the stage, but in the background, the troupe members underline this displacement; if they had vacated the stage, the performance would have ceased to frame the events transpiring. But as with the moment when soldiers came to the defense of the performance, the spectators seem not to enter into the frame of the performance but to exceed or go beyond it. The frame is not broken so much as it is exposed as having an outside, a space in which the spectators act, and the actors can only spectate. Here again, the distance and difference of solidarity is performed by the distance and difference between spectator and actor.

Acting like Spectators (Agents Provocateurs and Invisible Actors)

In this final section of a chapter dedicated to spectatorship, I want to take up the problem of the passive spectator, as conceived by a particular vein of political theater history and practice, but also the problem embedded in one of its contemporary, and quite persuasive, critiques. This problem involves a failure to account for the relationship between "action" or "activity" and "acting." If a common concern of politically committed theater makers is the "activation" of the spectator, it is in quite varying degrees that this activation is conceived of as requiring the spectator to act in the way an actor acts. Similarly, when Jacques Rancière insists, in the title essay of *The Emancipated Spectator*, that the spectator is always already active and acting, and that she need not move from her seat to be so, it is entirely unclear to what extent he accounts for acting of the sort that happens onstage.

While the overtly problematic practices of the Living Theatre, for example, have been discussed by contemporary historians, this has happened largely in the service of attempts to recuperate participation, by distancing it from its coercive manifestations. There remains a vested interest in understanding the spectator's activation or participation as constitutive of a less didactic or more democratic exchange between actor and audience, an interest that manifests in discussions of theatrical practice, particularly in comparison with performance. In Baz Kershaw's *Radical in Performance*, a discussion of *The Labyrinth*, a 1996 immersive performance by Colombian company Taller Investigación de la Imagen Dramática, is prefaced by, in order to mark its difference from, its bad object—the Living Theatre's *Paradise Now*. For Kershaw, the theater forecloses the possibility of a noncoercive participation (leaving aside the question of whether participation is desirable in the first place), where performance offers the possibility of realizing something more attentive to the individual within the process of collective meaning-making.[39] The distinction is a tenuous one—he claims that because *The Labyrinth* involved a space being made within a theater building, it avoided conforming to the effects of the performance venue. Yet, as Louis Althusser observes in his "Notes on a Materialist Theatre," when we go to the theatre, we are not positioned as an audience only once we are inside, in a darkened auditorium, pretending to be invisible—we go to the theater because we are already its audience.[40]

In fact, Kershaw's argument seems to mirror other attempts to distance contemporary practice from the embarrassing excesses of 1960s political theater, excesses that might best be understood with more nuance. Arthur Sainer points out, in his *Radical Theatre Notebook*, that the "more physically active role" of the audience in 1960s performance ought to be understood as on a continuum with the "traditional" theatergoing experience:

> [The spectator] always participates, the play is always in part dependent upon his perception of it. . . . "There are, in fact, as many Lears as there are spectators watching it, and for the same spectator a new Lear each time he sees the play. Part of Lear is where you are seated, what you have eaten—not only this evening but all your life—what the morning papers have warned you about, who your companion is."[41]

This is similar to the argument Jacques Rancière puts forward in "The Emancipated Spectator." Rancière's primary intent in this brief meditation on theatrical spectacle is to apply his concept of "the equality of intelligence" to the "paradox of the spectator," both, it seems, to contribute to an understanding of the dilemmas facing contemporary theater and also as a way to further elucidate his theory of radical equality. Recognizing in contemporary theater discourse and practice a desire to eradicate the perceived passivity of the spectator through strategies of inclusion and/or distancing, Rancière poses an alternative interpretation of the status of the spectator that views these strategies as misguided. Against the idea that the spectator must be *made* to act by that which she spectates, Rancière insists that the spectator is, in fact, always already acting, and that the form this acting takes is equal in value or legitimacy to the acting happening onstage.[42]

The problem, then, is shown not to be that the spectator is passive in comparison with the activity onstage, but that the discourse that positions the spectator as passive can only do so because it rejects the existence of what Rancière calls the "equal intelligence" of the spectator—her individual capacity or power to interpret what she sees and to resist the reduction of her experience to the automatic "effect" that the director or playwright claims to "cause." The existence of this individual capacity conflicts with the presupposition (which Rancière rejects) that theater is inherently communitarian and so must seek to rescue those passive community members stranded on the "bad" side of the actor/spectator divide. Interestingly, in making his argument, Rancière directs our attention to an image of the spectator that, like the images of soldier-spectators in *FTA!* and the Hope specials, has been captured by a filmmaker's camera and edited in such a way as to compose a meaningful scene of spectatorship:

> Let us simply observe the mobility of the gaze and expressions of spectators of a traditional Shiite religious drama commemorating the death of Hussain, captured by Abbas Kiarostami's camera (*Looking at Tazieh*).[43]

The presence of this "captured" spectator in the midst of Rancière's text, as an image edited and evidentiary, raises a question the philosopher never quite answers, but one which I consider central to the problem of political theater and activist practice: what is meant by *acting*? When Rancière describes the paradox of the spectator—namely, that the spectator is both necessary to theater and a "bad thing" to be—he explains that one reason for its negative associations lies in the fact that spectating is understood as "the opposite of acting: the spectator remains immobile in her seat, passive. To be a spectator is to be separated from both the capacity to know and the power to act."[44] But what, exactly, does "acting" mean in this context? Is the spectator to be granted—or to be recognized as already possessing—the power to act in the way that an actor acts? Despite how ready and fruitful this reference seems to be, Rancière is not speaking of a doubled process of signification when he speaks of acting. Which is to say, the activity and the passivity to which Rancière refers are not the activity of acting onstage versus the passivity of watching someone act onstage. Rather, activity for Rancière seems strictly to mean something like "work," which can, of course, characterize what an actor does onstage (and what a spectator does), but it does so without regard for the specificity of the activity of acting (or the specificity of other kinds of work, for that matter). In fact, we get a simple equation between the inside and outside of the theater space: "the spectator is discredited because she does nothing, whereas actors on the stage or workers outside put their bodies in action."[45]

What this formulation leaves out is the possibility—and the reality, given the set of practices with which Rancière is concerned—of acting as an actor acts, of bodies behaving in a certain way to signify that behavior, to make and signal meaning as meaning. Rancière does not recognize (or, at any rate, does not acknowledge) the doubled sense in which the spectator is already an actor—he acts and he potentially acts. Strictly speaking, this does not conflict with Rancière's central point. It does, however, complicate its significance. The opposition Rancière rejects between the activity of acting and the passivity of spectating is rejected because it does not account for the fact that the spectator is already active. But what if the spectator is not simply active or in action, but acting *as an actor acts*? What, then, is the nature of the action that the emancipated spectator partakes in? The actor onstage often (though not always) uses his body to signify another body. If this is the kind of acting we can attribute to the spectator, then the way one behaves, in this context, necessarily operates according to a different or more complicated logic than that of Rancière's emancipation, because it is not entirely owned or ordered by the spectator/actor, but is done to communicate—to transmit meaning interpretable by someone other than oneself. And it is done in or on a space that is understood to undermine the legitimacy or reality or efficacy of this communicative activity.

To put it another way, what Rancière here fails to acknowledge is the fact that inactivity, in the form of ineffectiveness, is often associated with the kind of acting that happens on a stage in front of an audience. To act as an actor acts is, in some cases, not to act (take action) at all. It is, as discussed in chapter 3, what Austin calls the "infelicity" of performative speech on stage. "Language," he writes, "in such circumstances is in special ways—intelligibly—used not seriously, but in ways parasitic upon its normal use—ways which fall under the etiolations of language."[46] The words and actions that might carry meaning outside of the theater lose their impact when framed by the stage. One does not really fight, marry, or place bets. As soon as we add this set of assumptions to the equation, we begin to get the sense that the anxiety about spectating Rancière identifies is actually a displaced anxiety about the status of activity on the stage itself, built upon the fear that the theater cannot do anything "real," and so is always in the position of depending upon its audience for any external, material effect. This is one way of understanding the motivating anxiety of political theater—it must mobilize its audience, because it does not believe it can go out into the real world itself. Political theater, for the sake of maintaining its claim to be political, must make its work the work of mobilizing spectators, precisely because spectators are not actors—they are not necessarily merely bodies signifying other bodies, as those on stage are or might be.

This logic is, of course, highly problematic, and performance studies as a discipline has, in large part, taken as its project the troubling of the opposition between the real and the representational, between the felicitous performance and the infelicitous one. In this respect, we find a clear affinity with Rancière's project of dismantling a similar opposition, which is necessarily an opposition that implies difference in value, between looking and acting. Yet, while performance studies interrogates the concepts of acting and performance to suggest that these are not practices or activities limited to the space of the stage, Rancière seems uninterested in the specificity of the terms he has put into play—indeed, he is uninterested in the actor, except insofar as the spectator is "also" one. But who or what is this actor? Any body in action? Or the theater's body in action? And even if the theater's body in action is also or *like* every and any body in action, isn't this understanding of acting deeply relevant to the argument that the capacity to act pertains to the spectator? As his slippery references continue, they begin to take on the sentimental tone of a rhetoric of self-empowerment, as when Rancière remarks that "[e]very spectator is already an actor in her story; every actor, every man of action, is the spectator of the same story."[47] The excess of the term's meaning is evident in this moment—he refers to actors in stories, developing together a narrative that exists . . . where? Onstage, it would seem, even as Rancière seems to make claims that extend beyond that space.

In contrast to the "mobile gaze" of the spectator Rancière identifies in Kiarostami's work, the spectators in Hope's specials are represented as entirely "immobile"—the editing process disciplines the gaze of the spectator into a strict and singular attention to the stage, which we access through an adapted shot-countershot. But this is, of course, not so much more disciplined than the spectator to which Rancière refers, as the latter's mobile gaze has likewise been produced for us: watch this spectator watching; watch this spectator not-watching. We, in turn, have no access to a mobile gaze in Hope's specials—or in the context of screened images more generally, when they capture our attention; we look where we are given to look, and we may or may not have our attention drawn to the visual access, and subsequent construction of meaning, the editorial process has facilitated. In contrast to the Hope specials' rhythmic screening of images of soldier-spectators, *FTA!* regularly confronts us with the borders we are required to cross, the potential and sometimes very real barriers to access that govern spaces of communication and representation. I gain, as a white spectator, entry into spaces closed to the white performers; when Black performers would attend meetings of Black GIs closed to white GIs, they brought cameras along. But in doing so, I recognize the heterogeneity of the "we" of the GI movement. I can position myself in relation to this "we" but not as a member of it. As with the scene in which we look at Fonda in profile, while she speaks to a group of people who are neither us nor the soldiers (and therefore clearly not-us), we are offered the possibility of deciding to include ourselves among those she addresses.

The Hope stage shows adhere to the premise that the spectator does not need to be made to act, and that he is, in fact, already engaged in an activity peculiar to him as a member of the Armed Forces. Moreover, the format of the show, and the fact that it was often presented in massive open-air amphitheaters, necessitates an attitude toward the spectator that allows for his gaze to wander. We can easily imagine soldiers at the far edges of a large audience listening intently one moment and conversing with a neighbor the next. The response of the soldiers to the presence of cameras, holding up signs that demonstrate an intent to communicate with someone in the home audience, demonstrates in no uncertain terms the activity of these spectators, which does not require their presence onstage. Indeed, this presence is not desired, except under the most carefully controlled of circumstances. When, according to war correspondent Richard Boyle, fifty military police had to be called in to protect the stage during the show in 1969, the problem was precisely the spectator's activity.[48] The editing-out of this incident illustrates the fact that the coercive treatment of the spectator occurs on the level of its representation to an audience that comes, in one respect if not in all, later.

In *FTA!*, in contrast, the disruption of the Yokosuka performance is included not because of the spectators who chose to disrupt the show, but because of those who came to the show's defense. My reading of the interruption of Sutherland's performance is complicated by the likelihood (or at the very least, the strong possibility) that the hecklers are provocateurs, in which case they are "acting like" spectators.[49] They are not there to spectate, but to disrupt the spectatorial experience, to participate in the spectacle. They put themselves on stage, first occupying only its edge, but with the intention, it seems, of moving toward its center. As James Harding explores in his research into performance and surveillance, the "radical reinvention of theatre" during the 1960s, while certainly in debt to activists who explored ever more creative and theatrical modes of protest, is also in debt to those who acted like activists—specifically, the special agents who infiltrated activist ranks to surveil, discredit, and intimidate their assumed comrades. Harding argues that we do not take sufficient account of the role played by the state in shaping activist practice via the ways in which it attempted to repress or discredit that practice. By quite literally theatricalizing life, undercover agents and provocateurs modeled a formal breakdown between the real and the not-real.[50]

As spectators take the stage in Yokosuka to defend the performance, we witness the way in which the figure of the spectator serves as an index between activity and passivity (even as we might want to complicate these terms), one that might at times be useful or productive, or even necessary to the construction of solidarity. If we consider, following Harding, that the thrall to activity, and its privileging in opposition to both passivity and acting, facilitated the covert "performances" of agents provocateurs because they "took action," we can recognize that the spectatorial defense of the FTA show reflects the crucial nature of the spectator as a position available to be occupied, against attempts to force the spectator to "act." If, indeed, these few young men (certainly two, and perhaps one or two more—it is difficult to discern in the film) were agents provocateurs, their task would likely have been to instigate a fight so that military police could justify entering an off-base performance venue and shutting down the show. The spectators appear to categorically refuse provocation—which is to say, they refuse to participate in anything other than the *activity* of spectating. When the spectators, then, appear onstage, they do so as spectators who want for the show to proceed—they take action but they also *resist* activity. In this way, the FTA's spectator-on-stage functions as a marker of the difference between spectating and acting. If the spectator is a "bad thing to be" because it is associated with a kind of unproductive passivity, if the spectator is to be eradicated or collapsed, then there exists no space in or from which it is legitimate to resist or avoid activity, or to participate in the activity peculiar to the spectator. Against this premise, the spectators choose the activity that will allow the performance to proceed—they choose to refuse to respond to threats of physical violence with physical violence. They disarm the agents provocateurs with a radical passivity that invokes the threat of a physical violence they do not then carry out. They return to their seats so the show can continue.

When Rancière's momentary reference to the image of the spectator produces the spectator as a figure—or object, or subject—we can observe, he reveals that the emancipated spectator is emancipated only insofar as he or she is the object of someone else's gaze. This gaze brings emancipation into being, claims its existence, defends its legitimacy, and so figures emancipation as a relation of solidarity, rather than as a position one can occupy on one's own. As Jodi Dean contends, "anyone—but not everyone—can be a comrade." It is the possibility of *not* being a comrade that makes the relation meaningful. When the hecklers take the stage, they misunderstand the scene—they think they can provoke the audience to action, starting a fight for fun, or, if they are plants, for the purpose of shutting down the performance. Certainly, in some other context this might've been possible. But the actors and the spectators are comrades, and they want the same thing, so they take up the task of the actor and the spectator respectively, but with the flexibility being a comrade requires.

If we can undo an activity/passivity bind that fails to account for the spectator not merely as already active but as, at least potentially, an *actor* who uses signs as signs of signs, a theatrical reading of early forms of GI resistance can take us one step further and reveal the possibilities of a tactically acting spectator. Because he is presumed to be "passive," the spectator can enjoy a kind of plausible deniability, escaping the category of the actor while also benefiting from activity performed under its cover. This shifts us from considering the spectator in *FTA!* to considering the ways in which GIs engaged in a form of spectatorial resistance outside of the space of the auditorium, in the midst of their everyday routines. From the overacting provocateur, we move briefly to the soldier-spectator who "merely" spectates, and in so doing, covers over the fact of his activity. While the provocateur must perform radical action, the resisting GI performs radical passivity.

In *Soldiers in Revolt*, David Cortright summarizes the ways in which GIs negotiated the limitations upon personal and political expression:

> In the totalitarian environment of the military, solidarity was expressed symbolically through long hair and afros, rock and soul music, beads and black bracelets, peace signs and clinched fists. The consequences of open defiance could be extremely harsh, and most GIs thus normally expressed their loathing for the military through more subtle means. Vast numbers of Vietnam-era servicemen participated in countless minor acts of sabotage and obstruction designed to clog the gears of the "Green Machine." Every unit had its examples of intentionally bungled repair or paperwork, of unexplained minor damage to equipment, of constant squabbling between certain GIs and the "lifers," of mysteriously appearing peace signs,

etc. The cumulative effect of thousands of such acts constituted the reality of the morale crisis.[51]

"Unexplained minor damage" and "mysteriously appearing peace signs"—these are incidents that are at once happening and not happening, in the sense that they are unascribable to a particular actor. Individually, they are insignificant; collectively, they function theatrically, signifying that they are signifying, acting as signs of signs. I categorize this as a kind of tactical acting because it takes advantage of the possibility of disavowal. The actors—by which I mean the men who cause "minor damage" and "clog the gears"—perform in absentia and then return to the scene to become their own spectators. The point is not to identify oneself as an individual undertaking an act of resistance, but rather to help facilitate the appearance of these acts, in part by seeing them, and, in so doing, to contribute to the collective survival of the unit. This appearance situates the GIs, as well as their superiors, as spectators, protecting the former from direct confrontation with the latter. In chapter 1, I described what was referred to as "working it out," a process by which soldiers and officers would arrive at a mutually agreed upon course of action. Viewed through the lens of spectatorship, "working it out" appears as the exposure of the subtly coercive premise underpinning practices that require audience participation: both practices enjoy the pretense that all are equal partners in a decision-making process, even as it is entirely clear, in either case, who is running the show.

In its most extreme instances, GI dissent manifested violently, in the form of "fragging." A neologism derived from "fragmentation grenade," fragging referred to the killing of one's officer. Just as important as the actual act of fragging was the fact of its threat:

> For every one of the more than five hundred reported assaults, there were many instances of intimidation and threats of fragging which often produced the same result. The unexpected appearance of a grenade pin or the detonation of a harmless smoke grenade frequently convinced commanders to abandon expected military standards.[52]

The "unexpected appearance" certainly reflects an instability associated with the theatrical—its at once real and not-real status. The grenade pin is threatening precisely because it poses an unverifiable and untraceable threat; dissociated from the actor, it offers the officer no way to discipline this sign of insubordination, as it might not be a sign of insubordination at all. And in accusing any individual or group of soldiers of planting the grenade pin, the officer would transform a potentially meaningless event into evidence of an extant resistance.

These tactics of visibility and invisibility, activity and passivity, pose a provocative contrast to the performance practices associated with radical and political theater during the period, which have in turn shaped activist discourse. They offer an alternative way of examining the relationship between performance and protest that develops during this period, and suggest that in the examples of untraceable acts of resistance we might identify a form of tactical acting that leverages the presumed passivity of the spectator in undertaking subversive activity and in protecting against its repression.

5

The Actor and the Activist

Jane Fonda is important because she is a celebrity, and unimportant because she is a celebrity. She is a revolutionary who happens to be an actress, and a movie star who happens to be a revolutionary.
—*Rolling Stone*

I'm not a revolutionary. I'm an actress with revolutionary politics.
—Jane Fonda

If Fonda's celebrity was necessary to the success of the FTA show, it also became the basis for her singular treatment as an antiwar activist following the end of the Vietnam War era. Highly recognizable, she could function as a stand-in for an entire generation of protesters and, by extension, a ready target for critics of the era's perceived excesses. What is most interesting about the collection of negative responses, then and now, to Fonda's vocal and active support for the GI and civilian peace movements is that they fall into two seemingly contradictory categories. Whereas right-wing narratives of Fonda-as-traitor tend to present Fonda as an activist who used her skill as an actress and her status as a celebrity to pursue a political agenda, narratives on the left tend to assume Fonda's inability to be anything other than an actress, directed (which is to say, manipulated) by forces (which is to say, men) beyond her control. In the case of the former, Fonda is endowed with agency, as evidenced in part by the fact that some of her most vehement critics continue to call for her to be tried for treason. In the case of the latter, Fonda is either identified as representative of a generation of activists who were only ever acting in the way that actors act, or she is separated out from the "real" (nonacting) activists in an effort to maintain the perceived legitimacy and authenticity of the movement as a whole.

Neither the right-wing nor the left-wing narrative adheres entirely to its primary premise, however, and as a result the two intersect in illuminating ways. Among the tens of thousands of results generated by a Google search for "Hanoi Jane Fonda traitor," many of the sites or comments charging Fonda with treason also disparage her political inconsistency, attributing her changing views and interests to her various romantic attachments. Representative in this regard is an introductory note to a video (posted on YouTube) featuring a montage of photographs of Fonda in Vietnam:

> JANE FONDA is solely responsible for what she said and did behind enemy lines. So, if you love Jane Fonda, then love her; but it doesn't change historical facts. Telling U.S. soldiers they are war criminals and the punishment is DEATH! Treason can also be punishable by DEATH. Jane's own daughter told her that a movie about Fonda's life should simply have a chameleon crawling across the screen, because Jane changes and molds herself to fit the man she is with at the time—whatever values and views he may have become hers. Jane herself admits that she was a "co-pilot" in her own life, so my assertion was and is correct. [. . .] It has not been fun watching a spoiled young woman subconsciously trying to both rebel against and obtain love from her famous father.[1]

The author of this text at once holds the actress "solely responsible" for her actions, citing "historical facts," and also reduces them to the status of a child's demands for attention. It is not so much that the two positions are incompatible, but that they betray a desire to render Fonda's activism doubly unreal: by refusing its legitimacy *and* insisting upon its punishment. Similarly, when, in his autobiographical "Hollywood Confidential," Fred Gardner implies that Fonda did not pursue a romantic relationship with him because she was "really looking for the Alpha Male of the movement," he reinforces the image of Fonda as premising her politics on romantic attachments, but also seems to suggest that she didn't so much adapt her politics from man to man (a common theme in disparaging coverage of Fonda's war years) as she sought out the men who best reflected what she already believed.[2] Here again, Fonda is rendered as at once calculating and oblivious. The ambivalence in either case reflects the instability that the figure of the actress introduces into assessments of political activity, as well as the uses to which this instability can be put, and the suspicion that arises from the difficulty of determining how, when, and by whom it is being used. In what follows, I put that use to use, assessing the assessments of Fonda's political activity, or *work*, as I will discuss, and considering what these imply about the relationship between acting (as an actor acts), popular discourse on activism, and the practice of revolutionary politics. My primary purpose is not to argue that Fonda, as an activist, was acting as an actor acts in any deliberate sense, but rather to show how the actress-activist became the troublesome subject it did.

In considering the many representations of Fonda as activist, I am building upon ground that has been well covered by others, particularly efforts to clarify what she did and did not do during her trip to North Vietnam in 1972. Mary Hershberger, author of *Jane Fonda's War* (2005), has carefully documented the campaign waged by the Nixon administration against the actress after her July 1972 trip to Hanoi; and Sarah King's master's thesis on the "Making of the Myth of Hanoi Jane" (2011) is an exceptionally detailed accounting of the development of that narrative.[3] Beyond these scholarly treatments, Fonda's autobiography, *My Life So Far* (2006), draws upon extensive evidence to dispel claims that she caused or condoned torture. Even earlier, in 2000, Snopes.com, a fact-checking website, published a lengthy investigation that categorized as "false" the claim that Fonda betrayed American POWs in North Vietnam. In short, the misinformation surrounding Fonda's visit to Vietnam has been thoroughly accounted for.

At the same time, these efforts at correcting the historical record have been largely overwhelmed by the claims' persistence; accusations that Fonda committed treason, or prompted the torture of POWs, began in 1973 but reached a pitch during the post-9/11 period, as the US entered into its deeply unpopular wars in Iraq and Afghanistan, and as the internet entered a phase marked by the rise of YouTube. Because these "afterlives," to borrow Kristin Ross's term, are my focus here, I find myself more dependent than I would like to be on an unstable archive of online content marked by a shifting political landscape. Videos and articles featuring Fonda-as-traitor seem to have been swept up in recent efforts to curtail the spread of right-wing conspiracy theories via the internet in general and social media in particular. While it might seem odd that a misrepresented event from fifty years ago would warrant this kind of corrective, it may simply be that the algorithm was scouring contemporary discourse for the very trope Fonda's detractors had helped to establish—that activists might also always be actors, trying to trick us into believing what is staged is actually real. This is precisely the premise of Alex Jones's claims, now fortunately costing him millions of dollars, that the parents of murdered kindergarteners at Sandy Hook Elementary School, or the survivors of the shooting at Margery Stoneman Douglass High School, were performing their grief for attention, or gun reform, or both.

That the "facts" exonerate Fonda is irrelevant to a discourse that presumes her disingenuousness. Fonda, as an actress, is incapable of not being an actress masquerading as an activist; which is to say, as an activist she must be acting. Later in this chapter, I will take up the proliferation of short, online videos that perpetuate the perception of Fonda as a traitor, but for now I want to emphasize that, in 2007, some thirty-five years after her visit to Vietnam, Fonda's legacy makes a star appearance in footage of conservatives counterprotesting an anti–Iraq War demonstration in Washington, DC. The fifty-second clip titled "Hanoi Jane!" shows a man holding a sign that says "COMMIE TRAITOR BITCH." A woman has just walked up to the sign holder and his fellow counterprotesters; she introduces herself to the camera and says, "He's going to explain to us why Jane Fonda is a traitor." The man does so: "Everybody's seen the pictures. The POWs told of the beating they got 'cause of what she done." He finishes or trails off (it's difficult to tell), and the woman steps in to clarify: "She turned in their Social Security numbers, is that right?" The gathered all murmur in the affirmative and confer on whether Fonda should go back to Vietnam. As they pose, per someone's request, for a picture, the woman says, "She'll go to hell anyway"; a male voice replies, "She's living in hell already."[4]

Fifteen years on from the march at which the footage was filmed, with the withdrawal of most US troops from Afghanistan and Iraq now complete, the right wing's fixation on Fonda seems to have lost some of its popular appeal. This is likely in part due to her new profile among younger activists and audiences who are less familiar with her trip to North Vietnam. The beginning of her long-running television series with Lily Tomlin, *Grace and Frankie* (2015–22), roughly coincided with her involvement in the Dakota Pipeline protests, which in turn gave way to her work on the climate crisis. She gained particular attention with the advent of her "Fire Drill Fridays," at which she was consistently arrested, beginning in 2019. Despite this new profile (or perhaps because of it), "Hanoi Jane" continues to serve the right as shorthand for the illegitimacy of any movement or issue with which Fonda is associated. A *Rolling Stone* article from March 2020 notes a "Fire Drill Friday" at which one of Fonda's detractors turned out to wave a "Hanoi Jane Lock Her Up" sign. (The phrase invokes not only the actress's earlier activism but also Trump's rallying cry against Hillary Clinton, such that the two women seem to mutually reinforce each other's purported criminality.) In June 2021, speaking on Fox News about protests against the Keystone pipeline, in which Fonda had been involved, Trump aide Stephen Miller brought up Fonda's visit to Vietnam and accused her of treason. The accusation amounted to nothing, not only because it referenced an event that had happened decades earlier but, more importantly, because Fonda's actions did not, in fact, constitute treason. And yet, Miller's remarks, like countless other passing references to Fonda's antiwar work, circulated widely. As a kind of persistent static, they keep a highly useful interpretation of the past in play, reanimating an image of the 1960s and '70s that is understood to pose a threat, by way of association, to today's activists.

The right's persistent and enthusiastic circulation of a fictionalized version of events has been complemented on the left by a marked indifference to what Fonda actually said or did, based on the belief that she was only dabbling in or playing at what she was doing anyway. The right takes her actions seriously to the point of fabricating them; the left, as I will explore, dismisses them as inherently unserious, regardless of what they may have been. These are both maneuvers that activate and reinforce a long history of identifying in the actor a unique, paradoxical threat: that the actor's actions are empty or meaningless, and that therefore the actor's actions may be *mis*recognized as meaningful if and when they appear in the guise of actual meaningful activity. We can trace the perceived threat of the actor back at least as far as Plato, who has Socrates banish "imitators" from the Republic. Not only are imitators problematic because they put us at a further remove from the truth, by producing an image of an image of an idea; they are dangerous because we may not know when we have encountered them, if we are "a simple creature who is likely to have been deceived by some wizard or some actor whom he met."[5] Therefore, in the Republic, Socrates proposes, "One man plays one part only [. . .] we shall find a shoemaker to be a shoemaker and not a pilot also, and a husbandman to be a husbandman and not a dicast [a citizen of the polis chosen to act as a kind of judge and juror] also, and a soldier a soldier and not a trader."[6] Actors, by definition, play more than one part—at the very least one beyond their own. An actor is a pilot who is a shoemaker who may also be a soldier, to the extent that he imitates the activities of any of these.

Jean Jacques-Rousseau, in his 1758 "Letter to d'Alembert," displays a similar set of concerns, as he enumerates and elaborates upon the reasons why a theater should not be established in Geneva. Rousseau is responding to Jean le Rond d'Alembert's contention that the concern most often expressed regarding the theater—that actors are of low moral character—might be remedied by imposing strict laws upon their behavior. D'Alembert attributes the "dissoluteness" of the actor to the "barbarous prejudice" he faces from his fellow citizens and suggests that, were Geneva to properly cultivate and regulate "a company of Actors worthy of esteem," it would become the seat of decent pleasures, and even serve as a model for the rest of Europe in this regard. Rousseau agrees to a point, in that he does not attribute fault to the actor himself, but rather to a profession that requires a man to sell himself. In a manner similar to Socrates's, he counterposes the many parts an actor must play falsely to the singular and true role he is meant to play, "that of man"; his fitness for the former serves as evidence of his abandonment of the latter.[7]

Plato and Rousseau are concerned with the actor who might, covertly, disrupt the smooth functioning of the state, and it is this concern we can find echoed in the claims of Fonda's right-wing critics. She claims not to have done what (they say) she did, and because she is an actor her lie might be mistaken for the truth. But what of the actor who *openly* attempts to disrupt the smooth functioning of the state? Which is to say, what of the actor who pretends to be an *activist*? On this point, Fonda's progressive critics, too, align with the philosophers: for just as the actor might pass as a reputable citizen and obscure the proper distribution of parts, so too might she pass as a reputable activist. In both cases, the actor disorders the presumed relationship between work and identity, authenticity and affect. The actor can "act like" a militant, but, in the political climate of the 1960s, "acting like" a militant increasingly required one first to be entitled to that activity, on the basis of a demonstrably authentic connection to a given struggle. This consisted, in part, upon one's preexisting relationship to work, and whether or not one was a member of the working class. Within the GI movement, key tensions arose on precisely this point, as student activists became involved in the civilian-led soldier-support network. As discussed in chapter 3, political work could be pointed to as evidence of one's distance from the working class. The paradoxical nature of this problem—that one must *be* a certain sort of person before doing the thing that would lead to an appearance of that being—is apparent in the deeply contradictory ways in which Fonda's activism was received. The actor-activist, then, is an easy target, made doubly so by the inauthenticity attached to the actor and suspected of the activist. Already associated with the inauthentic, her taking-of-action is readily categorized as acting, of the sort actors do, because we know she is capable of this kind of acting.

In attempting to write about the actor-as-activist, the terms immediately become convoluted, in a manner both productive and obfuscating. "Actor," of course, refers both to one who acts in the way that an actor acts onstage or in a film—that is, in a way understood as "not real"—and also to one who acts in the sense of taking ("real") action. Generally speaking, distinguishing between the two is not difficult, when presented in context; this is also the case with the verb "to act." Confusingly, however, the correspondence I wish to explore between the actor and the activist is not dependent upon nor reduceable to the doubled meaning of "acting" or "actor." Were two distinct words to exist referring on the one hand to acting as performance and the other to acting as taking action, the same problematic would still stand. When one takes action, what does it mean if one does so under the sign of performance? While we might simply explain away the problem by recognizing, following performance studies, all behavior as performance, in the twice-behaved sense theorized by Richard Schechner, among others, this does not do anything to guard against the very real and entirely effective ways in which the *language* of performance—acting, pretending, playing, etc.—is used against activists. Perhaps the activist's actorly acting is intentional and manipulative; or perhaps, as an actor, she is simply incapable of doing anything else. In either case, she is not who she says she is, and she is not really doing what she appears or claims or pretends to be doing. She is an actor, and, like an actor, she is acting like someone else.

If she is a celebrity-actor-activist, she is easy to discover: we recognize her face. She is as unmistakable as Fonda was in 1972 when she traveled to Vietnam, found her way to a North Vietnamese antiaircraft gun, sat on it briefly, and was photographed. But if the actor-activist is not a celebrity, we might not realize she is acting (instead of taking action), and so the actor-activist who is not a celebrity poses a threat to those who would premise the legitimacy of political action and protest upon the discernible and provable authenticity of its participants: among the real activists, someone might be acting like an activist but is, in fact, really (merely) an actor. Usefully for those who wish to discredit or dismiss the activity of activists, the very concept of the actor-activist (which appears as the shadow of the celebrity-actor-activist) produces the possibility that all activists are potential actors, temporarily passing as activists. Suddenly, the language of performance presents itself as an arsenal of accusations, able to transform actions into "actions" and historical actors into (merely) theatrical ones.

Although identifiable as an actress, the celebrity-actress-activist introduces into the sphere of activism the very possibility that one might act as an actor acts, and it is this problem that Fonda ultimately poses for those on the left. She is recognizable as an actress, but others might not be, and so her dismissal is an attempt to protect against the perception that acting might be happening here, in the midst of activity understood as legitimate and authentic. This is the same maneuver, perhaps, that Plato makes when, in the process of banishing the actor from the Republic, he nevertheless turns him into a figure resembling the celebrity, who is at once to be recognized (in both senses of the word) and also refused entry:

> When any one of these pantomimic gentlemen, who are so clever that they can imitate anything, comes to us, and makes a proposal to exhibit himself and his poetry, we will fall down and worship him as a sweet and holy and wonderful being; but we must also inform him that in our State such as he are not permitted to exist; the law will not allow. And so when

we have anointed him with myrrh, and set a garland of wool upon his head, we shall send him away to another city.[8]

The fallout from Fonda's antiwar work during the early 1970s illustrates a set of assumptions and concerns that pertain to the intersection of acting and activism. Examining the ways in which Fonda's various critics (Fonda herself being among them) have contextualized, dismissed, justified, or condemned her activism, I argue that the activity of acting is at once necessary and threatening to the practice of revolutionary politics.

A Scripted Woman

"A scripted woman." This is how Bill Belmont describes Jane Fonda when I visit him at his Berkeley office in March 2013.[9] Belmont had helped to organize the logistics of the FTA's Asia tour in 1972 in his capacity as Country Joe's manager. Once Joe left the FTA due to his disagreements with Fonda, Belmont tied up loose ends and also parted ways with the group. Though his involvement was primarily logistical—booking flights, renting equipment—he had occasion to interact with the troupe during the fall of 1971, as its members met and rehearsed in Berkeley. Often the performers, writers, and directors would meet at the house Country Joe shared with Robin Menken, his then wife and a writer and performer with the FTA, for rehearsals as well as consciousness-raising sessions. This was the period in which the FTA transitioned into a more explicitly and consciously feminist project, and it is within the context of a discussion of this dynamic more generally that Belmont refers to Fonda as "scripted."

What does this mean, exactly? On the one hand, Belmont intended the term in an entirely literal sense—he claimed that the FTA's publicist, Steve Jaffe, would write out for Fonda whatever she was meant to say at a given press conference. Apparently fearful that the actress would prove a liability, Jaffe prohibited her, according to Belmont, from interacting with the press on her own. When I expressed surprise that this would be the case, given that Fonda had been touring the country speaking at Vietnam Veterans Against the War events for months prior to the first FTA performance, I discovered Belmont was unaware of this history. So too was Country Joe, even as, in a separate interview, he had cited his own connection with the VVAW as evidence of a familiarity with and knowledge about the movement he did not feel the show's other participants shared. I will return to the idea that Fonda didn't know what she was talking about, as it is a charge not uncommon among Fonda's liberal-left critics. For the moment, however, I wish to focus on the fact that Belmont's turn of phrase clearly asserts more than an unusually dictatorial relationship between a speaker and a speechwriter. As a "scripted woman," Fonda does not exist except insofar as she is scripted. However, the script does not produce Fonda as a scripted woman; rather, Fonda's status as to-be-scripted produces the necessity of a script. That is, it would always already have been necessary for Jaffe to provide her with a script.

"Scripted" as it is used by Belmont (among others) diverges from an understanding of the script that might attend to its ambivalent fixedness in relation to (re)performance. For example, in developing the concept of the "scriptive thing," Robin Bernstein "understand[s] a script as theatre directors do: a script is a dynamic substance that deeply influences but does not entirely determine live performances, which vary according to agential individuals' visions, impulses, resistances, revisions, and management of unexpected disruptions."[10] In *Performing Remains*, Rebecca Schneider similarly foregrounds the script's futurity and its fundamental dependence upon what the actor (or viewer of the scriptive photograph) will do.[11] In both cases, the script transmits a set of necessarily incomplete instructions through space and time. In contrast to these, I want to examine how "scripted" functions when used as an accusation, one willfully uninterested in the flexibility the script might offer its interpreters. Mobilized in this way, the script's inherent capacity to be reclaimed, reworked, and even undermined is replaced with an irreducible externality. By defining Fonda as scripted, Belmont effectively collapses the temporal distance and difference across which the script usually encounters its interpreters and establishes in its place an existential difference and distance that refuses passage. Passage, here, suggests both a movement through space or time, but also the act of passing. Without the distance from his script an actor usually enjoys, Fonda cannot "make the script her own" in any significant way—she cannot pass between the script and herself and interpret it as an actor might, because that distance is presumed not to exist. If she could, we might then lose the ability to perceive the existence of a script. At the same time, she cannot refuse the script, because it is, always already, her own. She cannot pass as unscripted, which is to say she must appear to be following a script, even as following a script implies an effort to pass the words of someone else off as one's own.

If we understand the script, as Belmont's comment encourages us to do, as a measure or index of the difference between the actor and the character (broadly defined) she represents, then describing someone as "scripted" facilitates the claim that the person in question is not entitled or proper to such behavior, and that this person is therefore not "really" doing or saying what they appear to be doing or saying. This bind tightens the more one might struggle against it by attempting to become more knowledgeable or credible—which is precisely what Fonda did as she got involved with a succession of different movements (American Indian, Black liberation, antiwar, women's liberation). In my discussion with McDonald, it became apparent that Fonda's efforts to learn as much as possible about the GI movement were interpreted by some, including McDonald, as evidence of an inescapable inauthenticity. McDonald referred more than a few times to his own status as a veteran (though not of Vietnam) and his working-class background, emphasizing the credibility these gave him within the movement. At the same time, McDonald implicitly distanced himself from the label "activist," in particular by explaining that he wasn't "taking [this stuff] very seriously." He had "a pretty fun time" until his fight with Jane; "it was amusing." Fonda's earnestness here appears as a liability, as McDonald measures it against his own more casual—and so more authentic—approach to supporting the GI movement.[12]

While Belmont's comments about Fonda seem to use her status as an actress to discredit her activity as an activist, what is betrayed here is that the path of negation is indirect—Fonda is not inauthentic because she is an actress. Rather, as an activist with revolutionary leanings, she is inauthentic like (but not as) an actress, a fact detectable because of her recognizability. She is not only an actress, but a celebrity, and so she cannot "pass" as an activist. As a result, the fact of her attempts to "act like" (because she cannot be) an activist provoke an anxiety around the figure of the activist more generally—what if the activist, and especially the revolutionary activist, is only acting? What if she does not occupy the position (social, economic, political, race, gender, etc.) proper to the activist engaged in a given movement or struggle? What if she is merely pretending? And if she is not recognizable, because she is not a celebrity, then how would we know if she's acting?

My point here is to supplement and potentially complicate a reading of Fonda's reception as an activist that understands her status as an actress as the source of her dismissal. I want to argue instead that Fonda's status as an actress is not the source of her perceived inauthenticity, but rather a way of masking its actual source—her activism. While Belmont's description of Fonda as scripted appears to depend upon the fact of her being an actress, in fact it simply depends upon "actress" as a point of reference. The problem with Fonda was that she was acting like an activist, and that in doing so she was acting as an actor acts, but without the frame proper to that kind of acting. Defining her as scripted is a way of pinning the activity of acting to an absence of agency, as opposed to dealing with acting as a component of activist work. For acting does not necessarily undermine an assertion of agency, unless one's performance is compulsory. "Scripted" transfers the unsettling possibility that we might not know whether an actor is acting onto the actor herself; we know the actor is acting—but does she? This is a maneuver not unlike the one Rousseau makes when he establishes a firm distinction between the Actor and Orator, suggesting that we might always tell each from the other. The Orator "represents only himself; fills only his own role, speaks only in his own name, says, or ought to say, only what he thinks; the man and the role being the same, he is in his own place."[13] In contrast, "the Actor on the Stage [says] only what he is made to say." Rousseau, however, cannot quite manage to keep the two apart: that the Orator "ought to say" only what he thinks signals the ultimate impossibility of distinguishing between them, should the Actor decide to speak off the Stage and in the guise of anyone other than himself.

Like Rousseau's "ought to," Belmont's comment does something specific to the idea of the actress as activist—it expresses the desire for the actress/activist to be scripted, to conform to something that he or she is obviously, measurably, demonstrably not. Confronted with an unresolvable distinction between the actress and activist (because she is both), Belmont moves to resolve in favor of the actress not simply by claiming the existence of a script, but by making it inseparable from the actress. The desire for a script, on Belmont's part, is a desire for the order a script establishes between the speaker and the words spoken. Without a script, it becomes more difficult to make claims for any person's behavior, as we possess nothing against which we can measure them. In this way, we might think more generally about writing history as the process of producing a script that measures the identity of historical actors against the activities they undertook. The script has to be able to define who was who when they did the things they did—those who will be categorized as having been "just acting" appear as history's defeated; if they hadn't lost, the script would validate the legitimacy and authenticity of their activity. If however, history's actors successfully usher in a new state of things, they were simply ahead of their time in the way they acted. If they attempt to do so and fail, they were acting as though something impossible was possible—they were acting "as if," or as an actor acts. In attempting to disrupt the script, activists use what Jacques Rancière describes as the power "to put into circulation more words, 'useless' and unnecessary words, words that exceed the function of rigid designation." He continues:

> [T]his fundamental ability to proliferate words is unceasingly contested by those who claim to "speak correctly"—that is, by the maters of designation and classification who, by virtue of wanting to retain their status and power, flat-out deny this capacity to speak.[14]

The script, as both a measure of speaking correctly and as means of assigning "parts," participates here in the disciplining of this proliferation, recognizing in its excess a challenge to the premise that all possible roles or parts have been accounted for.

Ultimately, what most struck me about Belmont's remark was not its seeming absurdity in the face of substantial evidence to the contrary, but the fact that the activist as "scripted" appeared to be a theme running through his thoughts on the show and its participants more generally. Among the materials Belmont had thought to be in his files were letters written by Elizabeth Farnsworth, who had become a correspondent with the *PBS NewsHour* in the late 1990s. Belmont's particular interest in these letters stemmed from the fact that their existence was evidence of a past from which Farnsworth, he believed, would want to distance herself. Unable to locate them, Belmont described the letters, in particular the way they tended to begin and end ("Brothers and sisters," "Comrades," and "*Venceremos!*"), and offered them as evidence that Farnsworth—and by extension, others in the group—had been "having a really good time playing at being a revolutionary."[15] For Belmont, these phrases were transplanted by the letter writer from elsewhere, from other "real" struggles, and were, in very much the sense J. L. Austin describes, parasitic upon the language of authentic revolutionary struggle. McDonald expressed the same sentiment, describing the Filipino activists as "really, fully aware," in comparison with what he perceived as a "guided tour of celebrities in the danger zone."[16]

In fact, I had seen these letters before, in Elaine Elinson's files, and had copies of them with me, and so I knew what Belmont apparently did not: that the letters he truly believed he could not find were sitting in plain view on the coffee table in front of us in his Berkeley office. They had been written not by Farnsworth, who had never worked on the show, but by Elinson, who had made many of the arrangements necessary for the group's Pacific Rim tour. Farnsworth had been connected with the show only insofar as she had recommended Elinson for the job.[17] In her capacity as advance person, Elinson traveled to Hawaii, the Philippines, Okinawa, and Japan, corresponding regularly with Fonda and Parker, Alan Miller from the Pacific Counseling Service, Paul Lauter of the United States Servicemen's Fund, and Belmont as well, as spaces were rented, accommodations secured, and political conditions reported upon. In between "Brothers and sisters" and "*Venceremos*," Elinson's reports served a critical role in shaping the content of the show by providing the writers, directors, and cast with information about what sorts of issues might be of particular concern at a given base or within a given local community. Moreover, Elinson was not the first nor the only of the FTA's tour organizers to include these sorts of expressions; Louis Wolf, who worked with the GI movement in the Philippines, consistently signed off with "*Venceremos!*"

Leaving aside, for the moment, the potential usefulness of the kind of "acting" Elinson may or may not have been doing, as she concluded her letters, I want to focus on how "acting" functions for Belmont, through these two seemingly offhand descriptions. In the case of the Farnsworth/

Elinson substitution, Belmont had constructed a narrative surrounding these letters that depended upon the author being embarrassed, perhaps even threatened, by their existence. He had so thoroughly imagined Farnsworth as their author that even in the presence of the letters themselves, signed by Elinson (which I pointed out more than once), he maintained—because he believed it to be the case—that other, similar letters existed elsewhere, signed by Farnsworth. His belief in this fictional scenario had, in turn, manifested in more recent events that Belmont took as further proof of Farnsworth's participation and subsequent embarrassment. He described the flustered reaction he felt he had provoked in Farnsworth when, in a chance meeting, he reminded her of their mutual affiliation with the FTA. Though I cannot say to what extent Farnsworth was, in fact, flustered, it seems entirely possible that Belmont misread confusion as distress. Either way, his narrative offers a telling twist on the right-wing paranoia that sees a radical past lurking behind every influential or successful liberal: Belmont's desire to out Farnsworth presumes that the present-day liberal is not (as the right-wing position would have it) hiding her radical past in order to pursue the same agenda through subtler means, but is instead embarrassed by any evidence that she was not always the reasonable liberal she has become. Whereas the right might wonder whether the radical is knowingly acting now, Belmont insists that the "radical" was acting then, perhaps (and quite embarrassingly) without enough self-awareness even to recognize that she was doing so. Both constructions produce the activist-as-actor, but to entirely different ends. (This tension will return when I examine Godard and Gorin's *Tout va bien* and *Letter to Jane* alongside the many images and stories that together make up the Hanoi Jane narrative.)

If we read Belmont's reference to Fonda as a "scripted woman" in light of his description of Farnsworth (Elinson) as "playing at being a revolutionary," it becomes clear that "scripted" functions not only literally and metaphorically in relation to Fonda, but also as a more general way of describing activist activity that no longer corresponds, and so perhaps never corresponded, to the person of the activist. Farnsworth, because she ceased to act like a "revolutionary," was, then, in 1971, only ever "playing" at being one. Used colloquially, "scripted" suggests the state of being disconnected or distanced in some way from one's actions and words, through the mediating figure of the person to whom those words and/or actions "really" belong. They come from someone else or elsewhere—a director, a publicist, a propagandist, or the past and its imagined future—and so betray an inauthenticating association between the actor (in the sense of one who takes action) and the actor (in the sense of one who takes on a character distinct from themself). Belmont's insistence upon Farnsworth as the author of the revolutionary letters seems to emphasize the role of celebrity (albeit of a lower order) in identifying the infelicity of the activist. Apparently (for Belmont), Farnsworth's distress at being reminded by Belmont, in a chance encounter in the office building their companies share, of her connection to the FTA stemmed from the feeling that she had been recognized. The celebrity is, if nothing else, able to be recognized.

What also became apparent both in my discussions with Belmont and with McDonald was that, despite their perceptions of Fonda, neither contested the idea that the show had been a success. Thus, the disconnect was not between intentions and actions, but specifically around the question of whether or not the activity undertaken by the group in the service of its stated intentions was proper to those undertaking it. Put another way, Belmont seemed less concerned with whether or not the group had had its intended effect—of bolstering and emboldening the GI movement, which he believed it had—than with whether its members were or were not entitled to the language and gestures they used. Identifying Fonda and others as "scripted," whether directly or indirectly, appears to be the basis for focusing, in the present, not on the impact of the show but upon the "inevitable" failure of revolutionaries, who are not, and never were, *really* revolutionaries, to realize permanent, structural change.

Going Off Script

Perhaps Belmont, in projecting onto Steve Jaffe a fear of Fonda's speech, is retroactively ascribing to Fonda-in-1971 remarks she would not make until later. If so, Belmont would not be the first to misremember, willfully or otherwise, the course of events. Len Chandler, interviewed in 2022, recalled with frustration that Fonda's trip to Vietnam had eclipsed the opening of *FTA!* and prompted its disappearance at the time of the film's release. However, at the time of the film's premiere, the controversy surrounding her visit had not yet developed. Indeed, the timeline separating Fonda's trip to Hanoi from her transformation into Hanoi Jane is significant precisely insofar as it has been obscured. Events from the period have come to constitute a kind of mythic time that allows for the attribution to Fonda of many, and often contradictory, acts of betrayal, treason, and treachery. That these circulate in relation to a handful of photographs underlines the centrality of the actress's image, which is to say her recognizability, in ascribing intent, agency, or the lack thereof. The photographs remain as objects of proof, even as the stories to which they are often attached (and so "prove") have been discredited and debunked.

So what actually happened?[18] Several months after concluding the FTA's Pacific Rim tour, and just weeks before the premiere of *FTA!* in New York and LA, Fonda traveled alone to North Vietnam. She was not the first American peace activist to visit the war zone, though she would undoubtedly become the most infamous. Between 1965 and 1972, nearly three hundred US citizens traveled to Hanoi, carrying humanitarian supplies and looking, writes Mary Hershberger, "for alternative information about the war at a time when the American media largely presented the official view from Washington."[19] Fonda went in much the same spirit, with the specific goal of documenting the damage done by US airstrikes to the dikes protecting the Red River Delta—airstrikes the US had flatly (and falsely) denied. She also met with US prisoners of war, as many others before her had done, and delivered letters sent to them by their families.[20]

During her two weeks in North Vietnam, three events occurred that precipitate, albeit latently, the Hanoi Jane narrative. First, Fonda spoke to American pilots over Radio Hanoi. (She was not the first American to have done so.)[21] Since arriving, she'd been viewing the heavy damage inflicted by American bombs on homes, hospitals, and fields, and she decided she wanted to ask the pilots if they understood what they were doing. The first broadcast was done live, and, in her autobiography, Fonda describes conjuring her audience before her: "I see in my mind the faces of the air force pilots I have met. I feel as if I am talking to men I know."[22] After the first broadcast, Fonda was given a Sony tape recorder, and each morning she "sat down and spoke from her heart about what she had seen the day before."²³ These recordings, too, were broadcast over Radio Hanoi. Although they prompted accusations of treason from members of Congress, the attorney general ultimately found that Fonda had not violated any statutes and that she would not be prosecuted. The chairman of the House Committee on Internal Security, who had studied the transcripts, stated in a congressional hearing that Fonda had asked the pilots "to do nothing other than to think."²⁴ The chair also, in questioning a representative of the Justice Department, emphasized that Fonda seemed to have been singled out from among the many US citizens who had visited North Vietnam and even broadcast over Radio Hanoi. The representative confirmed that only one other person had been investigated (and was also ultimately found not to have broken any laws).

The second relevant event was Fonda's twenty-minute meeting with seven POWs in Hanoi. The brief encounter is described simply in her autobiography: she told the men that she was against the war and had come to photograph the damage done to the dikes. Several of the prisoners told her that they, too, were against the war, and expressed their fear that if Nixon was reelected it would "go on and on." Fonda recalls that one prisoner, Navy captain David Hoffman, raised his arm up and down over his head and asked Fonda to tell his wife that his arm had healed, which she did when she returned to the US. She described the appearance of the men as "healthy and fit." Though they "seem[ed] genuine," she recalls recognizing that the men may have been lying to protect themselves.²⁵

Third and finally, there are the photographs, taken on Fonda's last day in Hanoi. During a visit to a military installation, she sits on an antiaircraft gun—just where a gunner would've sat to take aim at planes overhead.²⁶ Yet while these several black-and-white shots of the same moment have undoubtedly become, and firmly remain, the catch-all image²⁷ for Fonda-as-traitor, the infamous photographs did not initially cause much of a stir in the press. Fonda's broadcasts over Radio Hanoi, likewise, were not well-known in the months immediately after she made them, even as the Nixon administration explored the possibility of charging Fonda with sedition. The photograph was a latent signifier, sutured into the popular imaginary by the cathexis that was and is Hanoi Jane.

Jane Fonda sitting on an antiaircraft gun in North Vietnam during her visit in 1972. This is only one of a number of slightly different photos capturing this moment that circulate as basically identical. There are also a number of doctored photos that circulate alongside these, often without any acknowledgement that they have been altered to show Fonda making gestures or facial expressions that suggest she is pretending to shoot down US planes.
Photo credit: Nihon Denpa News/AP.

Though the government started investigating Fonda in the fall of 1972, the "Hanoi Jane" narrative actually only took hold in April 1973, with an inflammatory statement Fonda made during Nixon's Operation Homecoming. To give a bit of context: according to her autobiography, Fonda felt the administration's heavily publicized characterization of the POWs as war heroes was disingenuous. In her autobiography, she cites internal documents (since released) that suggested accounts of torture had been exaggerated by the military in service of Nixon's reelection campaign. Fonda also felt that to single out the returning POWs for such celebration was a disservice to all the other men who had done tours of duty in Vietnam.[28] Perhaps most important to an understanding of why Fonda took such a hard line on the question at hand is the fact that David Hoffman, one of the POWs with whom she had met in Hanoi, claimed on national television that he had been tortured into meeting with Fonda.[29] Fonda saw Hoffman's story as a personal attack set within a larger effort on the part of the Nixon administration to generate support for a brutal escalation of the bombardment of North Vietnam by claiming that the torture of American POWs had been systematic and ongoing. In a 1973 article in the *New York Times,* Fonda told a reporter that she did not believe the claims of some of these POWs that they had been tortured by the North Vietnamese: "I'm quite sure that there were incidents of torture . . . but the pilots who were saying it was the policy of the Vietnamese and that it was systematic, I believe that's a lie."[30]

Despite substantial evidence to support the premise that, at least since 1969, the North Vietnamese had not systematically tortured POWs, and despite evidence contradicting Hoffman's specific claim, Fonda's comments prompted a swift and hostile response. This included death threats and public denunciations, and continued largely unbroken until the events of Watergate began to unfold, when, Sarah King notes, Fonda's criticisms suddenly found company in the myriad others directed at the Nixon administration.[31] This did not mark the end of the attacks, however; they would continue, and continue still, as an internet search for the words "Fonda" and "Vietnam" put together makes clear. Not only did Fonda's comments about POW torture fold back onto her visit to Hanoi, they also folded over into a fictional world in which Fonda deliberately prompted the torture of the POWs she met there.[32] This particular story seems to have originated in the late 1990s, likely initially in response to ABC's plan to honor Fonda on its program *A Celebration: 100 Years of Great Women.* Though even among Fonda's most ardent critics the story is now recognized as untrue, it continues to circulate widely, usually with a disclaimer along the lines of "it's not true, but it might as well be," on the many, many websites devoted to exposing Fonda as a traitor who still needs to be tried, found guilty, and executed.[33] The story goes like this: when Fonda visited with POWs in Hanoi, the captured American servicemen each slipped her a small piece of paper as she shook their hands. On these slips of paper, the men had written their Social Security numbers, intending that Fonda should let the US military and their families know that they were still alive. Fonda then immediately turned the slips of paper over to the North Vietnamese, who punished the prisoners with brutal torture. The most common account claims that three of the four men with whom Fonda met died as a result; the fourth, Corrigan, was the only one who lived to tell the tale. In a way, this seems an unsurprising conflation of her comment (which many perceived as intentionally hurtful to POWs and veterans more generally) with Hoffman's claim. The right-wing narrative of Fonda's traitorous activities has been constructed almost entirely in reverse; and even among those, like Belmont, who remain sympathetic to the antiwar movement (if not to Fonda in particular), the story begins and ends with her trip to Hanoi.

Going Off Screen

One of the most remarkable aspects of Fonda's status as anti-icon is that it develops almost simultaneously on the left and the right alike. The same infamous visit to North Vietnam produced the two images that sit, separately and differently, at the heart of the Hanoi Jane narrative and of *Letter to Jane: An Investigation about a Still*, a short film by Jean-Pierre Gorin and Jean-Luc Godard. *Letter to Jane* is built around a photograph of Fonda published in *L'Express* magazine in 1972. In it, she appears to be listening to a person whose back is turned toward the camera, his or her face hidden by the brim of a hat. Further away, we see a second face, that of a Vietnamese man, whom Godard and Gorin identify as a revolutionary. The revolutionary is standing behind Fonda and to her left; he is not in her field of vision. Fonda looks as though she is listening intently to the person we cannot see—her expression is serious, her head is bent forward slightly, and a camera hangs from her neck.

At the outset of *Letter to Jane*, Godard and Gorin explain that the photograph of Fonda with which their "letter" is concerned is also being used in publicity materials for *Tout va bien*—a different film in which Fonda had starred—in place of an image from *Tout va bien* itself. Much of the beginning of *Letter* is taken up with stating and restating this point. As the film progresses, *Letter to Jane* repeatedly shows us the *Express* photograph, as Godard and Gorin meditate upon its meaning.[34] They are concerned, they tell us, with the question of the role of the intellectual in revolutionary struggle. While the *Express* photograph is the visual focus of the film, it is not the only photograph we are shown, though we are shown only photographs. We see stills from *Tout va bien*, mostly featuring Fonda, but we see also her co-

The *Express* photograph of Fonda in North Vietnam in 1972 that Godard and Gorin use in *Letter to Jane*. Screen capture from digital video.

star, Yves Montand, and the (actors playing the) sausage factory workers from the same.³⁵ Occasionally what appear to be images of North Vietnam flash before the viewer, usually underscored by revolutionary choral music, introduced at a volume that makes it difficult, briefly, to hear Godard or Gorin.

Letter to Jane is certainly less well-known than the Hanoi Jane stories and images, and indeed it would be an overstatement to suggest that the brief film has significantly impacted popular perceptions of Fonda. Fonda herself has downplayed its relevance to any discussion of her politics or her career; it does not appear in her autobiography, and David Zeiger recalls that, when asked about *Letter to Jane* at a screening of *FTA!* in 2009, Fonda responded simply and dismissively that "Godard is a Maoist."³⁶ However, the film is significant insofar as it is an appropriately frustrating representation of the attitude toward Fonda that would come to dominate among her left-leaning critics: that she should've kept her mouth shut, both because she has nothing to say and because her speech causes problems. Though the message at the end of the film is somewhat more general—*Americans* must keep their mouths shut—this directive has been delivered to Jane, as a proxy for all those who speak, presumably, from a position of ignorance. The film stages her (desirable) silence, as throughout, the filmmakers speak directly to Jane, posing an "assembly line" of seemingly unanswerable questions to the actress who cannot answer. They directly ask Jane to come and answer "directly," even as they tell us that the questions are not for the actress but for the photograph, or for the "function of Jane."³⁷

It is this "function" that the filmmakers sought to exploit in *Tout va bien*, by scripting Fonda and the film as a whole such that she appears always to act like the actress she is. She is hired to be the actress who plays a character, but not so well that we might cease to be able to identify the difference between the two; her celebrity ought to have been a guarantee against this possibility. And yet this is precisely what Fonda disrupts when she finishes filming *Tout va bien*, leaves Paris, visits Hanoi, and then returns to Paris via the pages of *L'Express*. Immediately after the end of the FTA tour Fonda flew directly from Tokyo to Paris to play herself playing an American journalist trapped overnight in a worker-occupied sausage factory. This was despite an unsuccessful attempt to pull out of the project: in her autobiography, Fonda claims that, after she got word to Godard that she was no longer interested, a man close to the director came to her house and threatened her with "bodily harm" if she wouldn't do the film. Fonda had been excited to work with Godard, but was unaware, until she received the script for *Tout va bien*, of the polemical turn his filmmaking had taken.[38] Moreover, she was becoming increasingly outspoken about sexism and had expressed interest, in a piece she authored for the *New York Times*, in working primarily with female directors.[39] However, as Fonda was key to securing funding for the film, Godard and Gorin refused to release the actress from her commitment.

Fonda was also key to the film conceptually, as *Tout va bien* is built around Fonda-as-actress. In addition to Fonda's *skill* as an actress, she is needed as a "real star," so that, as Gorin puts it, the film might put into conversation "contradictory traditions of acting" and expose the fact that "the real stars are not Jane Fonda and Yves Montand but the twenty extras who play workers in the factory sequence."[40] In this, it is easy to hear the idea that the real star is the *historical* actor, as opposed to the film actress, who is a quote-unquote "real star." Thus, when the *Express* photograph appears, reflecting Fonda's attempted foray into the space of something like the historical actor, she disrupts, for Godard and Gorin, her ability to play the supporting role of "real star" to the real stars in *Tout va bien*. Suddenly, the work Godard and Gorin need Fonda to do as "actress" in *Tout va bien*—which is in part the work of making her work appear as not-work or other work—is compromised by the work the actress does as a militant. Because the surplus value, so to speak, of the work of the actress (whether financial or political) cannot be realized until the film reaches an audience, Fonda's visit to Vietnam, and the use of her status as a film star to do work as a militant activist, constitutes what Michel de Certeau (and the French more generally) call *la perruque*, and which he identifies as a "tactic." Literally translated as "the wig," *la perruque* refers to the work one does for oneself on company time: it is "the worker's own work disguised as work for his employer. It differs from pilfering because nothing of material value is stolen. It differs from absenteeism in that the worker is officially on the job."[41] When Godard remarks that "you were with them after being with us," and then later wonders whether starring in *Klute* (in which she played a prostitute) was "the right way to go to Vietnam," it is difficult not to hear a charge of promiscuity.[42] The solution is to render Fonda's relationship to her appearance in Vietnam identical to her appearance in *Tout va bien*: across the board, she's been selling herself.

Letter to Jane, then, is a response to Fonda's *perruque*: the work she did at the expense of the work she was meant, by Godard and Gorin, to do. This appears on multiple levels. On the one hand, *Letter to Jane* is concerned with the way in which Fonda's attempts to pass as a militant degrade that category; they want to be sure she does not pass, and so they draw our attention to a photograph in an effort to elaborate just how thoroughly she is a performer. They refer to the expression on her face as "that of a tragic actress," and link it, via stills, to several cinematic antecedents including an expression on her father's face in *Grapes of Wrath* (1940) and one on John Wayne's in *The Green Berets* (1968). By this logic, Fonda is merely reproducing, even as a kind of unavoidable inheritance, a preexisting tragic expression, and this reveals that she is not—and could not be—actually listening and responding to her Vietnamese interlocutor. One way of answering this charge on Fonda's behalf would be to claim, simply, that Godard and Gorin are wrong: Fonda is not acting here, but *actually* listening, and that the expression on her face has nothing to do with her skill as a performer. However, once one is familiar with the story of her trip to Vietnam, it is hard, suddenly, not to imagine that she treated *Tout va bien* as a kind of training—would it have occurred to her to broadcast over Radio Hanoi, had she not only months prior performed the very same skill, as Susan the radio journalist? Had she perfected a listening expression in the process of "listening" to the workers in the factory? Or was she, when she ought to have been acting (as an actress acts), really listening to the actors who were not really, as Godard and Gorin would have it, acting? Knowing, alongside the story of her trip to Vietnam, the story of her attempt to withdraw from the film, it is likewise hard not to read, in an early scene, her contempt for the situation as a whole: as Susan, the radio journalist, she records something she has written for broadcast. When she concludes, the producer (or technician—it's unclear) tells her it's a wrap. She mutters "yeah" and smiles wryly. Every time I watch this scene, I cannot help but hear that "yeah" as directed at Godard. She writes, in *My Life So Far*, that "[d]uring the filming, I kept my head down, staying under the radar, showing up on time, and keeping to myself on set to avert outright hostility between Godard and me." Perhaps under the cover of "Susan," Fonda forces Godard's camera to capture *covert* hostility—another bit of *la perruque*.

La perruque takes on a particular valence when it involves the actor, who works to appear other than she is, because the ability to distinguish between the work done for the employer versus the work done at his expense is confounded by the ever-present possibility that the one might actually be the other. Indeed, the actress herself might not realize she is engaged in theft, or worse, she might use our awareness of that possibility to escape punishment should she be found out. Rousseau's attempt to separate the actor out from his behavior betrays this irresolvable fear:

> I know that the Actor's playing is not that of a scoundrel who wants to cheat, that he does not intend to be really taken for the person he represents or to be believed to be affected by the passions he imitates, and that, in presenting this imitation for what it is, he renders it entirely innocent. And I do not precisely accuse him of being a deceiver but of cultivating by profession the talent of deceiving men and of becoming adept in habits which can be innocent only in the theater and can serve everywhere else only for doing harm.[43]

The Actor, it seems, might try to be good but, by the very nature of his profession, is predisposed to fall victim to his own abilities, when tempted by other factors. This is why Rousseau spends a great deal of time explaining that the problem with the plan for a theater at Geneva is an economic one. Via a quite detailed analysis of the costs involved in mounting a season of productions, he contends that Geneva would not provide a sufficient audience—and therefore, sufficient income—to support the expenses of running a theater. As a result, performers would be supported "at the expense of the public." He means this, it turns out, doubly, as he expects that the Actors will inevitably practice offstage the skills (of thieving) they learn upon it. A similar dynamic is at play in the figure of the revolutionary activist, whose activity is temporally doubled back upon themselves. Instead of a physical space—a stage—that one can either be on or off, the activist escapes a temporal location. She is often treated as if linked to and located in the past, yet she is also subject to the passage of time, during which the relative failure of her efforts will have become an established fact. This fact reaches back and infects the past with its certainty and inevitability, transforming the activist into the actor who knows—and so measures—the infelicity of her actions from the very moment she undertakes them. She knows she is speaking and acting outside of the real and in the wrong time, but she persists in speaking and acting anyway.

The repetition marking *Letter to Jane*—the repetition of Fonda's (first) name, the repeated appearance of the same photograph—extends to the term "really," which Godard and Gorin use with striking frequency. They explain that they wish to "really ask questions" and "really think," and that they are "really upset." The appearance of the term ought not to be taken as wholly without an intended irony or distancing, and yet its use feels not terribly precise. Whether *Letter to Jane*'s repetition of the term "really" is calculated or not, and whether this repetition is intended to undo its own surface emphasis, the film nevertheless expresses an investment in identifying or defining what might be "really real." To be "really" real is to undermine the category of the real even as one intends to shore it up, as to be really real is to *act* real, in a way that seeks to correspond to the real by being "really" it. That is, the need to be really real inflects the real with the problem of acting.

J. L. Austin, via a single and uncited reference in Bourdieu's *The Field of Cultural Production*, supports this point, and provides what can almost operate as a counter to Austin's own assertions that the performative fails when it is spoken by an actor and/or onstage. Bourdieu writes:

"[E]ssences" are norms. That is precisely what Austin was recalling when he analyzed the implications of the adjective "real" in expressions such as a "real" man, "real" courage or, as is the case here, a "real" artist or a "real" masterpiece. In all of these examples the word "real" implicitly contrasts the case under consideration to all other cases in the same category, to which other speakers assign, although unduly so (that is, in a manner not "really" justified) this same predicate, a predicate which, like all claims to universality, is symbolically very powerful.[44]

The "not-really" Austin associates with acting and speech onstage—with the space of performance—here resurfaces as the very site of a truth-claim's interrogation. The word "really" is completely empty, meaningful only when it can be attached to categories that are already defined, already in play. But when it is attached to one of these categories, it engenders a false sense of authenticity by deflecting any questions pertaining to the authenticity of the category itself onto whether or not such and such pertains to that category—that is, is an authentic or even exemplary member of that category. The "really" implies and is implied by the "not-really."

The anxiety present in the implied doubled use of the root word "real" suggests that, in attempting to reduce Fonda to her function as actress, *Letter to Jane* inadvertently confirms the source of this anxiety. There, in North Vietnam, Fonda is "really acting," begging the question of what she might have been doing when she was "really acting" in *Tout va bien*.[45] The constellation formed by *Tout va bien*, *Letter to Jane*, and the interviews Godard and Gorin gave in relation to these films clearly delineates directing as the site of politics and acting as a relatively unproblematic tool to which a director has access. That is, the actor does not appear to have the capacity to do anything to the politics of a film that is not already known and intended by the director. Godard extends this explicitly to include the directing done by those involved in revolutionary struggle:

> I'm not the director in Hanoi. We can only direct her in Paris. We asked Jane to come to France in order to act in something staged by us, which was titled *Tout va bien*. Two months later, the North Vietnamese asked her to come and play in something they staged, which was entitled "Victory over America."[46]

By positioning Fonda as equally directed in either case, Godard effectively avoids the question that might be asked of his own work: in comparison with the real, authentic, revolutionary directors in Hanoi—is he *really* directing?

This is not to say that the kind of acting that happens in *Tout va bien* is irrelevant. However, the acting is reducible, it seems, to the person of the actor. This is made clear at the outset, when the film establishes the fact that Fonda and Montand are the means by which funding has been secured. Fonda and Montand (and especially Fonda) are present as celebrity actors, who, explicitly inscribed in the film on this basis, will only ever act precisely as the director intends. The director intends not for them to act in a certain way but to be who they already are. And since they are the very "characters" they are meant to be, they are incapable of not acting in the manner appropriate to that preestablished being. As mentioned above, Gorin explains that the real stars are "people who had never acted." Implied in this statement, I would argue, is that these people are "people who have never acted" because instead they work.

What appears significant is not the acting that is done, but the fact of who is doing the acting and the extent to which these people are or are not only recognizable as actors insofar as they are taking action within a frame that transforms all action into acting. When the workers describe to Him and Her (the "names" of Montand and Fonda's characters) what life is like at the factory, the film cuts to shots of the jobs to which they refer. In each brief vignette, Fonda or Montand appears as one of the workers. Significantly, however, they are not made to stand out, and in fact, in my experience watching the film, it took a moment before I realized they were present in the scene. They are dressed in the same uniforms as the other workers in the scene, mixed in among them and engaged in the same productive activity. After the initial recognition, of course, the viewer looks for Fonda or Montand in each subsequent shot; they are now immediately identifiable.

In his discussions of acting and of directing, I would argue that Godard exposes a double standard with regard to these two different types of aesthetic practice, acting and directing—the former appears to be something that does not have a correlative in the worker's daily life, whereas directing does. In his interview with Kolker, he posits the scenario of a worker making a film of his vacation; this, for Godard, is an inherently political film. He refers, not unlike Rancière, to the capacity for anyone to direct his or her life.[47] Acting, however, appears to be impossible without the figure of the director. The problem, then, with Fonda is that she exposes the fact of acting precisely where Godard and Gorin are most at pains to reject its presence—within an antiwar, anti-imperialist political discourse. Fonda, as the celebrity-actor-activist, betrays the already unstable categories of artist or intellectual and worker—the very categories that the revolution will obliterate, but which, it seems, must remain stable until after the revolution has ushered in the new conditions that will establish the legitimacy of transgressing them. Kristin Ross describes this as the "peculiar combination of literalism [...] and utopianism" characteristic of Maoism in the 1960s and '70s, such that activists simultaneously championed the "disappearance of a difference between intellectual and manual labor" and also valorized this difference, by identifying the worker's fixed (and specifically manual) relationship to labor as the source of an authentic, practice-based politics.[48] What Ross calls the "overdetermined figure of the 'barefoot doctor,'" engaged in "an embodied critique of specialization," shares much with the figure of the actor, insofar as both refuse Socrates's injunction to play one part and one part only. But when the actor as such attempts to "go to the people," Rousseau might ask whether she isn't practicing offstage the art she learned upon it, and so raise the uncomfortable (for Godard and Gorin) question as to whether acting isn't what everyone is doing anyway.

Despite its notable distance and difference from right-wing attacks on Fonda, *Letter to Jane*'s political maneuver nevertheless enjoys the persistence of something like the Hanoi Jane myth, insofar as it activates and exploits similar investments in authenticity and legitimacy. A number of web videos are notable for the uncanny resemblance they bear to *Letter to Jane*, as they are strikingly similar to the minimalist and propagandist style of the Godard/Gorin indictment. A predictable photomontage is set to music, with or without snippets of text attributed to Fonda and/or editorial commentary. Some of these are so similar as to beg the question: why make one's own? While individually quite brief, the sheer volume of right-wing "letters to Hanoi Jane" means they function not unlike the repetition and duration of *Letter to Jane*. The same pictures appear, sometimes intercut with stills from other films—never *Tout va bien*, always *Barbarella*—or images of death and destruction in

Vietnam, and overlaid with text. The text, in a departure from *Letter to Jane*, typically takes one or more of three forms: some videos include the actress's own voice, from her broadcasts over Radio Hanoi in 1972. Others include printed text within the video itself, scrolling over and commenting upon or captioning the images. And all are supplemented by separate commentary: often the video's creator posts an explanatory note along with the video. Even when this is not the case, viewers' comments pile up, many of them consisting of only two or three words (most of which I am not interested in reproducing here).

Although these videos are premised upon a desire to present the viewer with evidence, like *Letter to Jane* they appear to go beyond what is strictly necessary to achieving this end, as they screen the same images again and again. For example, in "USA HISTORY SHOWS HANOI JANE #1 TREASONIST TRAITOR-1," "walter kurtz" has used every preset fade, cut, or dissolve available in a basic digital editing program to transition between photographs of Fonda and grizzly images of the war; the four-minute montage is set to Haydn's decidedly upbeat Symphony no. 94 in G Major.[49] There is pleasure here, a pleasure in looking that is simultaneously a pleasure in showing, which betrays, I would argue, an attempt to assert control over the *subject* of a photograph by demonstrating control over the photograph itself as an *object*. Kent Jones comments upon this dynamic in a "letter" he writes "to Jean-Pierre and Jean-Luc," included in the liner notes of the Criterion Collection reissue of *Tout va bien*. After quoting Gorin explaining that to understand Marx one must remember that he was "jerking off all the time," Jones tells the two men, "It must be said that the pleasure is mostly yours, but we get our share of it too."[50]

Of Fonda's value, Gorin and Godard are also determined to get their share. Gorin describes the decision to make a film built around the photograph of Fonda:

> So we thought it was a good opportunity to show that it was possible to make a feature-length picture, featuring the Vietnamese war, featuring Jane, featuring the North Vietnamese, and featuring our views on these things. It was done in one day—of course, the writing took two weeks, but the shooting was done in one day, the editing took another day, the processing another day, and the money is made back in one day, here.[51]

In this way, they respond to Fonda's *perruque* by cutting her out of the production process altogether, recouping what was lost (politically, financially) by paying her nothing for her appearance—which is to say, her work. They made a movie "featuring Jane" without Jane. Undoubtedly, it is in part the gendered specificity of Fonda's body, like the enlisted status of the servicemember in Hope's specials, that facilitates the erasure of her agency and, even, presence, insofar as it is taken as a given.[52] She is understood as a "function," rather than as a political subject whose subjectivity might complicate the use to which her body can be put. When Godard and Gorin invoke Fonda's role as a prostitute in *Klute* and imply that her activist work is simply another form of narcissistic promiscuity, they rely upon the assumed sexualization of her body, rather than recognizing the political valence of this assumption. We see the same problematic at work in an incident I've described in chapter 3, when Jules Feiffer proposes a sketch featuring Fonda dressed like one of "Hope's girls." When the women involved in organizing the FTA's inaugural show at the Haymarket Coffeehouse object to this premise, Feiffer dismisses them as unable to see the satire. What they can see, and what Feiffer, apparently, cannot, is the way in which such a sketch would require Fonda to work against herself, offering her body as a kind of currency to a political project that fails to consider the relationship between imperialist and sexist forms of exploitation and oppression. The same failure besets Godard and Gorin. We might describe Hope's specials as featuring a similar kind of exploitation of the (stolen) image—in the specials, the soldier is present, in an edited form, while someone speaks at once to and for him. His image is placed before us, over and over, such that he becomes evidence of his own fixed relationship to the world. He sits; he watches; he laughs. He cannot be or do anything else, because should he be able to absent himself, the entire project of US imperialism will collapse. These are the terms the state sets, and so it is striking, on a formal level, that Godard and Gorin adopt this premise, this fixity, in service of their own revolutionary politics.

The FTA, in ways both deliberate and—probably—accidental, disrupted this dissociation of the material reality of the actress from her ability to "function" politically, refusing the short-term benefits of sexualizing Fonda's appearance on stage in service of the longer-term project of building solidarity based on the specificity of its actors' and spectators' lived experience. Occasionally this caused problems—as I mentioned in chapter 3, Fonda recalls hearing that some soldiers, disappointed at her physical appearance in the show, ripped down their *Barbarella* posters in protest (prefiguring, in a sense, the gleeful dismemberment of the actress's image in *Letter to Jane*). At the same time, Fonda's refusal to perform appropriately made her available in a much more specific way to her spectators, facilitating a relation of solidarity rather than mere support. I mentioned in chapter 2 a soldier who spoke with reporters after one of the FTA's first performances; he showed them a photograph he'd taken in Vietnam, a graphic image of a woman murdered and left with her genitals exposed. He says he thinks he should show it to Jane; that she should "know about it." The soldier's impulse feels, at first, confused, maybe even gratuitous or hostile—why, precisely, does he wish to show this to Jane? The article doesn't tell us. But from within this ambiguity, the range of possible reasons communicates the complexity of solidarity, its embodiedness, and its imperfect dependence upon mechanisms of communication and affect that cannot be "authenticated" in any clear sense.

I hear in this a rebuttal to Godard and Gorin's letter, and their disinterest in what Fonda might "really" hear when she "looks like" she's listening in the image from *L'Express*. What posture of listening would communicate authenticity? What if listening is always already a performance when we listen to those who are not otherwise understood as engaged in legitimate speech? What does the soldier with the photograph want from Jane? To be seen, it seems, and to be heard. Can she respond without performing? Isn't her performance already a response? Would Fonda "really" listening to this soldier look different from the image in *L'Express*? Like the letter's writers, I find myself piling up questions, though not for the image itself, but for its interrogators. Why see only the actor here? Why not see also the *activity* of listening, and wonder whether perhaps it isn't always a performance? Wonder whether modeling the very *possibility* of listening isn't, in fact, at least *a* role of the intellectual in the revolutionary struggle? Where Godard and Gorin seek a kind of purity, via an expulsion of the actor from the scene of radical left politics, in order to protect against the illegitimacy of the revolutionary who acts as an actor acts, I propose "acting" as a way of understanding a political practice of seeing and hearing that which is not meant to be seen or heard.

Critically, this is a practice that can reproduce itself, and therein lies its strength. Fonda attempts to "see" and "hear" in North Vietnam; the FTA (and other civilian antiwar activists) attempted to "see" and "hear" the GI movement; the GI movement attempted to "see" and "hear" the antiwar soldier and, by extension, the antiwar civilian. All of these instances of seeing and hearing could themselves become the seen or the heard, through photographs, footage, films, underground publications, mainstream newspapers, and so on. Each instance depends on retransmitting its transmission, being seen or heard again. When Godard and Gorin refuse to see Fonda "really" listening, but instead see only the (infelicitous) activity of the actor, they preclude the possibility, on Fonda's part, of precisely the kind of intentional political communication they themselves engaged in through their work as the Dziga Vertov Group and, more specifically, with *Letter to Jane*.

Between Paranoia and Embarrassment

A final image of listening: at one point while Fonda is in Hanoi, she and her guide Quoc are driving down a country road when suddenly their driver tells Quoc a raid is coming. Fonda is surprised: "I hear nothing, but then my ears haven't been trained as theirs have in endless war." Quoc tells Fonda to get into the nearest "manhole"; these have been dug every fifty feet or so along the road for the purpose of offering protection from air raids. As she hobbles toward one (she had broken her leg during a layover on the way to Hanoi), Fonda is abruptly assisted by a Vietnamese schoolgirl who drops her rubber strap of books on the ground and ushers the two of them into a tiny hole where they are pressed tightly together. The raid begins, and Fonda describes the noise of the bomber, the "thud" of the bombs, and the sudden silence when the raid is over. It feels, she writes, like a dream. When she emerges from the hole, she sees plumes of smoke in the distance, and she begins to cry, saying "over and over to the girl, 'I'm so sorry, oh, I am so sorry, I'm so sorry.'" And then:

> She stops me and begins speaking in Vietnamese, not angry, very calm. Quoc translates: "You shouldn't cry for us. We know why we are fighting. The sadness should be for your country, your soldiers. They don't know why they are fighting us."

More remarkable than this account, perhaps, is what Fonda writes next. She explains that she has thought about this experience for thirty years: "Out of the blue some schoolgirl gives me this foxhole analysis about the war being our problem, not theirs? Unbelievable as it may seem, it really happened—and it could not have been staged. There was no way to know that our car would have to stop when it did because of the air raid, no way to have planted that girl right then."[53] Of course, by telling us the event could not have been staged, Fonda prompts me, at least, to consider whether, after all, it might have been. Not that the bombs were staged, or that Quoc brought her to this spot, knowing a real raid was imminent, and had arranged for a schoolgirl to be at the ready to escort Fonda to a manhole. But, perhaps, that this girl had memorized these "lines" such that she could deliver them should the opportunity present itself? Or, less specifically, that she saw an opportunity to make an affecting, impromptu speech and she took it?

In her description of this encounter, Fonda betrays her reasonable fear that someone will accuse her of misrepresenting, or perhaps misunderstanding, something fake as something real. She anticipates our suspicion and makes it her own, emphasizing that she had no part in the performance, whatever it was or wasn't. This dynamic continues in her account of the damning moment from which the photograph of Hanoi Jane would emerge. She writes, "It is possible that the Vietnamese had it all planned. I will never know. If they did, can I really blame them? [. . .] If I was used, I allowed it to happen."[54] Fonda acknowledges here what is precisely the case—that the actress is, by definition, a figure to be used for purposes other than her own. It is her awareness of Godard's intent to do the same, once she receives the script for *Tout va bien*, that prompts her to try and withdraw from the project. When she cannot, she engages, almost without trying, in the practice of *perruque* described above. Even Fred Gardner, whose frustration with Fonda is apparent in his "Hollywood Confidential," acknowledges "use" as her consistent reality:

> The way people related to Jane Fonda—try though she might to be plain Jane—was not pleasant to observe. Everybody wanted something—money, an appearance, a favor, a quote, a picture, a connection, a mention, an endorsement. At the same time, they bombarded her with charges of "elitism" designed to maximize her guilt.[55]

When I interviewed Fonda, I was struck by the way in which her memory of the FTA corresponded so precisely to the narrative of the events she provides in *My Life So Far*. Even prior to the interview, she had expressed doubt as to whether or not she could tell me anything more than what she had already written there. When I received her email to this effect, I was surprised—my research had raised countless questions, none of which were answered in the brief twenty pages or so covering the tour in her autobiography. In addition, when I had spoken to other of the FTA's performers and organizers, they had consistently referred to Fonda as the person I needed to speak to—they expected that what they did not remember, she certainly would. She did not, though she did eloquently give voice to much of what I already knew. I recognize this now as a form of protection against this persistent use, a masterful self-scripting that retains control.

Fonda's slight expression of paranoia in her book, driven by the impossibility of determining always when and if she is being used, departs distinctly and importantly from the anti-theatrical revisionism that followed the tumult of the 1960s. While Fonda has referred to herself as "messed up" during the early 1970s, she has not generally distanced herself from her activism through the language of performance. Among the many accusations leveled against her, it is only the photograph(s) for which Fonda has apologized; she stands behind the broadcasts over Radio Hanoi, and though she regrets that her comments regarding the torture of POWs were hurtful to many veterans, and though she believes she should've expressed her perspective on the matter differently, she maintains that that controversy was basically fabricated by the Nixon administration. However, even as Fonda takes full responsibility for the existence of the Hanoi Jane photographs, she recalls the moment they were taken as one in which it would've been helpful to have something like a director:

> A traveling companion, someone with a cooler head, would have kept me from taking that terrible seat. I would have known two minutes before sitting down what I didn't realize until two minutes *afterward*.

Instead, she is by herself:

> Someone (I don't remember who) leads me toward the gun, and I sit down, still laughing, still applauding. It all has nothing to do with where

I am sitting. I hardly even think about where I am sitting. The cameras flash. I get up, and as I start to walk back to the car with the translator, the implication of what has just happened hits me.[56]

The moment Fonda ceases to act like an actress, by failing to consider how the scene she is playing will appear to others, is the very moment she acts in a way she identifies as fundamentally contrary to her political beliefs. Had a director been present and reminded her of her role, she would not have appeared to be something she insists she was not—a traitor, an enemy of American pilots. She would not have "sent a message that was the opposite of what [she] was feeling and doing."[57]

This refusal to draw a line between acting and sincerity is in contrast to many of the narratives that have subsequently been constructed concerning the era's activism, in the US and elsewhere. Kristin Ross, in *May '68 and Its Afterlives*, makes apparent, for example that the postmortem defanging of the French May '68 happened through the development of a discourse that emphasized the ways in which students were not sufficiently entitled to the activities they undertook. Though the words "theater" and "performance" do not appear in her book, her analysis is, arguably, an exploration of the idea that May '68 was the work of people behaving a lot like actors. This is (and was) an idea advanced both by the movement's critics and by its participants, though to decidedly different ends. Representative of the former is Raymond Aron, who provided the most influential conservative critique of May '68. The following is a description of Aron's account, which Richard Wolin gives in his *Wind from the East*:

> Although the insurgents repeatedly paid lip service to the ideals of the French revolutionary tradition, these allusions were largely rhetorical. They remained on the plane of citation or pastiche. The sixty-eighters were aping their eighteenth- and nineteenth-century progenitors. The May events were a grandiose instance of revolutionary pantomime. Hence, the chasm between the revolt's rhetorical dimension and the actors' real intentions, which were "reformist" rather than "revolutionary." Aron recognized that the May insurrection represented not the culmination of the French revolutionary tradition but its last dying gasp.[58]

Rife with the language of performance (aping, pantomime), Aron's interpretation (via Wolin) insists that, in France in 1968, people were not acting as they were supposed to act. For Aron, then, May '68 can appear as the site of illegitimate and unnecessary chaos. Like Austin's actor, forbidden the power of performative speech, the protestors of '68 could not do or say anything real because they were acting like people from the past.

On the first point, that '68 saw people acting in ways they were not supposed to, Ross notes that Aron is completely correct. In *Afterlives*, she explores "the forms and practices developed during May that went about 'denaturalizing' past social relations—and, in so doing, disrupting 'the police' as a kind of logic that assigns people to their places and social identities, that makes them identical to their function." She describes, in a manner that echoes Socrates's injunction to play one part and one part only, "the vehemence with which militants at the time refused to see themselves [as students], resisting attempts to be identified with any one function."[59] The difference between the analyses provided by Ross and Aron (and Wolin), however, is that Ross identifies in May '68 not only a refusal to accept "assigned roles, places or functions," but the breakdown of the very *means* by which one usually determines whether a person is acting in the way they "ought."[60] That is, May's activists weren't acting out of character, but rather against the very idea of a character to which one might be assigned and which is then assumed to restrict the range of behaviors in which one can legitimately engage.

Besides figures like Aron, equally vigorous repudiations of accidental theatricality come from those who count themselves among the activists who acted (appropriately) while the revolutionary play was happening, but who politely left the stage when the curtain came down. Consider, for example, the ways in which some "reconstructed" student participants in the movements of the 1960s in the US have framed their subsequent turn away from such projects as a turn away from a kind of playacting and toward a more sober, mature, anti-nostalgic, anti-idealist perspective. *Destructive Generation*, by Peter Collier and David Horowitz, seethes with frustration that during the 1960s no one, apparently, was who they said they were: "It was a time when a gang of ghetto thugs like the Black Panthers might be anointed as political visionaries, when Merry Pranksters of all stripes could credibly set up shop as social evangelists spreading a chemical gospel."[61] In other words, people were not being recognized according to their true nature. The book narrates its authors' own awakening from this theatrical dream, but this awakening, of course, is a real one, as distinct from the "*epiphanies*" (emphasis in the original) Collier and Horowitz attribute to the "lost boys and girls" of the 1960s.

It is not worth spending much time on *Destructive Generation*, as a petty and patronizing (and frequently sexist, racist, and homophobic) washing of hands. The book does, however, illustrate the way in which the most extreme version of the far-left-turned-right trajectory is driven by a deep embarrassment over that most embarrassing of activities: acting without knowing it. To distance themselves from the infectious space of performance, Collier and Horowitz insist upon defining the boundaries of the stage, so that they might corral all offending actors onto it and seal it off—in particular, they do not want to be mistaken for those "middle-aged activists with gray sideburns and sagging bellies" who continue to protest American imperialism. They do not want to be perceived to be living out of time, in the past, speaking from a theatrical—which is to say, unreal—space. The actor, when he appears offstage, assumes a category of behavior to which he is not considered entitled—he is not really doing or saying what he appears to be doing or saying. Thus, such behavior does not place him in the category of a person to whom that behavior "legitimately" pertains, but instead marks him as behaving illegitimately, because he is not in the proper "place." He may be pretending, or mimicking certain types of behavior, but his actions and words are invalid because they are not his own—they are not real because they are not *really* his.

Conclusion

A Refusal

A kind of representational overreach might always be necessary in the practice of activism that seeks radical or revolutionary transformation. Activists are always working from within the conditions they seek to change, and so, like actors on a stage, they propose the existence of a reality that is not (yet and may never be) real. Perhaps this is why a quote attributed to Vladimir Lenin seems to suggest (though no doubt unintentionally) that revolutionary time disrupts historical time in a way not unlike what happens when we go to the theater to see a play: "There are decades where nothing happens; and there are weeks where decades happen."[1] The staged play, for its part, offers hours "where" months, years, and decades happen, presented to an audience by actors occupying a presumably fictional, temporary space-time. This kind of acting facilitates the representation of the past and the future within the present, and the presence, here, of elsewhere.

In a similar manner, revolutionary acting proposes and performs an alternate present and the future that might follow from it. Yet while at the conclusion of a play the actor typically and easily rejoins the temporal and spatial registers occupied by her audience, the *revolutionary* actor, faced with conclusion—a return to historical time, synonymous with defeat because it is not the continuation or fulfillment of revolutionary time—must decide whether or not to refuse this conclusion. If she accepts the conclusion, that conclusion retroactively marks all that had come before as merely historical, theatrical entertainment. If she refuses, and continues to act "as if" an alternate present was then (and so is now) still possible, she may be charged with acting as an actor acts, but as one who, embarrassingly, hasn't realized the play is over.[2]

The necessarily theatrical practice of radical or revolutionary politics becomes the grounds on which protest movements, theatrical or otherwise, are accused of inauthenticity and illegitimacy. This explains so much about how we've written our histories of 1960s radical protest and political theater, as well as why, when we recover the missing pieces of those histories, things look the way they do. Antiwar GIs were obscured as not real GIs, and they took up practices that resisted this premise; the FTA staged solidarity between soldiers and civilians, beginning and transforming and ending according to the needs of the movement; it was erased as popular entertainment relative to the legacies of the period's experimental theater and then, as activism, suffered the same fate as the movement to which it was attached; and Fonda's activism with and on behalf of antiwar soldiers, which presumed and performed the possibility of solidarity, was distorted and erased through concerted efforts to represent her as anti-soldier—a project facilitated by the erasure of those soldiers themselves.

All this suggests that a theory of theatricality must inform our efforts to see and understand past radical movements. Without it, we might unwittingly give ground to a discourse that positions efforts to attain legibility—for grievances, injuries, erased identities—as, by definition, inherently fake. History is written by those whose past actions contributed to—were born out by—the then-future, our present. On the other side are those who acted as though things might follow a different path; the way they acted *then* is admittedly not compatible with the present, but this incompatibility is compressed and transformed by the succession of events into something entirely different: an incompatibility with the "then-future" that today appears foolish and naïve. The revolutionary activist was/is engaged in this kind of acting, and so is continually at risk of being made ridiculous in retrospect, by locating the decisions made and actions undertaken by the activist in the "wrong" time. Activists are at risk, always, of being charged with acting. Even worse, it seems (and this is the anxiety about the actor characteristic of the left) the historical acting activist must have been, in some critical sense, insincere. Given the way things turned out, they must've known all along that what they were doing wouldn't work, and so they were indulging in a kind of fantasy, a pastiche, a reenactment of earlier, *actual* revolutionary movements.

No one makes this claim more volubly than the people who "were there," but who now, it seems, wish they hadn't been, or at least not quite in the way that they were. A relatively recent example can be found in John B. Judis's "Warning from the '60s Generation," published in the *Washington Post* in January 2020.[3] The subtitle announces the source of Judis's authority: "I was a '60s socialist. Today's progressives are in danger of making my generation's mistakes." Judis begins with a compelling analysis of why and how our contemporary political context might favor progressive causes in comparison with the Vietnam era. He seems, at first glance, to agree with the substance of the demands progressive activists are making today, but is concerned with *how* these demands are being made. Relatively quickly, however, it becomes clear that the problem *is* the demands themselves, because they are, for Judis, the "how" as much as the "what." Some are "perfectly reasonable" or "entirely justifiable," but others go too far: calls for police abolition instead of reform, for open borders instead of "a path to citizenship," for free abortion on demand instead of "safe, legal, and rare," for reparations instead of some other option that acknowledges that most white people's ancestors showed up after the Civil War. Judis implies that he isn't rejecting these demands on the basis of their substance—indeed, he takes no position on the demands themselves—but on the basis of their *appearance*, because he is concerned other people won't like them. His argument against reparations is that it has been "rejected by broad majorities of the electorate." He doesn't like the "quasi-religious" hand-waving in DSA meetings, because he's worried other people might think it's weird. He seems, finally, embarrassed to see people behaving as sincerely as perhaps he once did about things that didn't come to pass and that, because they didn't, never could have. He doesn't want revolution because, as the '60s proved, revolution is impossible, and it is very embarrassing to want something that is impossible. Now firmly on the side of wanting what's possible, he wants to elect Democrats, and these awkward activists are getting in the way because they refuse to acknowledge what he is certain they must know deep down—that their demands are absurd. And yet they insist on making them anyway.

A concern with proper appearances masks, I would argue, a much greater anxiety: that the true extent of the 1960s' radical character will be recovered and used to inform contemporary movements and to facilitate a more politically sophisticated and historically informed organizing practice. The claim that certain demands are unreasonable or hard to justify is premised not upon any kind of material analysis, but upon the presumption that *other people* will not immediately or spontaneously perceive such demands to be reasonable or justifiable. What this ignores is the possibility of persuasion, of making the hard argument *for* reparations or open borders, rather than simply conceding to the ideological status quo that insists these are unreasonable demands. This is not impossible. Such arguments *were* made—in speeches and in writing, but also in practice by activists working to build solidarity, to demonstrate the ways in which the liberation of one is bound up with the liberation of all—and they can be made again. Occupy, for example, produced a class analysis with its rallying cry of "We Are the 99%" that snuck a Marxist definition of the "working class" back into popular activist discourse. This analysis—which is to say, the premise that there are two primary economic classes, and that the vast majority of people fall into one rather than the other—cannot be seriously challenged. To be sure, on the left debate raged over whether such an analysis diminished the lived experiences of marginalized peoples by lumping them in with groups—white men, in particular—that are unquestionably less oppressed. But far from undermining the overarching premise, these debates worked to sharpen the analysis, to provoke the kinds of reckonings that also marked the key movements of the 1960s, from Black liberation to activism against the Vietnam War to the struggle for Indigenous rights. In a word, Occupy reintroduced the concept of "solidarity" into contemporary US activism, no small feat considering the systematic dismantling of the labor movement that has taken place over the last fifty years, the right-wing transformation of identity politics into a basis for division rather than a radically accountable practice of collective action, and the redefinition of "working class" such that it refers not to a person's relationship to their own labor but to how much money they make. In response to the political quickening Occupy facilitated, and its ability to explain material reality, reformed '60s activists like Judis sidestep the analysis and go after the rhetoric, suggesting that we can't take people seriously if they are going to say "we demand the impossible" (which is precisely what Judith Butler did when they took the "human mic" at Occupy Wall Street back in 2011).[4] Instead of responding to the substance of their demands, it is the seriousness of those making the demands that is challenged—their legitimacy, their "authenticity," their chosen tactics.

I think this comes from a place of fear, an anxiety over what might follow from taking the "impossible" seriously. If, instead of dismissing "extreme" demands as rhetorically irresponsible, we consider whether they might in fact be entirely reasonable and justifiable, we might then find that they are, and we might feel compelled to make them. Doing so would involve the precarious task of trying to traverse the massive chasm separating a world that could hear and meet those demands from our own. To extend my metaphor perhaps a bit further than I should, we have to walk out onto the stage and try to represent a different world there, and then insist, against all odds, that it is a *real* one we could inhabit if we wanted to. This is easier said than done. During my own involvement in Occupy, while I was a graduate student in Providence, Rhode Island, it was easy to feel, at times, like I was indulging in some fantasy that had no place in the present, because what could we really achieve? People had all sorts of different ideas about what we should be doing—building a sustainable, long-term, anarcho-utopian community among the tents in the "People's Park"? Occupying Brown University's campus to demand they pay property taxes? Hosting reading groups and teach-ins on radical history, economics, forms of oppression, and/or strategies of resistance? If you cannot draw a straight line from what you are doing now to the future you hope your present actions will produce, it is quite easy to feel like you are engaged in some form of make-believe, even if you are deadly serious about all of it. And if, in the end, we fail in our efforts at radical transformation, we are revealed to have always only ever been mere actors—now subject to erasure and ridicule, to being made a cautionary tale.

Judis never invokes the activist-as-actor in so many words, but she is nevertheless on the scene, and in her most familiar form. He begins his article with Tom Hayden in 1969, and the piece never really gets past 1970 in its discussion of all that went wrong. It is strange, then, that the image of Hayden included—in fact, it is the only image associated with the '60s, as all the others are of Elizabeth Warren, Bernie Sanders, and their supporters—shows him sitting next to Jane Fonda, whom Judis never mentions in the body of his essay. Here is the caption in full: "Tom Hayden, a founder of Students for a Democratic Society, talks with actress and activist Jane Fonda in 1972. Hayden thought that if the '60s left could win over blue-collar workers, it would have the basis for a revolution." Now, one could reasonably make the claim that Fonda's appearance here isn't meant to signify anything—she just happens to exist in an image that is connected, by the article, exclusively to Hayden. It's a familiar image, I've seen it elsewhere. But when pushed on a bit this premise becomes absurd. Why use this image of Hayden? Why place Fonda on the scene and then say nothing about her? The inclusion is so striking that I wonder whether the point of the photograph is, in fact, to show *Fonda* rather than Hayden—she is the cautionary tale incarnate. Arguably, Fonda signals far more to far more people than Hayden does in connection with the narrative of the 1960s that the author is advancing. Fonda, more than Hayden, represents the "mistakes" of the 1960s, most infamously her Hanoi Jane moment in North Vietnam, but also more generally her involvement in multiple issues and movements, her unbridled enthusiasm, her puddle-jumping through the defining matters of the era (as some would have it). She is, to borrow from Barthes, the article's *punctum*, or something like it, betraying the anxiety that underpins Judis's insistence on publicly scolding "'60s socialists" for not knowing how it was all going to turn out. His effort to encourage today's progressives to "learn" from the 1960s by eschewing that which he fears will be impossible betrays the problem of acting as it pertains to revolutionary activist practice—the fact that it is at once necessary and also always a destabilizing threat.

Reshaping our historical narratives such that they do not prescribe to the past an inevitable future might offer a powerful shift in discourse to activists in the present by suggesting the possibility of responding to accusations of inauthenticity, not by accepting the terms of the accusation and pleading innocence, but by reclaiming the precarious practice of acting—as an actor acts and without any guarantee that we will avoid acting at the wrong place, in the wrong time—as an activist activity. This might cut against the embarrassment we (are told to) feel when we attempt a kind of precarious identification with people whose struggle we know is linked with our own, but whose relationship to that struggle is markedly and critically different—we have to learn to be, sometimes, the civilians who yell "fuck the army" and, at other times, the soldiers who can hear civilians say it. I do not mean here to diminish criticism of, for example, white people taking up the statement "I am Trayvon Martin," or other problematic forms of "performative allyship." There is

The image of Fonda listening to Tom Hayden included with Judis's article for the *Washington Post*.
Photo credit: Associated Press.

an important argument to be made that such expressions can paper over difference and risk indulging in a kind of liberal politics that has nothing to do with solidarity. Unless statements like these seek to advance the material or class analysis capable of revealing the ways in which racism upholds a capitalist system that exploits people of all races, though to infinitely varying degrees, they are indeed empty and parasitic. It is very much the point, as Featherstone and Dean explore, and as the FTA and the GI movement demonstrate, that the successful expression of solidarity depends entirely upon the practical work of movement-building.

And here's the thing—none of us can ever be totally sure that we've done the work necessary to say "Fuck the Army." There will always be a reasonable fear—of embarrassment, of seeming fake, of being an actor pretending to be an ally. This, I would suggest, is the real "warning from the '60s generation": that we must not be more afraid of seeming fake than of pursuing liberation. When I look at the FTA—the sometimes clumsy sketches, the overearnest documentary, the footage of Fonda seeming a little self-righteous—I see how and why one might become embarrassed. Things didn't totally work out. But the show for me is instructive, and the project of examining the correspondence, the work, the debates, the transformations—this is what reveals the *practice* of solidarity, of seeing and helping others see what isn't meant to be seen. The actor does this also, insofar as they propose the existence of a world that contests the fixedness of our own. In a moment characterized by countless crises, then, the actor might turn out to be just the kind of figure we need: someone who occupies the present but also refuses to be bound there; who expends resources on building a world even though it is certain to end; who plays not one part but many. The actor, by definition, tells us there is something to see here and insists that deliberate, even theatrical, acts of representation are legitimate because they are necessary.

ACKNOWLEDGMENTS

The worry with a book like this is that I've missed something—someone I didn't get to speak to, a document I never saw, some detail or incident that would transform the history I've written and the conclusions I've drawn. It's all certainly possible, and any errors or elisions in this book are my own. As for what this book gets right, I am indebted first and foremost to the FTA's actors, organizers, champions, and critics who gave me their time and attention, and many of whom opened their homes and personal archives to me. Thank you to Michael Alaimo, Nina Serrano, Barbara Dane, Country Joe McDonald, Rita Martinson, Len Chandler, Bill Belmont, Jane Fonda, Howard Levy, Yale Zimmerman, Vivian Gornick, Holly Near, Alan Myerson, Robin Menken, and Paul Lauter. Of the countless stories I heard during these many months, only a few have made it into this book, but all of them have become integral to my understanding of the show and its significance.

David Zeiger has been an invaluable source and thoughtful respondent, tolerating my many questions and requests for documents and images and information, connecting me with other people I might want to talk to, and, finally, reading the whole book and providing detailed feedback on matters both big and small. I was also fortunate to spend time with Elaine Elinson, who turned out to be my most important source of archival material, and an equally important source of encouragement and enthusiasm. I appreciated (really!) her cautious response to my initial inquiries—she wanted to make sure I had good intentions before providing me with the stacks of letters and itineraries she'd held onto over the years. I passed the test, and it is now hard for me to imagine how I would've proceeded without her help. Early on, my archival search was assisted considerably by Derek Seidman, who passed along a trove of newspaper coverage of the FTA that he'd gathered in the course of writing his own dissertation on the GI movement. Thanks to Jeff Machota at the National Office of the Vietnam Veterans Against the War for his help, and to Fred Lonidier and Alan Pogue, two of the GI movement's photographers, for letting me use their work.

My advisor and committee chair at Brown University, Patricia Ybarra, saw the earliest iteration of my research on the FTA, and it was with her encouragement that I found I could use this one little show as a way into the many larger questions about theater and politics that I wanted to ask. Rebecca Schneider and Nicholas Ridout were exceptionally thoughtful and engaged committee members, and their support for this project has extended well beyond the few years I was a doctoral candidate. At Brown I also found a community of fellow students whose creativity and collaborative spirit made scholarly pursuit a real pleasure, many of whom remain valued interlocutors: Michelle Carriger, Michelle Castañeda, Hans Vermy, Coleman Nye, Christine Mok, Elise Morrison, Eleanor Skimin, Jim Dennen, and Patrick McKelvey. At NYU Abu Dhabi, I was fortunate to talk shop with Mark Swizlocki, Katherine Williams, and Deb Levine. At City College in New York, my colleagues in the Department of English, especially Dan Gustafson and Robert Higney, generously welcomed me into their ongoing writing workshop and provided invaluable feedback on my work. At Temple University, I have been blessed with exceptionally kind and supportive colleagues, as well as curious and engaged students, all of whom have, in various ways, made it possible for me to complete this work and get it out into the world. My thanks especially to David Ingram, Lynne Innerst, and Fred Duer, to the very inspirational Ziggy McKenzie for their puppets and activism, and to the graduate students who went on strike in the spring of 2023 and did the beautiful work of winning.

I've benefited immensely from the decade's worth of discussions Sonja Kuftinec and John Fletcher have facilitated at the American Society for Theatre Research conference, and from spending time thinking with the other participants in these working groups. I am grateful to Jazmin Llana for her herculean efforts organizing the Philippines site(s) of the 2015 dispersed Performance Studies International conference, and for accepting me as a participant on the several-weeks-long journey across the big island of Luzon. The theorization of solidarity I advance here relies heavily on my experiences on this trip and the conversations about political activism and the history of the Philippines I was fortunate to have with my fellow travelers. The book benefited as well from the feedback I received during the 2017 Harvard Mellon School for Theater and Performance Research, and I am grateful to Martin Puchner for facilitating this opportunity. My thanks to Sarah King and Franny Nudelman for their scholarly generosity and to Jessie Kindig for her insight and advice.

Deep gratitude to Brian Herrera for championing this project, and for helping me see how it might in fact be more expansive in its reach and intervention that I had considered. He and Robin Bernstein offered exceedingly helpful feedback at critical points, and I am so pleased that, together with Stephanie Batiste, they felt my book was a good fit for the Performance and American Cultures series. I am grateful as well for the editorial support of Eric Zinner at NYU Press. My thanks to all those who helped shepherd the book through the publication process, and particularly to my readers, whose insight and suggestions improved the book immeasurably.

I was hopeful this book would be legible beyond an academic audience, and I am indebted to several friends-turned-readers for their feedback and enthusiasm on this point: Margaret Scott, Sam Hopkins, and Paul Hubbard. Speaking of Paul, I owe a massive intellectual debt to the many community and student activists I have worked with since 2006, as it has been my experiences in these contexts that have given rise to many of the questions this book explores. Among them are my Rhode Island comrades, especially Paul, Brian Chidester, Shaun Joseph, Mary Rapien, Chris Murphy, Mayra Paulino, Greg Morse, Paige Sarlin, Melody Monaghan, John Brown, Ian Georgianna, Luke Lattanzi-Silveus, and Chris Mastrangelo, and my collaborators at Brown, especially Molly Little, Gavriel Cutipa-Zorn, Ruhan Nagra, Francesca Contreras, Michael Becker, and Alysha Aziz. There are many more comrades I could and should name, but I have to trust that they know who they are.

A very special kind of thanks to Paige Sarlin, who has been tireless in offering every kind of guidance and support—intellectual, political, emotional, academic. Nicholas Ridout also requires a second mention, for being an intermittent collaborator and constant example of the kind of scholar I want to be. Our work making the odd performance has had a profound impact on my thinking about theater, politics, solidarity, and the role of the intellectual in the revolutionary struggle. Jessica Pearson's encouragement throughout has been absolutely sustaining. I am indebted to Eileen O'Brien for her friendship and for her help with the practical realities of being a working mother. My parents, Martin and Lisa Goss, have provided me with decades (decades!) of love, encouragement, comfort, and confidence, and that's really all anyone can hope for. My partner Andrew Starner has been editor, counselor, and the most incredible, tireless cook. He has read these words a thousand times, and they are so much better for it. For all of this and more I cannot thank him enough. My children, while steadfastly refusing to create the conditions that might be conducive to finishing a book, have been supportive and sustaining in other ways. I'm glad they're here.

NOTES

INTRODUCTION

1. "Red and Red," 1971, unpublished script, private collection.
2. "The Playing Field," *FTA!*, directed by Francine Parker (1972; New York: Docurama, 2009), DVD.
3. Robert Neubert, "Antiwar Revue Draws GI Crowd," *Rolling Stone*, June 24, 1971, 12.
4. In *The Spitting Image*, Jerry Lembcke carefully traces the development of this particularly potent narrative, noting that in part it was created retroactively and with the participation of protesters against the Gulf War, who drew a line between their own pro-soldier protests and the "anti-soldier protests" of the Vietnam War. Jerry Lembcke, *The Spitting Image* (New York: New York University Press, 2000), 24.
5. From a speech given by Agnew on October 19, 1969, denouncing the Moratorium demonstrations. Quoted in "Spiro Agnew's Barbs," *Christian Science Monitor*, Oct. 22, 1969, 18.
6. In 1971, during a trip to North Vietnam, Fonda was photographed while seated on a North Vietnamese antiaircraft gun. This, along with public statements the actress made about the torture of American POWs, gave rise to rumors that the actress had deliberately caused the torture of POWs she had visited while in Hanoi. These events are discussed in chapter 5.
7. Following the colloquial usage of the terms, I often refer to groups of men enlisted in any branch of the Armed Forces as soldiers or GIs, though it would be more accurate to refer specifically to soldiers, sailors, airmen, and/or Marines. When I use these latter terms, I am referring exclusively to men enlisted in that particular branch of the military. My use of the plural forms of soldier and GI typically refer exclusively to men (though they may be from a mix of branches); when I refer to servicemembers, this is meant to signal the inclusion of women enlisted in the Armed Forces.
8. David Zeiger, *Sir! No Sir!* (Los Angeles: Displaced Films, 2005), DVD.
9. David Cortright, *Soldiers in Revolt* (Chicago: Haymarket Books, 2005); Col. Robert D. Heinl, Jr., "The Collapse of the Armed Forces," *Armed Forces Journal*, June 7, 1971, http://msuweb.montclair.edu/~furrg/Vietnam/heinl.html.
10. Both *Restaging the Sixties: Radical Theatres and their Legacies* (Ann Arbor: University of Michigan Press, 2006) and the *New Radical Theatre Notebook* (New York: Applause, 2000) are representative in this regard, as are a number of books devoted to individual groups and artists from the era who are still making work today.

11 I credit Jon Rossini and Patricia Ybarra's article "Neoliberalism, Historiography, Identity Politics" with inspiring this line of thinking. *Radical History Review* 112 (Winter 2012): 164, doi:10.1215/01636545-1416223.
12 Harry Elam, Jr., *Taking It to the Streets* (Ann Arbor: University of Michigan Press, 2001), 133.
13 Andreas Malm, *How to Blow Up a Pipeline* (London and Brooklyn, NY: Verso Books, 2021).
14 For a related discussion of how the memory of the Vietnam War has affected the commemoration of other events, including subsequent US wars, see David Kieran, *Vietnam Forever* (Amherst: University of Massachusetts Press, 2017).

CHAPTER 1. SEEING THE ANTIWAR SOLDIER

1 Founded in 1941 at the request of President Franklin D. Roosevelt, the USO brought together six civilian organizations to handle the on-leave recreation of the men in the Armed Forces: the Salvation Army, the Young Men's Christian Association (YMCA), the Young Women's Christian Association (YWCA), the National Catholic Community Service, the National Travelers Aid Association, and the National Jewish Welfare Board. Providing recreation for the troops had as much to do with keeping them *from* certain activities as it did providing them with others. Which is to say, the USO was one among a number of organizations and government agencies charged with preventing the spread of venereal disease among enlisted men.
2 Bob Hope was one of the USO's earliest and most popular performers, as he toured to troops stationed at home and abroad during World War II, and later during the Korean War. Hope, who was trained in the tradition of vaudeville, was already known at the time of his first USO appearance, in 1941, for his work on radio and television. His tours for the USO, however, would become the single most defining aspect of his career, and an exceptionally lucrative one at that. Hope contested this, in part by claiming that he paid for the tours himself. See Margy Rochlin and Ira Glass, transcript of "Act Two. Live on Stage by the Sword, Die on Stage by the Sword," from "Hearts and Minds," episode 200, *This American Life*, originally broadcast Nov. 30, 2001, www.thisamericanlife.org.
3 "Typhoon Jane," *Time*, Jan. 3, 1972, 71.
4 Raymond Coffey, "USO Viet Shows Hurt by Antiwar Sentiment," *Los Angeles Times*, Sept. 10, 1970.
5 Charles Thompson, *Bob Hope, Portrait of a Superstar* (New York: St. Martin's Press, 1981), 143–44. See also Ian Wright, "Vietnam: An Army of Doubts," *The Guardian*, Jan. 8, 1970.
6 Thompson, *Bob Hope*, 143–44.
7 Heinl, " Collapse of the Armed Forces."
8 Morris Janowitz, "Voluntary Armed Forces and Military Purpose," *Foreign Affairs*, Apr. 1, 1972, 2014, www.foreignaffairs.com.
9 *Marine Corps Gazette*, quoted in Cortright, *Soldiers in Revolt*, 3.

10 Cortright, *Soldiers in Revolt*, 36.
11 Ibid., 35.
12 Fred Gardner, "Hollywood Confidential: Part II," *Viet Nam Generation Journal and Newsletter* 3, no. 3 (1991), www2.iath.virginia.edu.
13 Drummond Ayers, "War Disillusions Many G.I.'s in Vietnam," *New York Times*, Aug. 4, 1969.
14 During the Vietnam War, those drafted served two years, while those who enlisted served three. A tour in Vietnam was typically one year; if a GI had fewer than six months left after returning from a tour in Vietnam, he would typically be discharged. So while some soldiers would've returned home after a tour and become, by definition, antiwar veterans rather than antiwar soldiers, many did continue to serve in the military.
15 Cortright, *Soldiers in Revolt*, 50.
16 Ibid., 55. See also James Lewes, *Protest and Survive: Underground GI Newspapers During the Vietnam War* (Westport, CT: Greenwood Publishing Group, 2003). Lewes's work on GI newspapers led to the creation of a digital archive, the GI Press Collection. Hosted by the Wisconsin Historical Society, it provides access to thousands of pages of newspapers and other documents related to the GI movement.
17 Cortright, *Soldiers in Revolt*, 53.
18 For a thorough historical account of the coffeehouse movement, see David L. Parsons, *Dangerous Grounds: Antiwar Coffeehouses and Military Dissent in the Vietnam Era* (Chapel Hill: University of North Carolina Press, 2017).
19 Cortright, *Soldiers in Revolt*, 54.
20 Sam Lebovic, "'A Breath from Home': Soldier Entertainment and the Nationalist Politics of Pop Culture during World War II," *Journal of Social History* 47, no. 2 (2013): 7, doi:10.1093/jsh/shto82.
21 Parsons, "Setting Up Shop: Coffeehouses Land in America's Army Towns," in *Dangerous Grounds*.
22 Ibid., 28–29.
23 Gardner, "Hollywood Confidential: Part I," under the heading "The First GI Coffeehouse," *Viet Nam Generation Journal and Newsletter* 3, no. 3 (1991), www2.iath.virginia.edu.
24 Cami Rowe persuasively and helpfully explores the ways in which veterans of the US wars in Iraq and Afghanistan navigated the problem of the antiwar soldier's legibility, and particularly their efforts to distinguish themselves from activist veterans in the Vietnam era. Rowe reads this choice as evidence that members of Iraq Veterans Against the War (IVAW) succeeded where antiwar Vietnam veterans failed: in "destabilizing" the identity categories that, she writes, led soldiers to be seen as "the enemies of those opposed to the Vietnam War." That they were not, in fact, widely seen in this way suggests that the historical erasure of the GI movement and its civilian supporters has had a significant impact on analyses of contemporary activist practices. Cami Rowe, *The Politics of Protest and US*

Foreign Policy: Performative Construction of the War on Terror (London and New York: Routledge, 2013).
25. Richard Moser, *The New Winter Soldiers: GI and Veteran Dissent during the Vietnam Era* (New Brunswick, NJ: Rutgers University Press, 1996), 111–12.
26. Lembcke, *Spitting Image*, 152.
27. Moser, *New Winter Soldiers*, 104.
28. Ibid., 105.
29. Ibid., 106.
30. Lembcke, *Spitting Image*, 4–5.
31. This action is captured in the film *Different Sons* (1971), Jack Ofield, director, with Vietnam Veterans Against the War and Volunteer Professionals of the New York Film Community. Internet Archive.
32. Moser, *New Winter Soldiers*, 108.
33. Ibid., 109. This moment also appears in *Different Sons*.
34. Ibid., 108.
35. Mary Hershberger, *Jane Fonda's War* (New York: New Press, 2005), 29.
36. In *Fighting Sleep*, Franny Nudelman offers compelling and moving analyses of both *Different Sons* (which documents Operation Rapid American Withdrawal) and *Winter Soldier* (which documents the Winter Soldier Hearings). She also reads the "rap session" as a politically committed therapeutic process, one that aligns it with some of the ideas I am exploring here about performance, authenticity, and visibility. Franny Nudelman, *Fighting Sleep: The War for the Mind and the U.S. Military* (New York: Verso Books, 2019).
37. Moser, *New Winter Soldiers*, 112–16.
38. Ibid., 114.
39. David Parsons discusses this in *Dangerous Grounds*, 89.
40. Cortright, *Soldiers in Revolt*, 172–73.
41. Parsons, *Dangerous Grounds*, 90.
42. Cortright, *Soldiers in Revolt*, 76.
43. Ibid., 14.

CHAPTER 2. STAGING THE MOVEMENT
1. Jane Fonda and David Zeiger, "Interview," *FTA!*
2. Homer Bigart, "Court Martial," *New York Times*, May 21, 1967.
3. Cortright, *Soldiers in Revolt*, 52.
4. Ibid, 61. See also Parsons, *Dangerous Grounds*, and Simeon Man, "A World Becoming: The GI Movement and the Decolonizing Pacific," chapter 6 in *Soldiering through Empire: Race and the Making of the Decolonizing Pacific* (Oakland: University of California Press, 2018).
5. Thomas Kiernan, *Jane: An Intimate Biography of Jane Fonda* (New York: G.P. Putnam's Sons, 1973), 329.
6. "Anti-military Movement Entertainment Presented to Active Duty Military Personnel" Committee Exhibit No. 60, US Congress, House Committee on Internal

Security, *Investigation of Attempts to Subvert the United States Armed Services*, Part 3, 92nd Congress, 2nd Session, 1972, p. 7497.
7   Gardner, "Hollywood Confidential: Part I," under heading "Enter Jane."
8   "Anti-military Movement Entertainment," 7497. In her autobiography, Fonda specifically identifies Ken Cloke, Mark Lane, and Donald Duncan. Jane Fonda, *My Life So Far* (New York: Random House, 2005), 223.
9   Richard Stacewicz, *Winter Soldiers: An Oral History of the Vietnam Veterans Against the War* (Chicago: Haymarket Books, 2008), 233.
10 Jerry Parker, "An Antiwar 'USO' to Tour U.S. Bases," *Philadelphia Inquirer*, Feb. 18, 1971.
11 "1971," *Bob Hope: The Vietnam Years (1964–1972)* (Portland, OR: R2 Entertainment, 2004), DVD.
12 "Hope Responds to Fonda," *Variety*, Feb. 18, 1971.
13 James Wooten, "500 GIs at Debut of Antiwar Show," *New York Times*, Mar. 15, 1971; Paul Berg, "Gung-Ho for Peace," *St. Louis Post-Dispatch*, May 2, 1971, p. 14.
14 Gardner, "Hollywood Confidential: Part I," under the heading "First GI Coffeehouse."
15 "An oleo strut is a vertical shock absorber on the underside of a helicopter, and as one guy put it, 'This place (the army) is such a bring-down we needed something to absorb the shock.'" Barbara Dane, *The Guardian*, July 30, 1968, http://sirnosir.com.
16 Arthur Sainer, *The Radical Theatre Notebook* (New York: Avon Books, 1975), 70.
17 Gardner, "Hollywood Confidential: Part I" under heading "First GI Coffeehouse." See also Parsons, *Dangerous Grounds*, chapter 1.
18 Berg, "Gung-Ho for Peace." (This statement was reproduced, in part or in whole, in many of the articles covering the press conference.)
19 Parker, "An Antiwar 'USO.'"
20 "Anti-war Performers Want Show Like Hope's," *San Francisco Chronicle*, Feb. 17, 1971.
21 Parker, "An Antiwar 'USO.'"
22 Wright, "Army of Doubts."
23 "Kitty Mitty," unpublished script, 1971, private collection.
24 Country Joe McDonald, interview with the author, Berkeley, CA, Oct. 24, 2012.
25 Parker, "An Antiwar 'USO.'"
26 Judy Klemesrud, "His Happiness Is A Thing Called 'Joe,'" *New York Times*, August 2, 1970, http://www.nytimes.com/movie/review?res=9E01EFDB153EE336A05751C0A96E9C946190D6CF.
27 This included the part Gene Hackman would come to play in *The French Connection* (1971). (Richard Rys, "Exit Interview: Peter Boyle," PhillyMag.com, Apr. 21, 2008, http://www.phillymag.com/articles/exit-interview-peter-boyle/).
28 Klemesrud, "His Happiness."
29 William Buckley, "A Talk with Dick Gregory," *Boston Globe*, Dec. 11, 1970.
30 "Panther Rally—June 7th: Dick Gregory to Speak," *Sun Reporter*, June 6, 1970.
31 David Gelber, "'But Dick, They Are the 82nd Airborne,'" *Village Voice*, Mar. 18, 1971.

32 Leticia Kent, "It's Not Just 'Fonda and Company,'" *New York Times*, Mar. 21, 1971.
33 Pamela Howard and Larry Kleinman, "Antiwar Troop Entertainment?," *New York Post*, Feb. 16, 1971. Also quoted in Lacey Fosburgh, "Antiwar Troupe Formed to Tour Bases," *New York Times*, Feb. 17, 1971, and Joseph Modzelewski, "A Thinking Man's GI Tour?," *Daily News*, Feb. 17, 1971.
34 "Court Denies Fonda Show Request," *Fayetteville Observer*, Mar. 10, 1971.
35 "Troops Protest Ban on Jane's Troupe," *Daily Variety*, Mar. 10, 1971.
36 "Court Denies Fonda Show Request."
37 Michael Kernan, "For Whom Bella Toils," *Washington Post*, Mar. 10, 1971.
38 "Jane's War Parody Draws 'Stowaways,'" *Evening News* (Newark, NJ), Mar. 15, 1971. Also printed (without the final paragraph) as "500 Cheer Antiwar Performance," *Evening Outlook*, Mar. 15, 1971.
39 Michael Kernan, "GI Movement: A Show to Call Its Own," *Washington Post*, Mar. 15, 1971. (A shortened version of this article—which did not include the quote cited here—also appeared in the *New York Post* under the title "GIs Were the Stars of Jane & Co.")
40 "500 Cheer Antiwar Performance."
41 Ibid.
42 Kernan, "GI Movement."
43 Berg, "Gung-Ho for Peace."
44 Kernan, "GI Movement."
45 Kent, "It's Not Just 'Fonda.'"
46 Irwin Silber, "About the GI Movement," liner notes to Barbara Dane, *FTA! Songs of the GI Resistance*, Paredon Records, 1970, p. 3, http://media.smithsonianglobalsound.org.
47 "White Blues Singer: Blonde Keeps Blues Alive," *Ebony*, Nov. 1959, 149–54.
48 "Anti-war Revue Box Office Smash," *Fayetteville Observer*, Mar. 15, 1971.
49 Gelber, "'But Dick.'"
50 Gardner, "Hollywood Confidential: Part II," under the heading "FTA Show."
51 Kenneth Reich, "Jane Fonda's Antiwar Show Scores Hit Near Army Base," *Los Angeles Times*, Mar. 15, 1971.
52 Kernan, "For Whom Bella Toils."
53 Michael Kernan, "GIs Were the Stars of Jane & Co.," *New York Post*, Mar. 15, 1971.
54 Ibid.
55 Wooten, "500 GIs at Debut."
56 Kernan, "GI Movement."
57 In the *Village Voice* and the *Evening Outlook*, respectively.
58 Kernan, "GI Movement."
59 Kent, "It's Not Just 'Fonda and Company.'"
60 Stacewicz, *Winter Soldiers*, 232.
61 Kate King, "Drawing on Experience: Peers Salute 'Beetle Bailey' Creator Mort Walker," Stamfordadvocate.com, Sept. 7, 2010, www.stamfordadvocate.com.
62 Kernan, "GI Movement."

63 Fonda's public turn toward feminism began during the summer of 1971; she had, however, responded derisively to reporters at the February press conference who had asked whether she would appear in a bikini. She credits her introduction to feminism to Terry Davis, whom she met and talked with when she visited the Oleo Strut coffeehouse for the first time in early 1970.
64 "Jane Fonda Would Tour GI Bases with 'Peace & Love' Anti-war Unit," *Variety*, Feb. 17, 1971.
65 Cortright, *Soldiers in Revolt*, 85–86.
66 Ibid., 106.
67 Millie Pease, "Fort Ord GIs Dig Jane's Anti-war Show," *Watsonville Register Pajaronian*, May 10, 1971.
68 Kevin Howe, "Antiwar Show Packs 'em in," *Monterey Peninsula Herald*, May 10, 1971.
69 Neubert, "Antiwar Revue."
70 Howe, "Antiwar Show Packs 'em in."
71 Cortright points to *P.O.W.* as an example of a civilian effort that directly sparked GI organizing; the newspaper was actually started by a civilian collective, and "within a few months, a new GI group emerged, the 'United Soldiers Union.'" Cortright, *Soldiers in Revolt*, 79.
72 Neubert, "Antiwar Revue."
73 Ibid.
74 Cortright, *Soldiers in Revolt*, 111.
75 Alan Farley, interview with Robin Menken, Pacifica Radio Archives, Nov. 8, 1972. Internet Archive.
76 Jay Goode, "Jane Will Visit Hood 'If Invited,'" *Killeen Daily Herald*, Sept. 17, 1971
77 Ed Jeffords, "Jane Fonda vs. the Army," *Tacoma News Tribune*, Aug. 4, 1971.
78 Susan Vaneta Mason, ed., *The San Francisco Mime Troupe Reader* (Ann Arbor: University of Michigan Press, 2005), 58.
79 Nina Serrano, interview with the author, Oakland, CA, Oct. 21, 2012.
80 Schutts, "We Say No to Your War!: The Story of the Covered Wagon GI Coffeehouse, Mountain Home Air Force Base, Idaho, 1971," master's thesis (Boise State University, 1994), 89, www.jeffrschutts.ca.
81 Ibid., 95.

CHAPTER 3. SAY IT!
Epigraph: Holly Near on joining the FTA show, in "Holly Near: Singing for Our Lives," season 33, episode 4, of the PBS series *American Masters*, www.pbs.org.
1 Dick Brukenfeld, "Where There's Hope, There's Fonda," *Village Voice*, Nov. 25, 1971.
2 Ibid.
3 "Anti-war Salute to GIs Rocks the Lincoln Center," *Daily World*, Nov. 23, 1971.
4 Jay Goode, "Show Features Antiwar Skits," *Killeen Daily Herald*, Sept. 19, 1971. For coverage of the controversy, see also "School Board Drops Curtain on Fonda," *Killeen Daily Herald*, Aug. 11, 1971; "Antiwar Group Files Suit against KISD," *Killeen Daily Herald*, Aug. 27, 1971; Jay Goode, "Battle over FTA Show

Goes to Court Friday," *Killeen Daily Herald*, Sept. 5, 1971; Judy Cartwright, "Show Will Go On, Antiwar Group Says," *Temple Daily Telegram*, Sept. 17, 1971; Richard Hill, "Jane's Antiwar Revue Heads for Hood Stand," *Dallas Times Herald*, Sept. 17, 1971.

5 Bob Heaton, "Jane's JAM Session: A Super-Amplified Military Protest," *San Antonio Light*, Sept. 21, 1971.
6 "Jane Fonda: 'I Want to Work with Women,'" *New York Times*, Oct. 31, 1971.
7 Peter Ainslie, "Eye View," *Women's Wear Daily*, Nov. 19, 1971.
8 Belmont remarked, in an interview in 2013, that in fact Joe probably also departed because he was making a significant amount of money touring independently, playing at colleges and elsewhere, and the tour interfered with doing so. Bill Belmont, interview with the author, Berkeley, CA, Mar. 27, 2013.
9 Farley, interview with Menken.
10 David Featherstone, *Solidarity: Hidden Histories and Geographies of Internationalism* (London: Zed Books, 2012), 37.
11 Ibid., 16.
12 Ibid.
13 Ibid., 246.
14 Jodi Dean, *Comrade* (New York: Verso, 2019), 67.
15 Ibid., 66.
16 Evan Johnston, "Let's Be Comrades," *Spring*, May 19, 2020, https://springmag.ca.
17 Gardner, "Hollywood Confidential: Part 1," under header "The First GI Coffeehouse."
18 Gardner, "Hollywood Confidential: Part I," under header "Enter Jane."
19 Cortright, *Soldiers in Revolt*, 53.
20 Gardner, "Hollywood Confidential: Part 1," under header "Enter Jane."
21 This is not to say that civilians were not sometimes oblivious to the realities of enlisted life. In Japan, Michael Alaimo recalls "movement people" (not members of the cast) encouraging GIs to disobey curfew in order to see the show. "They would say 'it's illegal, so stay,' and I just got frantic telling Jane and Donald, 'I was in the military, there's no rights, you can't tell them to disobey like that.'" In a separate context, peace activist Fred Halstead describes being "taken aback to find that a common approach among Japanese peace activists toward American GIs was to encourage them to desert." For Halstead, this was at once an ethical question—the penalties for desertion were extremely harsh—and a strategic one: "An antiwar GI could do far more for the antiwar cause [. . .] than he could in exile or as a fugitive." Fred Halstead, *Out Now! A Participant's Account of the American Movement against the Vietnam War* (New York: Monad Press, 1978), 127.
22 Paul Lauter to "Everyone concerned with USSF show Pacific Tour," July 30, 1971, p. 2, private collection.
23 Louis Wolf to Alan Miller, Paul Lauter, Sid Peterman, "Re: Show in RP," Sept. 10, 1971, p. 2, private collection.

24 Meejuna (?) et. al. for Haymarket Square to Jules Feiffer with draft reply by Feiffer, ca. March 1971, Jules Feiffer Papers, Manuscript Division, Library of Congress (106.00.00).
25 Fonda, *My Life So Far*, 275.
26 It's worth pointing out that, while Fonda always appeared fully clothed, several articles (two in Killeen, in particular) included in their description of the actress the fact that she wasn't wearing a bra. The *Daily World* even printed a photograph that appears to have been included because Fonda's nipples are prominent, and her fingers, which she points away from herself at chest level, draw attention to this. While today a form of undress that would be categorized more readily as "sexy," at the time it seems clear that not wearing a bra registered as political, and so sexually undesirable.
27 No title, AP Newsfeatures, New York, Nov. 1971, private collection.
28 Ibid.
29 Vivian Gornick, "Jane Fonda's Political Vaudeville Show," *Chicago Tribune*, Apr. 9, 1972, http://search.proquest.com/docview/170265036?accountid=9758.
30 Serrano, interview with the author.
31 Farley, interview with Menken.
32 Gornick, "Fonda's Political Vaudeville."
33 "The Tacoma People" to "the FTA Show Cast," ca. Aug. 1971, private collection.
34 McDonald, interview with the author.
35 Featherstone, *Solidarity*, 21.
36 It would be reasonable to wonder why the title of this book is *F*ck The Army* and not *Free The Army*. Originally, I'd hoped the title might be *F- - - The Army*, but for various reasons this turned out to be impossible. In deciding whether to use "Free" or "F*ck," I was faced with what felt like a terrible choice. The point of "F- - -" was the undecidability, the ambiguity, and the plausible deniability. To choose "F*ck" was to do definitively and perhaps with a sense of impunity what I am arguing can only be done under specific circumstances, and never with a guarantee that the expression will be received in the spirit it was meant. But to choose "Free" seemed to concede to the premise that under no circumstances should I write or say such a thing. So I chose to "say it," because I'd rather risk the failure of the performative than preemptively foreclose its possibility altogether.
37 "On the World Stage," *FTA!*
38 Heaton, "Jane's JAM Session."
39 Kernan, "GI Movement."
40 "On the World Stage," *FTA!*
41 A description of the events at Firebase Pace in October 1971 appears in "GIs at Pace Say Hell No to Night Patrol," *The Bond* 5, no. 10, www.sirnosir.com.
42 "A Brand-New Day," *FTA!*
43 Pease, "Fort Ord GIs."
44 "Kitty Mitty," mid-1971, unpublished script, private collection.
45 Farley, interview with Menken.
46 Lustbader to Elinson and Sid Peterman, Nov. 2, 1971, private collection.

47. "The Movement's Moving On," *FTA!*
48. "Kitty Mitty."
49. Gardner, "Hollywood Confidential: Part II," under header "What the GI Movement Accomplished."
50. Kernan, "GI Movement."
51. "Insubordination," 1971, unpublished script, private collection.
52. Featherstone, *Solidarity*, 18.
53. Ibid., 161.
54. Miller to Paul Lauter, USSF offices, Jane Fonda, Francine Parker, and Sid Peterman, memo, Aug. 5, 1971, private collection.
55. Elinson to Francine, Bill, Ellen, "Hawaii Hall," Oct. 19, 1971, private collection.
56. Elinson to Francine, Nina, Paul Lauter, Alan, "Hawaii," Oct. 18, 1971, private collection.
57. Elaine Elinson, "Show Schedule/Preliminary Hall Details," Oct. 18, 1971, private collection.
58. Ben Wood, "Jane Fonda Brings Campaign against War to Honolulu," *Honolulu Star-Bulletin*, Nov. 24, 1971.
59. Cortright, *Soldiers in Revolt*, 112–13.
60. Philippines sketch, 1971, unpublished script, private collection.
61. Melinda Paras for Kabataang Makabayan to Alan Miller, Barbara Dane, FTA personnel, "Re: Pacific Tours and the Philippine Situation," Oct. 13, 1971, private collection.
62. Wolf to Alan Miller, Paul Lauter, Sid Peterman, "Re: Show in RP," Sept. 10, 1971, private collection.
63. Most coverage of the show in the Philippines mentions the sponsorship of the PASA, as in "Jane Fonda Show Opens Tomorrow," *Philippines Herald*, Nov. 27, 1971. Alaimo described the luncheon and swim meet in an interview.
64. Elinson to Belmont, Parker, Miller, Lauter, "Re: Philippine situation, Baquio hall," Nov. 6, 1971, private collection.
65. *FTA!*
66. "Jane Fonda Refused Formal Entry Permit," *Daily Yomiuri*, Dec. 9, 1971.
67. "Decision on Fonda Group Is Likely Today," *Japan Times*, Dec. 9, 1971.
68. Kyoichi Nakamura, "Jane Fonda Arrives for Antiwar Rally," *Mainichi Daily News*, Dec. 8, 1971.
69. Elinson to Parker, Belmont, Alan, Lauter, "Tokyo," Oct. 24, 1971, p. 3, private collection.
70. Ibid.
71. Elinson ("Guess Who") to Francine, Alan, and Paul, "Misawa," Nov. 13, 1971, private collection.
72. Elinson to Belmont, Parker, Alan, and Lauter, "Philippines," Oct. 27, 1971, private collection.
73. Paras for Kabataang Makabayan to Alan Miller, Barbara Dane, FTA personnel, "Re: Pacific Tours and the Philippine Situation," Oct. 13, 1971, private collection.
74. *FTA!*
75. "Jane Fonda Joins Dull Strike," *Okinawa Morning Star*, Dec. 16, 1971.

CHAPTER 4. ENLISTED AUDIENCES AND EMANCIPATED SPECTATORS
1 "Remembering Bob Hope's First USO Show," *USO Blog*, May 6, 2010, http://blog.uso.org.
2 Thompson, *Portrait of a Superstar*, 111.
3 David Zeiger, interview with the author, Silver Lake, CA, Mar. 29, 2013.
4 USSF Staff, "Dear Comrades," 1970, letter in GI Press Collection 1964–1977, Wisconsin Historical Society.
5 Paul Lauter, interview with the author, Hartford, CT, Oct. 29, 2013.
6 David Zeiger, "Finally, after 35 Years in Exile, FTA Is Back," accessed March 7, 2014, www.sirnosir.com.
7 For a close reading of both films, see Nudelman, *Fighting Sleep*.
8 Judith Johnson, "Bob Hope's Vietnam Christmas Tours," Historynet.com, Dec. 23, 2009, www.historynet.com.
9 *Bob Hope: The Vietnam Years*.
10 I should note here that, in speaking about the Hope specials, it would be misleading to refer to servicemen and women, as the latter are almost nonexistent in footage of the audiences, unless specifically acknowledged within a given context. With the FTA, however, a conscious effort was made by the show to connect with servicewomen, and also with military wives and local women's groups. This is reflected in *FTA!*, as attention is paid to including footage of women in the audience and interviews with women. To mark this difference, I generally do not use male and female nouns and pronouns when referring to Hope's audience (instead using exclusively male pronouns), but I do typically do so when referring to the FTA's.
11 Timothy White, "The Road Not Taken, Bob Hope without Laughter," *Rolling Stone*, Mar. 20, 1980, http://archive.rollingstone.com. See also Margy Rochlin's interview with Hope on the radio program *This American Life*. Rochlin and Glass, transcript of "Act Two. Live on Stage," from "Hearts and Minds."
12 White, "Road Not Taken," and Thompson, *Portrait of a Superstar*, 143.
13 "1971," *Bob Hope: The Vietnam Years*.
14 Ken Bell, *100 Mission North* (Dulles, VA: Potomac Books, 2003), 144. Many of the customer reviews for Hope's *Vietnam Years* DVDs are written by people who identify themselves as audience members:

> I went to Vietnam in 1965, saw the show in ChuLai, and when it was broadcasted in the states, my family saw me for the first time since I had left. I looked for years for a film of this show, and when the DVD came out, purchased it, and saw what they saw for the first time. It's a wonderful collection from Bob's collection, and if you were there and attended one, it will bring back memories. In the ChuLai show, several people pictured in the audience never made it home. During the performance, they stop for a moment, then continue on. Too many people were sitting on top of an outhouse (6 hole) and it collapsed. This is a wonderful collection for those who remember . . . (Robby Robinson "Globetrotter," "Family saw me at the ChuLai Show," Ama-

zon.com customer review of *Bob Hope: The Vietnam Years (1964–1972)*, Feb. 22, 2014, http://www.amazon.com/review/RWQQ7FJHHMY44/ref=cm_cr_pr_perm?ie=UTF8&ASIN=B00030ANYU&linkCode=&nodeID=&tag=).

15 "1964," *Bob Hope: The Vietnam Years.*
16 "1971," *Bob Hope: The Vietnam Years.*
17 "Fonda Blast Military," *Daily Yomiuri*, Dec. 22, 1971.
18 "On the World Stage," *FTA!*
19 Ibid.
20 Ibid.
21 The sketch is "Kitty-Mitty."
22 "On the World Stage," *FTA!*
23 Ibid.
24 "The Playing Field," *FTA!*
25 "A Brand-New Day," *FTA!*
26 "1966," *Bob Hope: The Vietnam Years.*
27 "No One Knows," *FTA!*
28 "1970," *Bob Hope: The Vietnam Years.*
29 "Act Two. Live on Stage," from "Hearts and Minds," *This American Life.*
30 "A Brand-New Day," *FTA!*
31 There is one exception to this absence of the soldier-performer that I have found: in Hawaii, it seems that a GI guerilla skit performed; interestingly, the content was very similar to the FTA's blackout sketches (Elinson to Parker, Belmont, Alan, and Lauter, "Tokyo").
32 "A Racist War," *FTA!*
33 "1967," *Bob Hope: The Vietnam Years.*
34 Ibid.
35 "Actor's Remarks Lead to Fisticuffs," *Japan Times*, Dec. 12, 1971.
36 "Save Our Soldiers," *FTA!*
37 Len Chandler, interview with the author, Los Angeles, Mar. 8, 2022.
38 "No One Knows," *FTA!*
39 Kershaw, *The Radical in Performance*, 195–99.
40 Louis Althusser, "The 'Piccolo Teatro': Bertolazzi and Brecht, Notes on a Materialist Theatre," *For Marx* (London: Verso, 2005), 149–50. Writes Althusser:
   the performance is, fundamentally, the occasion for a cultural and ideological recognition [that] presupposes as its principle an essential identity. [. . .] Yes, we are at first united by an institution—the performance, but more deeply, by the same myths, the same themes, that govern us without our consent, by the same spontaneously lived ideology.
41 Sainer is quoting himself here (Sainer, *Radical Theatre Notebook*, 69).
42 Jacques Rancière, "The Emancipated Spectator," *The Emancipated Spectator* (London: Verso, 2009), 1–23.
43 Ibid., 13. *Looking at Tazieh*, which has been screened in London, Brussels, and Paris, and at the Edinburgh International Festival in 2008, is best described as a

ninety-minute multimedia installation. A center screen or television plays footage of the *tazieh* (a Shiite religious ritual that commemorates, through reenactment, the martyrdom of the Imam Hussein) Kiarostami staged live for audiences in Rome and Taormina, Italy, in 2002 and 2003. On two larger screens flanking the smaller one, footage plays of Iranian Shiite spectators watching a rural production (or potentially multiple different productions) of tazieh during Muharram, when the plays are commonly staged. This footage has been edited such that the reactions of the spectators appear to correspond to the events unfolding on the center screen's "stage."
44 Ibid., 2.
45 Ibid., 12.
46 J. L. Austin, *How to Do Things with Words* (Oxford: Oxford University Press, 1962), 22.
47 Rancière, "Emancipated Spectator," 17.
48 White, "Road Not Taken," 51.
49 Joe Roach proposed this possibility during a presentation at the Yale Performance Studies Working Group, and it was mentioned by Michael Alaimo as well. Alaimo also believes that a member of the FTA's cast or crew must have been an informant, as conversations that happened in hotel rooms in Japan made it into FBI reports. Michael Alaimo, interview with the author, Los Angeles, Oct. 18, 2012.
50 James Harding, "Undercover Surveillance Operatives: Bigotry, Bathrooms, and Environmentalists" (working group paper, annual meeting of the American Society for Theatre Research, Dallas, November 2013). For more elaboration of Harding's theory of the thespian/espionage connection, see James Harding, *Performance, Transparency, and the Cultures of Surveillance* (Ann Arbor: University of Michigan Press, 2018).
51 Cortright, *Soldiers in Revolt*, 22.
52 Ibid., 46.

CHAPTER 5. THE ACTOR AND THE ACTIVIST
Epigraphs: T. Findley, "Jane Fonda: So What's George C. Scott Done?," *Rolling Stone*, May 25 1972, 42–44; M. Campbell, "32 Years Wasted, Jane Fonda Says," *Atlanta Constitution*, Aug. 6, 1972.
1 "SWSSimpson" (username), "In the Words of Jane Fonda," YouTube, posted July 1, 2006, http://www.youtube.com/watch?v=QOnG71EgAm4. This video was accessed in 2011. It is no longer available online.
2 Gardner, "Hollywood Confidential: Part I," under header "Enter Jane."
3 Sarah King, "Making of the Myth of Hanoi Jane" (master's thesis, University of Waterloo, 2011), https://uwspace.uwaterloo.ca.
4 "prettypaperpusher" (username), "Hanoi Jane!," YouTube, posted Mar. 19, 2007, http://www.youtube.com/watch?v=ogQEU_5K6O0.
5 Plato, *Republic*, Book X, in Bernard Dukore, ed., *Dramatic Theory and Criticism, Greeks to Grotowski* (New York: Holt, Rinehart and Winston, 1974), 22.
6 Plato, *Republic*, Book III, 17.

7. Jean-Jacques Rousseau, *Letter to d'Alembert and Writings for the Theater*, vol. 10 of *The Collected Writings of Rousseau*, ed. and trans. Alan Bloom, Charles Butterworth, and Christopher Kelly (Lebanon, NH: University Press of New England, 2004), 309.
8. Plato, *Republic*, Book III, 18.
9. Bill Belmont, interview with the author, Berkeley, CA, Mar. 17, 2013.
10. Robin Bernstein, *Racial Innocence: Performing American Childhood from Slavery to Civil Rights* (New York: New York University Press, 2011), 71.
11. Schneider, *Performing Remains*, 163.
12. McDonald, interview with the author.
13. Rousseau, *Letter to d'Alembert*, 310.
14. Jacques Rancière and Davide Panagia, "Dissenting Words: A Conversation with Jacques Rancière," *Diacritics* 30, no. 2 (Summer 2000): 15. These are the two reasons Rancière gives for defining humans as "political animals": because they can produce an excess of words, and because these words are contested by those who claim to "speak correctly."
15. Belmont, interview with the author.
16. McDonald, interview with the author.
17. Elinson, interview with the author.
18. For a comprehensive account, see Hershberger, *Jane Fonda's War*; Fonda, *My Life*; and King, "Making of the Myth."
19. Hershberger, *Jane Fonda's War*, 75–76.
20. Hershberger documents the many trips made by American peace activists into enemy territory during the war, as well as the US government's attempts to stop them. Mary Hershberger, *Traveling to Vietnam: American Peace Activists and the War* (Syracuse, NY: Syracuse University Press, 1998).
21. Hershberger, *Jane Fonda's War*, 118.
22. Fonda, *My Life*, 305.
23. Hershberger, *Jane Fonda's War*, 86.
24. Fonda, *My Life*, 324. See also: *Hearings before the Committee on Internal Security*, House of Representatives, 92nd Congress, Second Session, Sept. 10 and 25, 1972 (Washington: Government Printing Office): 7552.
25. Ibid., 315.
26. As I was writing this passage, I was trying to figure out whether it is correct to say someone is "seated on" an antiaircraft gun; it turns out, if you Google "antiaircraft gun pilot's seat," the third image (though I was not searching for images) is one of the "Hanoi Jane" photographs of Fonda.
27. Though there are multiple photographs, including some that have been doctored to make it appear as though Fonda is squinting through the gun's sight, it is appropriate to speak of the *image*, singular, to the extent that the photographs (including those doctored) have all effectively come to circulate the same meaning.
28. Fonda, *My Life*, 325–27.

29 Hershberger, *Jane Fonda's War*, 149. ABC, NBC, and CBS all covered Hoffman's allegation.
30 "Jane Fonda Grants Some P.O.W. Torture," *New York Times*, Apr. 7, 1973.
31 King, "Fonda's Antiwar Activism," 103.
32 This story and others, along with a compilation of evidence refuting them, appear on the website Snopes ("Hanoi'd with Jane," Urban Legends Reference Pages, *Snopes*, June 14, 2013, www.snopes.com).
33 For example: "Traitor Jane Fonda," 26th Marine Regiment – Vietnam: History and Photo Project, http://www.26thmarines.org/janefonda.html.
34 Jean-Luc Godard and Jean-Pierre Gorin, *Letter to Jane*, special edition feature included on *Tout va bien* (1972; New York: Criterion Collection, 2005), DVD.
35 Jean-Luc Godard and Jean-Pierre Gorin, *Tout va bien* (1972; New York: Criterion Collection, 2005), DVD.
36 Zeiger, interview with the author.
37 Godard and Gorin, *Letter to Jane*.
38 Fonda, *My Life*, 278.
39 Jane Fonda, "Jane Fonda: 'I Want to Work with Women,'" *New York Times*, Oct. 31, 1971.
40 Robert Phillip Kolker, "Angle and Reality: Godard and Gorin in America," *Monthly Film Bulletin* 42, no. 3 (Summer 1973): 131.
41 Michel de Certeau, *Practice of Everyday*, (Berkeley and Los Angeles: University of California Press, 1984), 25.
42 Godard and Gorin, *Letter to Jane*. In fact, this works on two levels; it is not necessary to know that Fonda played a prostitute in *Klute* for the comment to seem to refer to a woman "being" first with one film/director/man and then another. The added dimension of *Klute*, and the question of whether starring in it was "the right way to go to Vietnam," suggests Fonda went to Paris and then to Vietnam not merely as a promiscuous woman, but as a prostitute. And the prostitute, as *Klute* makes clear, is an *actress*.
43 Rousseau, *Letter*, 309.
44 Pierre Bourdieu, *The Field of Cultural Production* (New York: Columbia University Press, 1993), 263.
45 The multivalence of the term confounds the dynamic characteristic of French Maoist politics in the late 1960s and early '70s, as described by Kristin Ross. Kristin Ross, *May '68 and Its Afterlives* (Chicago: University of Chicago Press, 2002), 96.
46 Kolker, "Angle and Reality," 132.
47 Ibid.
48 Ross, *May '68 and Its Afterlives*, 96.
49 "walter kurtz" (username), "USA HISTORY SHOWS HANOI JANE #1 TREASONIST TRAITOR-1," YouTube, posted March 11, 2012, http://www.youtube.com/watch?v=xOagtrbzJZ4. This video is now "private" on YouTube.
50 Kent Jones, "Letter to Jean-Pierre and Jean-Luc," liner notes to *Tout va bien* (New York: Criterion Collection, 2005), 14.
51 Kolker, "Angle and Reality," 232.

52   Ibid.
53   Fonda, *My Life*, 311–12.
54   Ibid., 316.
55   Gardner, "Hollywood Confidential: Part II," under header "The FTA Show."
56   Fonda, *My Life*, 316–17.
57   Ibid., 317.
58   Richard Wolin, *Wind from the East* (Princeton, NJ: Princeton University Press, 2012), 8.
59   Ross, *May '68 and Its Afterlives*, 206.
60   Ibid., 79.
61   Peter Collier and David Horowitz, *Destructive Generation* (New York: Free Press, 1996), 15.

CONCLUSION

1   In any reference to the quote I have seen (including as the title of an article in the *Journal of Hepatology*: http://dx.doi.org/10.1016/j.jhep.2013.12.002), it is attributed to Lenin; however, I have not been able to find a reference to a specific, printed source.
2   In her chapter on "The Police Conception of History," Kristin Ross notes that the "feeling that nothing happened" in May '68 is "frequently expressed today." Even in anniversary commemorations, she writes, "the viewer is most clearly left with the suspicion that 'nothing happened'" (*May '68 and Its Afterlives*, 20–21).
3   John B. Judis, "A Warning from the '60s Generation," *Washington Post Magazine*, Jan. 21, 2020, www.washingtonpost.com.
4   "smabiner" (username), "Judith Butler at Occupy Wall Street," YouTube, posted Oct. 23, 2011, https://www.youtube.com/watch?v=JVpoOdz1AKQ&t=4s.

INDEX

Abzug, Bella, 51
acting: and action, 146–49, 158–59, 177, 179, 192; and activism, 7, 10, 32, 154, 158–60, 163, 166, 191–92, 195–98; and sincerity, 187; and spectator, 119, 144–45, 148; anti-war Veteran as, 30–32; as an actor acts, 11, 15–16, 119, 144–45,154, 159, 163–64, 191, 196; plausible deniability of, 149, 211; revolutionary as actor, 79, 152, 162–63, 165–67, 177, 180, 187–88, 191–92; tactical acting, 10, 15, 20, 151; "the actress," 154–55, 159, 162–63, 168, 174–75, 178, 182–83, 185
activism: activist performance, 9; and authenticity (*see* authenticity); antiwar movement as anti-soldier, 1–2, 10, 37, 203n4; Black liberation, 2, 18, 48, 65, 72, 97–98, 118, 128, 146, 162, 194; campus/student activism, 26–27, 40, 195; Chicano activists, 72; Indigenous activists, 72, 101, 194; performative activism (*see* performative); revolutionary activist (*see* acting: revolutionary as actor); Veteran activism and protests, 12, 26–27, 118. *See also* VVAW, Operation Rapid American Withdrawal, Winter Soldier Hearings
agent provocateur, 147–49
Agnew, Spiro, 1
Alaimo, Michael, 44, 66, 73, 91, 104, 110, 130, 210n, 215n
All-Okinawa Military Employees Trade Union. *See* Zengunro

all-volunteer force, 35, 37. *See also* VOLAR (Project Volunteer Army)
allyship: 11, 26, 78, 198; "ally theater," 10; "performative activism," 10, 196
Althusser, Louis, 142, 214n
American International Pictures (AIP), 117
anti-imperialism, GI movement and, 2, 38, 100, 130; cultural imperialism, 108; FTA show and, 14, 86, 100, 102, 129; *FTA!* (film) and, 129
anti-sexism, 79, 82, 85–86, 93, 96
antiwar movement, 28–29; as anti-soldier, 1, 10, 29; Hollywood support for, 42
Arkoff, Sam, 117
Armed Farces Day, 2, 62–64
Aron, Raymond, 187–88
audience participation, 90–91, 120, 133–39, 142, 150
Austin, J. L., 88, 145, 165, 177–78, 188
authenticity, 7; discourse of, 7–9, 11, 13, 15, 119; inauthenticity of activists and activist movements, 10; of the antiwar soldier, 8; of the antiwar veteran, 27–33, 80, 119, 162. *See also* activism, acting

Baraka, Amiri, 5, 98
Barbarella (film), 41, 84, 180, 183
Barthes, Roland, 196
Beetle Bailey (comic strip), 59, 208
Beheiren (Japan Committee for Peace in Vietnam), 106–7
Belmont, Bill, 74, 160–67, 172, 210n
Berk, John, 51
Berkeley (CA), 64

219

Bernstein, Robin, 161
Berrigan, Fr. Daniel, 55, 58
Big Brother and the Holding Company, 62–63
Black Panther Party, 48, 188
Black Revolutionary Theatre, 6, 98
Boal, Augusto, 91
Bob Hope Christmas tours, 8, 17–18, 42–43, 46–47, 56, 64, 112; television broadcasts, 113–15, 120–21, 123, 126, 204n2
Boise State, 66–67, 209
Bonifacio, Andres, 105
Bourdieu, Pierre, 177–78
boycott, 65, 96
Boyle, Peter, 1, 45, 48, 54, 56–57, 64, 66
Bread and Puppet Theater, 4, 73
Broadway, 23, 66–67; "Broadway salute to the GI movement," 70
Brown, Les, 56
Bryant, Anita, 132–33
Buckley, William F., Jr., 49
Butler, Judith, 194

Caldwell, Ben, 98
campus activism. See activism
celebrity, 13, 41, 42, 48, 51, 58, 60, 116, 152, 159, 162–63, 167, 174
Chandler, Len, 62, 66, 73, 89, 129, 134–35, 139–40, 167
Chavez, Cesar, 96
CIA (Comedy In Action), 63
class: politics, 77–78, 86, 87; classism, 87. See also working class
Cleaver, Eldridge, 82
climate activism, 9. See also Fonda, Jane: climate activism
Clinton, Hillary, 156
co-presence, 114
coffeehouse movement. See GI coffeehouse movement
collective: action, 194; theater collective, 4, 7, 54, 75
Collier, Peter, 188–189

Committee United for Political Prisoners (CUPP), 49
Committee, The, 4, 44, 54, 56, 59, 62, 65–66, 74–75, 86
Communist Party of the Philippines, 103. See also Kabataang Makabayan
comrade: 77–79, 88, 149. See also Dean, Jodi
consciousness-raising, 22, 65, 72, 77, 96, 160
Cortright, David, 3, 4, 19, 21–22, 35, 36–37, 81, 102, 149
Curry, David, 28

Da Nang airbase. See Bob Hope Christmas tours
Dane, Barbara, 55–57, 82
Davis, Ossie, 70
Davis, Terrie, 209n63
de Certeau, Michel, 175
Democratic Socialists of America (DSA), 193
desertion, 19, 35
Different Sons (film), 118–19, 206n
director, 143, 167, 186–87; politics of, 174, 178–80. See also Godard, Jean-Luc
Donegan, Pamela, 71, 73, 91, 107
draft, 5, 37, 205n14; draft-dodging, 21. See also All-Volunteer Force
DSA. See Democratic Socialists of America
Dunaway, Faye, 70
Dziga Vertov Group, 184

efficacy: of theater and performance, 5, 41, 45, 122; of protest, 5–6
El Teatro Campesino, 5, 73
Elam, Harry, Jr., 5–6
Elinson, Elaine, 94; correspondence regarding Pacific Rim tour, 99–108, 165–66
elitism, 74, 85–87, 185
embarrassment, 100, 166, 187, 196, 198

Entertainment Industry for Peace and Justice (EIPJ), 42, 66
entertainment: politics of 13, 22, 24, 44, 51, 64, 67–68, 136; FTA as 8, 13, 39, 41, 45–47, 51, 58, 76, 80–85
experimental theater 44–45, 67, 104; legacy of 4, 192

FTA! (film), 116–119; rerelease, 110, 116–117, 167–168; response to Bob Hope Christmas specials, 38, 116, 126, 133; suppression of 14, 116; visit to Hiroshima memorial, 107, 140
FTA/Free Theatre Associates (troupe): changes to cast, 64–65, 70–73; historiographical erasure of, 3–9; original cast of, 54–56; schism, 66, 74–75
FTA (show): as counter-USO show, 45–47, 49, 56, 64, 83–84, 116; description of sketches, 75, 90–91, 93–98, 102, 108, 128, 130; script revisions 51, 54, 59, 83, 96, 97, 102, 108; domestic performances: Fayetteville, NC, 3, 42, 46, 49–50, 52, 54–56, 60, 62–63, 70, 83, 87, 99, 117; Fort Dix, NJ, 3, 23, 45, 74; Monterey, CA, 61–63, 92–93, 95 (*see also* Armed Farces Day); Tacoma, WA, 23, 44, 47, 64, 66, 75, 86–87, 209, 211; Boise State, ID, 66–67; Mountain Home, ID, 66–67; Killeen, TX, 45, 50, 65, 71; San Antonio, TX, 71–74, 90; Lincoln Center benefit, 3, 61–62, 69, 71–72, 74; tour of the Pacific Rim, 70; preparations for, 82, 85, 99, 101; politics of, 79, 110, filming of *FTA!* during, 116; Honolulu, Hawaii, 101–102; Philippines, 69, 82, 102–5, 108; Japan, 106–11, 127, 138–39, 210n21; Okinawa, 69, 109–10, 129, 134, 138
"FTA" (slogan), 11
FTA (song) aka "The Lifer's Song," 11, 57–59, 65, 89, 107, 109, 128
Farnsworth, Elizabeth, 164–67

Featherstone, David, 76–79, 88, 92, 98, 198
Feiffer, Jules, 4, 48, 83–84, 182
feminism: feminist movement, 72; and FTA show, 63, 65, 69, 75, 85–86, 89, 94, 160; Fonda and, 60, 85, 63n
Firebase Pace, 19, 91, 97
Fonda, Jane: and agency, 152, 163, 168, 182; as cautionary tale, 195–97; as celebrity, 152, 159; as elitist, 85–87; as surrogate for American public, 60, 173; climate activism, 156; comments on torture of POWs, 169–71 (*see also* "Hanoi Jane"); feminism, 86; filming of *Tout va bien*, 174–75; involvement with GI movement, 40–41, 50, 59; sexualization, 84, 175, 182, 217n42; "scripted woman," 160–63, 166, 186; support for political prisoners, 49; trip to North Vietnam, 1, 99, 167–72, 184–87
"Free The Army" vs. "Fuck The Army," 11, 59, 89–90, 96, 128, 196, 198, 211n36
Friedrich, Philip, 51
Fort Bragg (Fayetteville, NC). *See also* FTA (show): domestic performances
Fort Dix (NJ). 23. *See* FTA (show): domestic performances
Fort Hood (Killeen, TX), 23, 36, 82. *See also* FTA (show): domestic performances
Fort Jackson (Columbia, SC), 23, 39, 81
Fort Leavenworth (KS), 39
Fort Ord (Monterey, CA). *See* FTA (show): domestic performances
Fort Polk (LA), 23
"Fuck the Army" (slogan), 11, 89, 211n36

Garson, Barbara, 51
Gates Commission, 36. *See also* VOLAR (Project Volunteer Army)
Gerhard, Capt. Harry, 64
GI Alliance, 87. *See also* Shelter Half (GI coffeehouse)
GI Bill, 12, 26

GI coffeehouse movement: 20, 22–24, 36, 39–40, 44–46, 50–53, 55–56, 58, 65–67, 70–71, 80–83, 86, 101, 107, 117, 138, 182, 205n18; Covered Wagon (Mountain Home, ID) 66; Fort Dix coffeehouse (NJ), 3, 23, 45, 74; Haymarket coffeehouse (Fayetteville, NC), 23, 45, 50–53, 55–56, 70, 83, 117, 182, 203, 207, 211; Liberated Barracks (Waikiki, HI), 101; MC coffeehouse (Iwakuni, Japan), 107, 129; military "psychedelic" coffeehouses, 36; Oleo Strut (Killeen, TX), 23–24, 44, 207n15, 209n63; Shelter Half (Tacoma, WA), 23, 60, 86–87; The UFO coffeehouse (Columbia, SC), 23, 44, 81–82
GI movement, 3, 10, 20–22, 27, 34–38, 61–62
GI newspapers 2, 3, 21, 34, 68, 71, 75, 184; *Bragg Briefs* (Fort Bragg, NC) 52; *Liberated Barracks* (Waikiki, HI), 205n16
GI resistance, 18, 20, 22, 24, 30, 36, 38, 44, 51, 81, 149–51
Godard, Jean-Luc, 172–84, 217n42
Goodrow, Gary, 54, 56, 62
Gorin, Jean-Pierre, 172–84, 217n42
Gornick, Vivian, 85–86
Gould, Elliot, 48, 54
Gould, Josh, 23
Grant, Beverley, "Tired of Bastards Fucking Over Me" (song), 95
Green Berets, The (film), 175
Gregory, Dick, 3, 41, 48–49, 54–56, 70
Guerrero, Amado, 103
Guidote-Alvarez, Cecile, 105
Gulf War, 203n4

Halstead, Fred, 210n
"Hanoi Jane," 154–56, 168–70, 180–81, 185–86, 196. *See also* Fonda, Jane
Harding, James, 147–48
Hayden, Tom, 65, 80, 82, 195–97
Heinl, Col. Robert, 3, 18, 21
Henriques, Darryl, 66

Hershberger, Mary, 154, 168, 206, 216n
Hesseman, Howard, 62
hippie, 48, 53, 76
Hoffman, Capt. David (POW): allegations against Fonda, 169–72, 217n
Hollywood opposition to Vietnam War, 1, 42, 48
Hope, Bob, 113–114. *See also* Bob Hope Christmas tours
Horowitz, David, 188–189
Horvitz, Gary, 51
House Committee on Internal Security (HCIS), 21–22, 40, 169

identity, 87–88, 98; identity politics, 194; of soldier/veteran as antiwar; 10, 12, 27–29, 32, 34, 46, 80–81. *See also* authenticity, visibility
image: of soldier, 8, 24–32, 34–38, 43, 46, 72, 75, 125–129; of soldier-spectator, 17, 113–14, 116, 118, 121–22, 125–26, 135, 138, 143, 146, 148; of Fonda, 168–69, 172–73, 180–84, 195–97
inauthenticity. *See* authenticity
insubordination, 13, 19, 25, 35, 91, 97–98, 118, 151
internationalism, 82, 100; international solidarity, 14, 76, 107
Iraq Veterans against the War (IVAW), 205n
Iraq War, 10, 154–55, 205n

Jaffe, Steve, 160–61, 167
Johnson, Lyndon B., 27–28, 87, 120
Joe (film), 48
Jones, Alex, 155
Judis, John. B, 193–97

Kabataang Makabayan student organization, 103, 109
Kerry, John, 40
Kershaw, Baz, 142
Kiarostami, Abbas, 143, 215n

Kieran, David, 204
King, Dr. Martin Luther, 9
King, Sarah, 154, 171
Kline, Stephen, 81
Klute (film), 4, 40–41, 175, 182, 217n42

Laird, Melvin Robert (Secretary of Defense), 57
Lane, Mark, 207n
Lauter, Paul, 82, 117, 165
legacy, 5, 7
legitimacy, 10–15, 33, 37, 58, 60, 119–20, 152–53, 159, 164, 180, 194
Lembcke, Jerry, 27, 29–30, 203n, 206
Lenin, Vladimir, 191, 218n
Levy, Howard, 39, 41, 50
Lewes, James, 205n
liberalization policy, 36, 50
liberals, 166; liberal politics, 198
"Lifer's Song," 59
listening, 131, 172, 175–76, 183–84, 197
Lincoln Center benefit. *See* FTA (show): domestic performances
Lockard, Jay, 23
Long Binh Base (South Vietnam), 17–18, 123
Looking at Tazieh (film installation), 143, 215n
Loring, Gloria, 133
Lustbader, Ellen, 94–95

M*A*S*H* (film), 48
Malm, Andreas, *How to Blow Up a Pipeline*, 9–10
Marcos, Ferdinand, 103–4
Martin, Trayvon, 196
Martinson, Rita, 65, 73, 95, 107, 135
Marxism, 78, 194
Mason, Al, 62
May 1968, 187–88
McDonald, Country Joe, 64–65; criticism of Fonda and FTA, 47, 54, 74–75, 85, 87, 165. *See also* FTA (troupe) schism

Menken, Robin, 64–66, 75, 86, 93–95, 160
Mickelson, Donna, 23
Miller, Alan, 100, 165, 210, 212
Montand, Yves, 173–74, 179
Mooney, Paul, 71, 73
Moser, David, 3, 27–29, 30, 33–34
movement-building, 68, 72, 77
My Lai massacre, 25, 33, 35
Myerson, Alan, 44, 54, 56, 64, 74

NBC. *See* Bob Hope Christmas tours
National Mobilization Committee to End the War in Vietnam, 23
Near, Holly, 69, 71, 73, 84, 95, 139
Newton, Huey P., 49
Nichols, Mike, 48, 54, 84
Nixon, Pat, 90, 95
Nixon, Richard, 2, 27–29, 33, 35–37, 61, 83, 95, 118, 154, 169–71, 186; sketches featuring, 57, 90, 95
non-violence, 9–10
Nudelman, Franny, 206n

Obama, Baraka, 78
Occupy Wall Street (OWS), 77–78, 194–95
Occupy Providence, 195
Ofield, Jack, 206n31, 206n36
Okinawa. *See* FTA tour of the Pacific Rim, *see also* Zengunro
Open Theater, 73
Operation Desert Storm, 10. *See also* Gulf War
Operation Homecoming, 170
Operation Rapid American Withdrawal (RAW), 30–32, 40, 118, 206n36
organized resistance, 21, 24, 34–35, 61–62

Pacific Counseling Service (PCS), 99, 106, 165
Pageant Players, The, 45
Paine, Thomas, 30
Parker, Francine, 2, 65, 74, 86, 116–17, 138, 165

Parsons, David L., 4, 36, 205n
participation. *See* spectating as participation
patriotism, 1, 57, 136; GI as patriotic, 12, 21, 24, 32, 38, 43; patriotic dissent, 8
performative, 7, 41, 78, 87–89, 92, 98, 110, 145, 188. *See also* allyship
perruqe, 175–76, 182, 185
Peterson, Gypsy, 82
petition, 34, 50–51, 64, 102
Philippine Amateur Swimming Association (PASA), 104
Philippine Educational Theater Association (PETA), 104–5
pickets: as form of GI resistance, 21; at Bob Hope performance (GIs), 18; at Colonial Stores (GIs and lettuce workers) 96–97; of U.S. Army at Mt. Fuji (Camp Fuji Mothers), 107–8; of U.S. Army base on Okinawa (Okinawan base workers)
Plato, 156–57, 159–60
Pogue, Alan, 24
political correctness, 45, 47, 55
political theater, 11–12; of the 1960s, 3–8
POWs, 154–55, 169–72, 186, 203n6. *See also* Operation Homecoming
progressives, 9, 193, 196
punctum, 196

race, 13–14, 38, 66, 70–71, 80, 87, 96–98, 101, 163, 189, 198
radical politics, 7–8, 15, 83
Rancière, Jacques, 15, 141–46, 180
Raye, Martha, 46
"really," 177–78
recognition, 20, 22; misrecognition, 12, 93; sites of recognition, 24–26, 30, 37–38, 68, 80
revolutionary politics, 9; as theater, 41, 79, 191; "evolution of" 5–6. *See also* activism
rhetoric, 13, 194–95

Rivers, Johnny, 62
Roosevelt, Franklin Delano, 204
Ross, Kristin, 154, 180, 187–88, 217–18
Rossini, Jon, 204n
Rousseau, Jean-Jacques, 157, 163, 176, 180
Rowe, Cami, 205n

sabotage, 2, 60, 149–51
San Francisco Mime Troupe, 4, 44–45, 66, 73
Sanders, Bernie, 78, 195
Sandy Hook Elementary School, 155
Sainer, Arthur, 45, 142
Schechner, Richard, 158
Schneider, Rebecca, 161
Schutts, Jeff, 66–67
script and scripting, 69, 133–38, 160–67, 186
Seale, Bobby, 49
Second City, 48
Serrano, Nina, 65–66, 86, 107
sexism, 3, 6, 38, 65, 71, 74, 79–80, 84–87, 94–95, 174
Simone, Nina, 3, 69–70
simultaneity, 122, 124
Sir! No Sir! (film), 2, 81, 116
soldier, as worker, 2
soldier on stage, 133–38
soldier-spectator, 1–2, 60, 76, 113, 119–23, 125–26, 133, 135–36, 146, 149
solidarity, 76–80; as performative and theatrical 78, 87–89, 92, 98, 110–111; civilian-soldier, 75, civilian participation in veteran protest FTA show and, 69; distance and, 79, 90, 118, 141; precarity and, 88, 93, 97, 12
spectating as participation, 7, 38, 67, 91, 120, 133, 135–42, 150. *See also* Rancière, Jacques.
Stacewicz, Richard, 40, 59
Steelyard Blues (film), 61, 64, 74
strike, 2, 21, 109–10, 138
Sturdy, Don. *See* Howard Hesseman

Sutherland, Donald, 1, 4, 41, 42, 45–46, 48, 55–59, 62, 64, 73, 91, 95, 104, 116
Swamp Dogg, 55–56

Taller Investigación de la Imagen Dramática, 142
theater, 3–13, 141–46
theatricality, 7–8, 10–11, 28, 34, 79, 192; accidental, 188. *See also* solidarity, activism, acting
theatrical protest, 8, 10, 12, 34, 147. *See also* Operation Rapid American Withdrawal
Thompson, Charles, 17–18
Tolson, Lt. Gen. John J., 49–50, 54
Tomlin, Lily, 155
troop disaffection: denying evidence of, 25, 36
Trumbo, Dalton, 55, 138

Underground GI newspapers. *See* GI newspapers
United Service Organizations (USO), 17, 23–24, 38, 50, 113, 204n1, 204n2. *See also* Bob Hope Christmas tour
United Servicemen's Union (USU), 62
United Soldiers Union, 209n
Urgo, Joe, 59
USS *Constellation*, 63–64
USS *Coral Sea*, 102

Vadim, Roger, 64
Vadim, Vanessa 64
Valley Forge, 30. *See also* Operation Rapid American Withdrawal
vaudeville, 1, 5, 57, 105, 204n
Vereen, Ben, 66–67

veteran protest, 12, 30–35, 118; medal-returning ceremony, 34. *See also* Operation Rapid American Withdrawal, Winter Soldier Investigation, Vietnam Veterans Against the War, authenticity
Veterans of Foreign Wars (VFW), 30
Viet Cong, 1, 57, 99
Vietnam Veterans Against the War (VVAW), 26–28, 30–35, 40, 118, 161
violence, 97–98, 148, 149–51. *See also* nonviolence
visibility, 12–13, 19–21, 25, 27, 32, 36, 38, 41, 59, 61, 72, 76, 80, 83, 110, 151, 206

Wallach, Eli, 70
Warren, Elizabeth, 195
Watson Jr., James, 71
Winter Soldier Investigation, 32–33, 35, 118–19, 204, 206–8; Fonda's support for, 40
Winter Soldier (film), 118–19
"winter soldiers" (term), 30. *See also* Stacewicz, Richard; Moser, David
Wolf, Louis, 82–83, 102–4, 165
Wolin, Richard, 187–88
working class: definition of, 194; FTA's audience as, 75, 87; membership in, 158, 162
"working it out," 19–20, 150–51

Ybarra, Patricia, 204n
Yokosuka, Japan, 106, 138, 147–48
Yokota Air Base (Fussa City, Japan), 106

Zabriskie Point (film), 39
Zeiger, David, 2, 81–82, 116–18, 173
Zengunro, 109–10
Zimmerman, Yale, 66, 199

ABOUT THE AUTHOR

LINDSAY GOSS is a theater maker, cultural historian, and performance theorist. Her work explores how popular discourses of authenticity and identity shape the field of contemporary performance and activist practice. Her writing has appeared in *TDR*, the *Journal of Dramatic Theory and Criticism*, *Performance Paradigm*, *Contemporary Theatre Review*, *Performance Research*, and *Afterimage*. She teaches at the University of Melbourne in Australia.

www.ingramcontent.com/pod-product-compliance
Lightning Source LLC
Chambersburg PA
CBHW020405080526
44584CB00014B/1181